Financial Freedom for Beginners

How To Become Financially Independent and Retire Early

Nathan Bell

Disclaimer

All erudition contained in this book is given for informational and educational purposes only. The author is not in any way accountable for any results or outcomes that emanate from using this material. Constructive attempts have been made to provide information that is both accurate and effective, but the author is not bound for the accuracy or use/misuse of this information.

Table of Contents

CHAPTER ONE

Introduction To Financial Freedom

Guy and Tom are two friends who work together in a similar capacity under the same company. They both are alike and different, alike in the sense that they share the same responsibilities and duties, but different in their reactions and willingness to perform these duties. Guy is always ready to perform them, even when unforeseen circumstances arise; he is simply always prepared. However, Tom is the direct opposite; he is in a constant state of panic and crisis based on the complaint that he does not have enough funds to support these situations.

The subject of concern is, what creates this significant difference between these colleagues?

What Is Financial Freedom?

It is important to a lot of people or a vast majority of people that they can satisfy their needs or desire at whatever time it arises. However, many are not equipped with the mentality to actualise this desire; hence, the need for financial freedom.

The meaning of financial freedom is subjective to different people and the various situation they find themselves. For a teenager, financial freedom is independence from parents; it is them not having to depend on the income or allowances given by the parents. Therefore, teenagers might regard themselves financially free if they have their personal income which funds their lifestyle irrespective of the benefits provided by the parents. To a retiree, it is the freedom to have the desired lifestyle without the stress of bankruptcy because of the retirement plans or investments that have been set in place. To some people, it the ability to perform in a role they admire or remain self-employed without strain on their finances.

However, financial freedom, in general, refers to a lifestyle void of the concern or domination of income. In clear terms, it refers to the ability or status of a person to provide or support a need in whatever circumstance. It is a position where you are settled financially; any unplanned or sudden expense will not cause a dent to your financial state. It refers to a state of being economically independent without having to depend on salaries from employment. It is also important to note that financial freedom connotes a debt-free situation, that is; a person who wants to lay claim that he is financially free cannot claim that the money that funds his free state is from debt.

Financial freedom is not restricted to being able to only fund emergencies but also to find solace in the fact that your life after retirement has specific plans in place that would ensure financial stability and growth. It's a lifestyle that is dominated by money and a constant worry to make these funds.

It also entails the ability to retire early or quit a job simply because you have lost interest in that particular field but do not have a specific task that you are registered to at that specific time. It is the ability to afford a desired lifestyle without stress about the next paycheck. Therefore, you are in control of your finance and lifestyle instead of your financial state dictating a particular lifestyle it believes you can afford without collapse. It is the ability to work for cooperation or company based on the fact that you enjoy whatever role you are given and not because it is crucial to your finance.

The Means to Attain Financial Freedom

As stated in the above paragraphs, every individual seeks to attain financial independence and this state of finance has different meanings and interpretations to people. However, these people are expected to go through the same or similar steps to attaining financial freedom, hence, the reason for the subsequently discussed opinions;

- Set Goals: This is an essential principle to financial independence; every idea and investment needs motivation. Therefore, a set goal helps you to choose the right investment and employment options that would ensure you are moving towards a goal which leads to financial freedom. Also, these goals are advised to be in clear, specific and realistic forms because this would increase the possibility of achieving them. However, even after sustenance of a position where you no longer stress about money, has been reached, it is still important to live on or make a budget so that you do not overspend and return to your former stage. It is of primary importance to be purposeful about financial freedom.

- Make a Budget: it is vital to make a set budget; this would help to regulate your spending and ensure that the right percentage is invested in meeting your set goals. A budget is used to document the progress of savings and investments. This also helps to contain unplanned and unnecessary temptations to spend recklessly.

- Pay Loans: if you desire to have a financially independent lifestyle, it is essential to pay up or clear all loans; student loans, house loans or car loans. If this is not done, it would only consume or eat up the profits/interests of your investment. It is crucial to set up all financial investments on a fresh slate, so your desire for independence is not undermined by debt and the interests that overwhelm it.

- Register to an Automatic Savings Plan: There are various retirement savings plans made available for employees by their cooperation. For example; the 401(k)s made available for employees of private cooperation and Thrift Savings Plan available for federal government workers and members of the uniformed forces, gives individuals an option to have their savings automatically invested in a plan after their retirement. These plans contribute largely to financial freedom because of the matching contribution option that is contributed to your personal savings account and investment funds opportunities. Also, this particular option helps ensure that a specific percentage which has been registered by you is pulled from your salary and contributed to your investment before you start spending, and in some cases before tax deduction.

- Examine Investment Options: This is the central way to ensure financial freedom as every investment accommodates interest and growth based on the percentage and time it was contributed. It also provides individuals to choose an investment option that suits their situation as there is a variety of them. However, it is advisable to begin investing as soon as because its success and growth are based on the time contributed and time fixed and decided to be for withdrawal. Therefore, it is essential to examine investment options or hire a financial advisor who could assist based on gathered knowledge to decide on an option for your situation. Growth can be supported with a weekly, monthly or yearly or any comfortably consistent plan that would not affect the individual's lifestyle but improve and manage the growth of savings.

- Accommodate Bargains: In most cases, when individuals begin to make some percentage of wealth, they decide that there is no point behind negotiating goods they can afford at the stated price. However, this a financial sucking idea which prevents a lot of people from saving expenses if they had asked for or agreed to a bargain price. This is so because they find it an injury and their status and would not like to appear cheap. Therefore, it is important to negotiate since this could save them a considerable amount of money if they submit themselves to negotiate with these sellers. Although some people refuse to negotiate because they believe that, some businesses are not open to negotiation, this might be in fact true, but some small-scale businesses are available to negotiate the price of goods. Also, buying in bulk and consistently from one seller attracts discounts and creates a more relaxed atmosphere to accommodate discounts.

- Be informed: knowledge in financial freedom is power. To reach and sustain a stage of financial independence, it is essential to keep yourself updated about economic laws, rules and regulations as they apply to you. Ensure that you are updated on the changes and improvement in tax laws and the investment and interest options; this would help ensure that your investment is not at a loss, and you profit at full capacity based on whatever option you choose to be reasonable and valuable to your desires. Also, it is an essential defence to avoid people who would like to delude an investor from making crucial investment options or cheat you from making the necessary profit. However, to prevent this, it is advisable to employ the services of an advisor.

- Do Not Spend More Than You Earn: This is of critical importance in every financial step or journey; it is also of vital importance to the course of financial freedom. Although the idea of financial freedom is to afford whatever lifestyle you desire without the fear of the impact it would make on your finance. It is also of notable importance to highlight "live below your means." An individual who is in a constant hurry to spend the funds or income that should be contributed to the savings of the financial freedom would find himself in a never-ending journey. This does not mean that you should cut down or limit your spending or cancel spending at all, it merely projects the idea that an individual who is interested in financial freedom has to be able to distinguish between wants and needs. These needs have to be prioritised accordingly.

- Hire a Financial Advisor: In the preceding conclusions, it has been suggested that a financial advisor is needed; before and after the attainment of financial freedom. In cases, once individuals see that they have amassed so much wealth, they either invest or spend it wrongly, hence, the need to employ the services of an advisor. A financial advisor would help manage the wealth or funds that have been accumulated. An advisor could also be of help in ensuring that you subscribe to the right investment option and funds to minimise risks. Correspondingly, they help in determining a plan that would stabilise your freedom and also reasonable withdrawal plans for your situation.

Importance of Financial Freedom

It is the case that some people are not concerned about financial freedom, they are satisfied with the lifestyle of dependence on salaries and working for corporations because of their financial state, they are not concerned with the profits and interest from investing. However, apart from the benefits and advantages of financial independence, it also gives you the plan to schedule your day or time according to your desire. Your life is fixed with things that sincerely interest you. Therefore, you have the freedom of choice to select any of the following options;

There is no compulsion to work with or for a company, a financially free person has enough funds to identify a hobby as a job daily even though it might not provide as much as an actual job. The liberty to work based on the fact that you enjoy something rather than the necessity to fund your lifestyle.

It puts you in a relaxed and settled position or situation to do whatever you want. For instance, a financially free person who does not work for a company has the liberty and the funds to travel anywhere at any time without any impact on his status. However, someone else would have to apply for a break at the cooperation to attend to this. You have the liberty to plan your schedule and work at any time you desire. Financial Freedom does not only include being able to support your desired lifestyle. It also entails being able to assist and fund those who need this help.

Conclusively, the difference between Tom and Guy is that Guy has been able to identify with financial freedom to satisfy his needs while Tom is yet to recognise the steps and importance of this ideology.

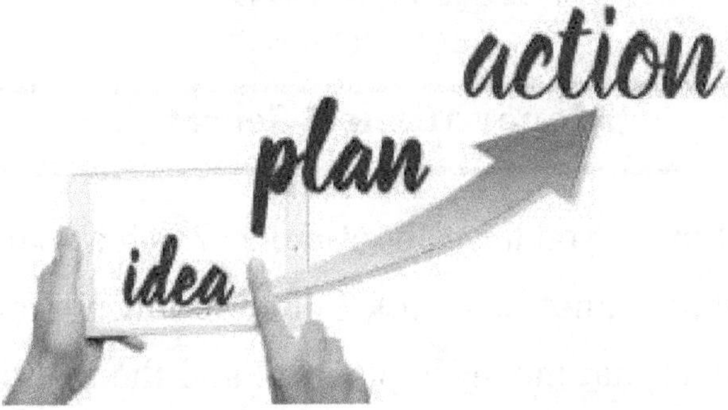
action
plan
idea

CHAPTER TWO

Money Mindset Secret

What conviction do you have about money? Is it a sparse idea or commodity that cannot be attained after so much effort? Or are you of the belief that money is plentiful and the reality of being wealthy is a fact that is possible? Well, the opinion that you have, or support is referred to as a money mindset. It is merely your way of thinking or view when it comes to issues about money, funds, wealth and finance. It is of crucial importance in locking into financial freedom. A lot of people are not aware that they have a role in deciding what manifests in their life based on their thoughts and opinion, your money mindset goes a long way in determining the position of wealth you find yourself. This particular factor can be traced back to the connection between the law of attraction and the law of manifestation. These laws are the primary tools that come to play in issues concerning your money mindset and reality. The law of manifestation states that you attract the reality that you desire for yourself. The events that manifest in your life are attracted to the opinions you embody concerning a particular subject matter. Therefore, if you think that there is a scarcity of wealth and it cannot be acquired no matter the amount of hard work and skilfulness put into it, you might find your finance stagnant and in a position of destitute. It is essential to believe that money is obtainable for it to be the reality or manifestation in your life.

Therefore, the concept of money mindset refers to your belief and opinion about the circulation and existence of money or wealth in the world and your community. However, your money mindset is not shaped by the salary or allowances that you receive, and it is formed based on opinions that you have read, seen and experienced over the years. Sometimes, you unknowingly develop a money mindset without knowledge that it exists. Money mindset is an essential determining factor in attaining the status of financial freedom, your chosen position or mindset also determines your stand or orientation in issues concerning finance and economic changes; it reflects in your discussion and attitude towards others when a question about money is brought up. However, two underlying mindsets control the wealth or finance of every individual, and they are the abundance mindset and the scarcity mindset.

The abundance mindset refers to a state of belief or understanding that wealth and money can be acquired; that is, attaining money is a reasonable and possible idea that is not as distant or as far-fetched as many people believe. The abundance mindset puts people who identify with it in an available position to identify with financial freedom; the laws of attraction and manifestation are at an advantage in their lifestyle and finance. The people with the scarcity mindset, on the other hand, believe strictly in the thought that money is sparse, and attainment of money or wealth depends on a vigorous search which you cannot ascertain that money would be acquired after such search. In most cases, they find themselves working hard and with an urge or the constant need to acquire wealth but making little or less money compared to those with the abundance mindset. It is important to note that a particular mindset is not dependant on the money you currently have but on a series of event and the conclusion you have unconsciously or unconsciously drawn; this is the reason for the possibility that some millionaires or head of offices are encompassed with the scarcity mindset. It could be as a result of various events, and it affects their investments negatively because of the fear it instils about risks. However, this does not mean that once an individual has identified with a particular mindset, he would solely depend on it for life. The remedies are some of the issues discussed in this chapter.

The important question at this point is how your money mindset is chosen or decided? The mindset you seem to identify or select is as a result of various factors. An individual might want to identify with either the abundance or scarcity mindset as a result of some situations or ideas highlighted in the combination of your personal choices, sometimes your unconscious thoughts or feelings made this choice a long time ago before you become aware of the existence of a money mindset. It is sometimes caused by the financial circumstances or situation an individual grew up with, a person whose parents or family were in constant disarray because of limited funds or unstable finance would probably identify with the scarcity mindset, to such person, attaining funds will always be a struggle rather than a pleasurable act.

Also, the economic or the financial state of the general public during an individual's growth is a factor in determining one's mindset. For instance, if Tom's community or country was in recession during his formation years, he believes and absorbs the ideology that there is little or not enough money to benefit the entire population. The money mindset is majorly determined during the childhood or growing stage because most opinions and ideologies are formed during these years.

The Effects of Your Mindset on Money

Sometimes people find themselves in favourable situations where money is always available to support every need and desire that arises. However, most people do not belong to this particular category. Whether an individual acknowledges it or not, the amount or percentage of money that you make or that you have in your account is as a result of the mindset you have subscribed. Therefore, it is essential to understand the importance and the effect of the money mindset so that it could be changed if it is identified as the factor of detriment on your road to financial freedom, and if this is not the case, it is essential to continue the abundance money mindset to attain and sustain a financially free state.

What are the effects of money mindset on your current financial state?

- It helps nurture financial freedom: a good (abundance) money mindset helps to attain the position of economic freedom and independence. Beyond achieving financial freedom is sustaining it and growing in a financially free state. This mindset helps to ensure that there is a manifestation of wealth and growth in your reality rather than the scarcity mindset, which would limit the wealth and funds received.

- It limits financial growth: the scarcity mindset is a massive barrier for growth. A person with a scarcity mindset does not necessarily have to be without funds, he could be wealthy to some extent, but he does not have any desire or curiosity to become aware of what exists beyond his current financial state. Therefore, a scarcity mindset could make individual comfortable in a position where he should ordinarily want to change or move beyond, as change is expected to be the only constant procedure in every individual.

- It determines your approach to money-related issues: A determinant in the way you talk, spend, live, and opinions you give in every situation about finance or any other subject matter is based on your mindset. As stated earlier, a person with a scarcity mindset would identify no reason or importance in making more funds or profit. However, an abundantly conscious person tends to identify the most valuable positions and ideas in a room so that he could invest and promote such a financial situation.

- It affects your business dealings: take, for instance, a situation where you would like to meet an investor to invest in your business or cooperation but your scarcity mindset that does not have total confidence in the idea that you are presenting. Most individuals find confidence attractive, and no one would like to invest funds in a business that the CEO feels has an indifferent feeling concerning. Therefore, it is not enough to stand between the scarcity and abundance mindset, to be financially free; an individual must choose abundance and be most confident in his choice.

- A scarcity mindset might be interfering with your goals and limiting your potential. Due to your constant fear of loss or "not having enough", many profitable business deals are not considered because an individual with a scarcity mindset is never ready to take risks. They are unaware of the fact that every investment growth or profit is made based on the ability to take chances on reasonable or potential business deals.

- An abundance mindset gives you an edge: it allows you to see and identify opportunities in situations or cases where others believe there is only limited profit. It gives you foresight because of the belief that benefit would be made in whatever situation or account that you invest. Therefore, you are more open compared to others with the scarcity mindset when it comes to investing in new ideas or businesses.

Your money mindset determines a lot of factors in your life; it determines your association, the places and events you attend, your response to issues and every other aspect of life

Steps to Attaining the Abundance Mindset.

You do not have to live in a loss for the rest of your life if you have been a victim of the scarcity mindset for some time. A scarcity mindset can be clarified when your lifestyle and expenses are based on your paycheck and amount of salary or income you get. With such a mindset, you might never have the ability or fierceness to participate in whatever interests because of the fear that you do not or will never have enough.

However, the abundance mindset is filled with various advantageous options and opportunities, and it considers every profit or advantage that could be acquired from investment deals which have been ignored or avoided by individuals with a scarcity mindset. A person with an abundance mindset would never consider the possibility that a business or investment might not be successful at its start-up stage; they are optimists when it comes to issues, ideas and thoughts that concern money. There are some necessary steps to shift from the position of scarcity to abundance to ensure financial freedom; identify your current mindset: to grow or move on from a particular mindset, it is important to own up to and acknowledge one's current stage of belief to proceed further. You have to be self-aware and conscious of this change or development, to ensure that you are mindful of the shift from scarcity to abundance.

- Research: If you are reading this, you have taken the first and most important step in shifting to the abundance mindset. It is essential to identify what kind of mindset you identify with by reading books and carrying out research on different money mindsets.

- Focus on benefits not losses: although most mindsets are formed during childhood or the teenage years, in some cases, it is formed during adulthood when you have a job. It is even possible that you grew with an abundance mindset, but due to some losses during your adult stage, there was a loss that sabotaged your entire belief of abundance. How then do you move forth from this? To grow beyond the scarcity mindset, it is of importance to identify the factor that established it in the first instance and move beyond this affair or circumstance. Therefore, it is important to focus on the profits that can be made when the loss has been forgone. Let go of every mistake that has been made in your finances to establish to release negativity and harbour positive energy.

- Budget: in every stage and decision towards attaining financial freedom, it is crucial to identify a direction or budget for the money made. A budget is a laid-out plan of funds that is spent on every aspect of an individual's life. How then does a budget contribute to the abundance mindset? It is essential to understand that saving or working for money without a significant plan can be aggravating when you believe you do not have any use for the wealth garnered. A budget is like a motivator that would give you a definite reason to identify with abundance. From the standpoint of a marketer, if he does not have a particular task or purpose of attaining money, he would feel indifferent about his financial situation, which resembles the scarcity mindset.

- Associate yourself with people of a similar mindset: in most cases, individual energy or esteem is drawn from those he surrounds or associates himself with; it is essential to associate yourself with people that identify with the abundance mindset to be of abundance. For development in every stage of life or a particular aspect, it is vital to consort people who have gotten this position right, to learn the appropriate procedures; fraternise with the right kind of people. In this case, it entails associating with other people who can be pinpointed to have the abundance mindset or similar values that you would like to assimilate.

- Reaffirm yourself: it is essential to have motivations or goals that would affirm the advantages and needfulness of the abundance mindset.

- Take note of your finances: it is important to have a ritual of examining the income and spending of your account, this would assist in sustaining your financial mindset; every individual grows based on the fact that whatever they have invested in has made some percentage of income.

- Avoid complaining: most individuals find themselves complaining about the circulation of money; this only contributes and hardens the scarcity mindset. Therefore, you have to avoid all negative positions and thoughts to ensure that there is no contributing factor to a scarcity mindset. As this is mindfully done, it establishes growth for an abundance mindset. Create a ritual to show gratitude to yourself, appreciate whatever stage of growth you have been able to attain.

To achieve financial freedom, it essential that this necessary change or step is carried out as it determines the profit and investment choices that an individual would be able to make. Disregard the opinion that some people are born with the abundance mindset; hence, their success and growth in finance; take note that your thoughts and ideas about money are something you can manage. You should be in charge of your money mindset rather than taking the principal role in your lifestyle.

CHAPTER THREE

Passive Income

Every individual has that one friend who is not interested in going through the stress of taking a job that would require a strict work ethic; you might not even have a friend as you are that person to someone else. Every person reaches that stage in life where no ideas or job are of possible interest to them, the only task they seem to enjoy or consider enjoyable are those that require little or no effort from them. In the technological era that the world has evolved into, most people are interested in the strenuous jobs that require total dedication and adherence to schedules or rules that do not fit their desires.

What is Passive Income?

Passive income refers to the money or salary gotten from a task or "job" you are not actively involved. Unlike any other job or income gotten, the passive income does not require a significant level of effort to attain or sustain the situation. As far as there is a passive income, there would surely be an active income, which differentiates these categories of income. The active income involves and requests active use of time and effort to generate income while the former does not. However, there is an advanced level of passive income which is referred to as the progressive income; it relates to income sustained by enforcing little or minimal effort into performing required tasks. Then, what advantage is gotten from passive income? The most obvious advantage and benefit of passive income is the fact that it exerts little or no energy from its participants; you are getting paid for doing activities and tasks that do not require your physical participation. However, some passive income tasks might be a bit demanding at its initial stage, but it becomes easy after. The basic principle of this idea is to earn while you do nothing. An example of this is rental property income. The second benefit is the tax option available under this decision; some taxing institutions distinguish between the different types of income and tax them appropriately, not generally.

In this objective, there are three main categories of income as recognised by the Internal Revenue Service (IRS), they are passive income, active income and portfolio income. According to the IRS, the passive income is gotten from three categories, which are trade, rental and passive activities which you do not significantly participate. The primary streams to generate passive income are through investment, real estate, trading, and blogging. Individuals who subscribe to this are usually huge supporters on self-employment rather than formal jobs. The subject of self-employment is the significant connection it has to financial freedom.

How Can Passive Income Be Generated?

If you have suddenly quit your job or you've been fired and plan to depend on your savings, it is only a matter of time before this savings finish. Even if you do not belong to any of these categories, but you desire to earn more than your salary, a passive income is an important aspect to be considered. You do not have to be necessarily jobless to make money passively; it could be regarded as a side hustle to enhance your financial status when added to your basic pay. The following are some of the ways passive income can be generated;

Although people project the passive income as profit acquired "while you sleep", this is a false representation of the entire idea of passive income. This particular community or set of people fail to identify or present the main constitute of passive marketing which involves the fact that you must have put in a specific percentage of work at the initial stage of the project. Either time or money has been greatly invested to finally put you in the position where you can earn "while you sleep." This mentality misleads people into delving into passive income without any necessary training or investment in their knowledge of the subject matter. Therefore, a lot of work has to be generated into the start-up to ensure a properly managed income.

Passive income entails contribution, without this, where is profit gotten? To ensure that you would consistently enjoy a healthy profit from financial income. It is important to note that that you would have to invest something in the idea that would generate this income. It could be time or money, depending on the business you decide to invest. Take, for instance, investment in dividend stocks; investment in dividend stocks exists in companies that pay a particular percentage of their profit to their shareholders or investors. To qualify for an idea like this, you must have invested a large amount of money in becoming a shareholder in that company. Also, an investment in real estate would require a substantial investment in funds and time in finding a property that would produce a large percentage of income. Therefore, profit is gotten from the rental of these properties.

Therefore, to generate a particular percentage of income through passive income, it is essential to understand that no money is earned fully. Although this might some seem to be the case since you have that friend that does nothing but looks to make a lot, you have to understand that some principles and effort has been laid down at a point in his passive income career for him to identify with this position.

Steps to Attaining Passive Income

Due to the discussion in previous pages, you have become familiar with some of the importance and measures to attaining a stable passive income. However, it is necessary to state these steps in clear and precise terms to ensure that every participant establishes a well-thought passive income that would provide him consistent profit in the long-term. It is possible to invest into passive income at a loss after the investment of time and money, to avoid this, it is vital to highlight and define the reasonable steps to be taken by anyone interested in passive income as an actual job or a side job.

- It is essential to have an idea: it is not strange to you at this point to learn that passive income provides you with a lot of options. However, it is crucial to research every opportunity and select the most suitable one. Interest is an essential factor in passive income; since you are expected to invest your time and money. If interest is absent at this point, you might become tired or weary while your profit takes time to grow. Therefore, in choosing your idea, you have to consider several factors that apply to your particular situation and the money you have in hand. If you have a significant capital to invest, real estate or dividend stock investment is a desirable option for you. Although you may not get the profit and interest at the exact time of contribution, the profit you would make after you have given the investment time to grow is incomparable to that contribution. Some of the ideas that can be considered by any participant are;

o Selling information: the technological stage that the world has reached has made the sale of products that contain specific information possible. Most people have become curios, highly to learn things; hence, the massive production in the information provided products, for example, e-books and audiobooks. Once the set-up process or effort to write a book has been covered, it is left to the participants to earn money while products are sold. However, to gain from this, you have to ensure that your products are not mediocre as there is a lot of competition in this aspect.

o Rental: although this idea might seem traditional to some people, real estate investment and ownership of property is an excellent way to make passive income. It does not exert as much effort as the above idea, but it requires understanding in the process and technique of real estate to avoid the loss of capital that has been invested. An individual who is familiar with the components and requirements of passive income through real estate investment can establish this idea as a reasonable and actionable source of income after retirement. According to John Graves who is an Accredited Investment Fiduciary, there are three requirements that must be satisfied to ensure the stability of passive income; you must be able to determine the profit you expect from the contribution made to the investment, you must have an idea of the total cost of the property and the expense required and also the financial risks that accompany owning the property as this factors would prepare you for every situation.

o Affiliate marketing: this might not produce as much profit as the already stated ideas, but it is a way of earning without inputting so much effort. What is affiliate marketing? It is a marketing technique whereby bloggers or marketers promote the products of a third party by posting the links to such products. How does this technique make money for you? If an affiliate link is posted on your site and a consumer clicks on the link, at this moment, purchasing products from the third party, you are entitled to a commission from the third party. The percentage gotten solely depends on the number of products that are purchased. However, success in passive income through affiliate marketing might take some effort because you would need to develop an audience for your site and create a stable percentage with consistent and reasonable content.

o Lending: Peer-to-peer lending involves lending money to people through a registered third party. The profit made from this idea is on the interest paid by the party that has been lent money.

- o Dividend stocks, High-interest savings account, Rent out an extra room or car, Display Ads
- Create a goal board: this is more of personal use to you than the business. It is not going to be easy to participate in passive income. However, it is essential to note the idea where you would like to invest, the profit rates of that idea, the percentage of contribution you would like to make and the profit expected at the time of return. It is essential to set these goals as it helps to motivate you during the time of discouragement; hence, it is most important to set your goals on paper. Studies have shown that goals written out by individuals become more actionable and reasonable to them than the ones that exist in their minds. Therefore, write out your goals and expound as much as you can on paper as this would assist in your investment.
- Plan your decisions and steps: after an idea and goal, the next step is to plan your choices and decisions to achieve these goals. Note, the decisions and necessary options that you will need to consider getting from one position in your goal plan to the next. Making plans for your goals at every single point would make them more realistic and actionable to you and everyone who might consider assisting you. Therefore, it is important not to set goals

arbitrarily and to understand what would be required from you to get to your desired stage of earning passively.

- Create an alternative plan: there are different situations; passive income could be some people's backup while some depend solely on passive income. To attain financial freedom, you cannot be dependent on only one source of income. Innovation is key. You have to invest and create other plans while you set actionable goals to reach a stable stage of passive income, the reason for this is that some passive income ideas are not usually successful all the time despite the time and money invested in it. It is merely the nature of the business, and this is the reason for the importance of knowledge and research on whatever topic you decide to invest. Therefore, if you plan to invest in dividend stock or start a blog, these ideas do not require you to quit your day job and depend solely on them. Instead, it is advisable not to be dependent on these businesses to have a reckless financial situation.

- Connect with successful people in that area: the importance of networking cannot be overemphasised. If you desire to become successful in a particular field, an essential idea or option is to investigate or research on those who have made significant income from such an approach. Apart from reading about them, it is important to connect and talk to these people to create an understanding of the requirements and the expectations you should have about a particular system. In every step of your relationship with them, it is important always to find the things they are doing that you are yet to integrate into your business ideas and goals. Inquire about their ideas and strategies and implement it as it may apply to your passive income situation.

Benefits of Passive Income

It quickens your financial freedom status by adding an extra stream of income to double the percentage of the contribution made to your savings. It helps to widen or eliminate the limit that has been put in place to control or restrict a particular budget plan. This also helps to actualise the reasonability behind the concept of a money mindset, as you are more conscious and have faith in plans or ideas when there are ideas placed in motion to project the basic principle.

Participants have an option to retire early, quit their job to participate in something they are genuinely interested. Some individuals are unable to apply to or participate in situations that they desire because those jobs might not earn them much, and their regular job is time-consuming. The passive income job allows them to participate in their desired position and make more than or close to the percentage gotten from active jobs.

It is an advantageous technique set in place for a situation where an individual suddenly loses his job. Many cooperation and businesses have to urgently let some workers go before the end of their contract due to various reasons. Many of these workers are in disarray at the loss of their jobs. This does not have to be the situation as you are not primarily affected in the time that exists during the loss of employment and the acquisition of another.

It creates an alternative plan for funds or income after retirement. Many workers are dependent on their Thrift Savings Plans and 401(k)s without considering the possibility that an emergency which could clear out these savings could arise. A retired individual interested in passive income, mainly, rental activities could rely or depend on the salary gotten from this source.

However, an individual who plans to contribute to this must have the virtue of patience. Every option available to generate passive income requires patience as a person cannot get wealthy or financially free from this income overnight. Therefore, an individual who is willing to remain patient overtime can be successful and attain financial freedom through any of the option offered by passive income.

It allows personal growth, a daily or permanent routine at a particular job can become repetitive, unnecessary and limiting. Passive income provides you with an option to add a new business idea that aids your financial and intellectual growth. Apart from this, it gives a lot of spare time to participate in activities that genuinely interest you at whatever desired time.

Not every individual appreciates his current job, and not all would attain financial freedom from their current jobs. Therefore, to hasten your attainment of the financial freedom status, it is essential to indulge the passive income ideas.

CHAPTER FOUR

Dividend Investing

Any individual who seeks to earn through passive income has to understand and appreciate the importance and strategy that involves dividend stock investment. One of the characteristics of financial freedom highlighted in previous chapters is the fact that you might not have to work with or for anybody to identify with the financially free status. Dividend stocks investing is one of the most profound ways to attain financial freedom and passive income. It offers a chance to earn a massive percentage of income apart from the regular gotten from your daily job. It involves getting profit from the value of the market you invested by buying shares.

What is Dividend Investing?

Dividend investing is an investment or passive income option that offers company or business shareholders a percentage of income or profit based on the investment made towards that particular business. Usually, the distribution of profit to shareholders can be paid in cash or into a reinvestment plan, and this could also be paid by increasing or handing out more shares to the individual instead of a cash payment made to the bank. Through dividend payments, a company or business dedicates a percentage of its profit to shareholders, and the other portion is devoted to the growth of the market to ensure a stable cycle of profit. There is no compulsion to pay dividends to shareholders or stockholders, it is merely the choice of the management to fund the benefit of their share through two primary options; with cash by depositing it to their account or the opportunity to reinvest it in the company's shares. However, there is no general rule to decide when dividends should be paid; this is determined based on the requirement and situation of each cooperation. In dividend investing, it is essential to be careful about the time you choose to invest and be critical of the cooperation or business you decide to invest; this is of notable warning especially to high-income investors. Every individual who decides to contribute or participate in dividend investing has to ensure that the company of interest is in a stable financial state, that is, there is an increase in stock rate, high production of reliable product or services and there is potential for growth in the products, company and management of such business. The opinion of dividends presented by each individual is subjective to their experience; dividends are good or bad depending on your investment strategy or approach. For profit to be paid to shareholders on the company's level, the management team agrees on a percentage of profit or gain that should be given or paid to the investors and that which should be reinvested in the company's stock, however, this decision by the management is merely a suggestion as it requires confirmation from the board of directors. After this procedure, the company is expected to announce the dividend rate, and payment is made to the shareholders.

It is important to note that dividend investing is meant for people of various groups, although some people might argue that dividend investing applies only to or it is only suitable for retirees, this is not the truth about this investment option.

Types of Dividends

In regular investing, the investor is not entitled to a percentage of profit; however, in dividend investing, the investor or shareholder is expected to be paid a particular interest of the capital invested. Furthermore, this payment is not restricted to a specific model; it does not have to be only cash payment. A company is allowed to pay an investor with cash, assets or an option to reinvest. The model of payment is left to the investor to choose, or not if the mode of payment or profit was clearly defined in the stock quote. Companies or businesses are allowed to make payment to their investors through any of the options discussed below:

- Payment by cash: The most known payment of dividends is by cash. These companies or businesses pay the profit of the investor's interest or dividends with money. The payment by cash mode entails the transfer and payment of cash or funds from the company's account to the investor's account; this does not confirm the idea that money can only be paid to the investor through a wired transfer. In some cases, the profit of the stock or investment is paid in cash.

- Payment by stock: stock refers to the total money or income that a company has gathered from shares bought by investors or shareholders. How then do you pay shareholders profit with stock? This particular payment is made by reinvesting their profit to purchase more shares in the company. It is mostly done in companies that offer the option of a Dividend Reinvestment Plan (DRIP) to investors. So, instead of converting their profit into cash and making transfers to their account, their benefit is further invested in purchasing more shares and increasing the profit that they would eventually get from their original investment.

- Payment by assets: In some instances, shareholders might not be interested in gaining cash or more shares as profit, especially in the case of companies that have a decline in their overall profit. They might not even have the ability to pay in cash due to this reason. Hence, the availability of payment by assets, no company is restricted to cash and shares payment alone. A company may pay with assets like real estate and investment securities.

- In some very uncommon situations, a company might decide to pay a "special" dividend. The special dividend is the kind of profit paid outside your regular contract of payment (regular contract of payment could refer to annual or quarterly payments.) The "special" amount is usually as a result of an extra boost in the total profit made by the company or business.

- There are other modes of the payment depending on the company invested in; an investor can be paid with shares a new company established by the original company invested.

Steps to Investing in Dividend Stocks

How do you ensure that you have gone through the right process to invest? What impact does dividend investing have on your financial status? What is the connection between financial freedom and dividend investing? These are some of the issues discussed in this section.

- Research: in every area of finance, research is vital to ensure that an individual is investing in a goal; profit, not a loss. To ensure that you invest in a reliable cooperation that pays a profit of shares to shareholders, it is essential to identify a company with high-quality products and a large company with financial stability. These sorts of companies are with the highest probability of paying dividends as they already have a stable financial status and capital to handle problems in the economy that might affect the profit, progress and finance of the entire company. They have enough experience to understand the right procedure and techniques that should be put in place. Also, the large accomplished companies are the best to invest in because they are aware of and practice other modes of maximising the shareholder's wealth. For instance, companies in the pharmaceutical's sector, oil and gas and banks are known to have stable dividend-paying platforms as people are always interested and in need of healthcare products and financial services. The best position to start your research is to create a list or identify the company or cooperation that appear or have been reported to have a stable financial status. After this, it is advisable to highlight the cooperation that you are interested in buying stocks. Also, ensure that you have enough funds to invest in such company to become a shareholder because a large part of being a shareholder is investing funds that help to build or support the financial state of a company or cooperation.

- Study the stock quote: the stock quote is the summary of the information of a company an individual should be aware of before investing. Therefore, if you are unsure about the stand of a company on the payment of dividends or to learn about the options available for dividend payments, the stock quotes should be considered to familiarise yourself with the policies of dividends payments of each company.

- Purchase the stock: once you have successfully carried out research and identified the company or business, you would like to invest. The next reasonable step is to purchase the shares of stock. This can be done personally by you to the company or through a broker. A broker is a mediator or an intermediary between a buyer and seller; therefore, a broker, in this case, acts a middle man between you and the management of the company you choose. However, not all companies offer the option to buy stocks directly through the company; some necessitate the requirement of purchase through a brokerage company or institution. Some businesses even require that a minimum investment between

$25 to $500 is made if an individual desire or insists on buying stock directly through the company.   To avoid this, an individual would have to register with a brokerage institution, or if it is the case that the company does not offer the option to purchase stock directly, the individual would still have to register. Some brokerage institutions or firms are Ally Investment. eTrade and TD Ameritrade.

- Subscribe to DRIP (Dividend Reinvestment Plan): in dividend investing, you have two options to attaining your profit; a cash payment into your bank account or reinvestment. To ensure the sustenance of financial freedom and independence, it is important to be a participant or to be registered under DRIP. This plan is an automatic investment plan that ensures that profit that could have been converted into cash and sent to your account is reinvested into more shares. It is most advisable to enrol in DRIP to ensure that an individual's finance grows with the companies. To subscribe to this reinvestment option, an individual has to contact their broker if registered by one.

- Keep tabs on your dividends: companies are not entitled to pay shareholders. It is a choice rather than a requirement. The implication of this is that companies or businesses can choose to eliminate, increase or reduce their dividends at any given time. Therefore, when you are always aware of the changes and progress made to your dividends by tracking your brokerage account, you can conclude if the percentage of profits has fallen below standard and decide the ideal time to sell your stock or shares.

Benefits Of Dividend Investing

After the necessary procedures of dividend investing has been complied with, it is important to ensure that an individual adopts a reasonable strategy in ensuring the growth of the stock. It is essential to diversify investment across different sectors or companies if it can be afforded. This is to ensure that the investment of an individual is not dependent on only one industry creating a crash or accident if there are any financial fluctuations to the company or that particular sector of the company. In the same vein, it is advisable to invest in companies or businesses across the world to avoid dependence on one specific government. Therefore, you can make a profit from different companies and avoid reliance on a particular government. There are various advantages to investing in the dividend investment option;

- It serves as a steady means of passive income: as established in the previous chapter of this book, passive income is significant to your financial status in life. It is necessary to have a side-job that provides a passive income in attaining financial freedom in some cases. In this situation, dividend investing is a beneficial kind of way to achieve passive income. This particular type involves a substantial investment of money to become a shareholder and you are entitled to income or profit as far as you remain a shareholder. This specific example of earning passive income is particularly attractive to retirees or people close to the retirement stage; it ensures that the retired does not have a significant a particular role in the company and they do not have to exert so much energy in attaining their income.

- Retainment of ownership: In some situations, an investment can be frustrating, primarily when you have invested in a company that does not pay dividends because all your profit is tied to stock. Therefore, the only way to access this profit is to sell your shares, as a result of this, forfeiting your percentage of ownership of shares of the company. This is not the case in investment in dividend stocks. Investment in dividend stocks gives the option to retain your percentage of ownership of shares as a shareholder while you attain the profit of the shares owned.

- Substantial profit: there is a higher level or percentage of gain available in dividend investment, unlike other types of investments. For instance, when you purchase a particular portion in shares of a company that does not pay shareholders profit, you that exact number of shares. However, in dividend investing, you are a given the option to either reinvest the profit of your shares to buy more or for it to be deposited into your account. There is no requirement that you withdraw funds from your account to buy more shares when you can easily reinvest profit from your current stocks to purchase more.

Payment of dividends seems to be a loss on the part of the company or business paying the profit of shares to investors. Therefore, why do these companies indulge the option of dividends when its not a compulsion or an issue of legality for them? No reason can be generally applied to all companies to be regarded as their reason for this. However, every company has a right peculiar to its situation.

Dividends help to sustain trust, although the companies do not have to pay for the profit of shares. They decide to do this to honour the expectations and desire of the investor. A company that pays robust and consistent dividends is more likely to attract a more substantial capacity of investors willing to invest than one that does not honour the desire of the public. The payment of dividends to investors portrays a positive financial image and status of the company. Dividends help to attract investors or shareholders. A starting company that can secure a substantial percentage of quality products which does not have enough capital or investors in assisting its establishment can declare a level of dividend. This declaration helps to attract potential investors into examining the profits that could be gained by them if they choose to invest in a particular business or company. The interest of potential investors can assist in growing the stock value of such company. Therefore, the companies, in most cases, need the help of the investors to grow their businesses, and these investors need the companies to increase their funds or money by offering them the opportunity to invest in their shares. Also, dividends help to reduce the impact of a financial fluctuation or disability of the stock market on the investors, as a result of this reducing the risk of loss.

How does Dividend Investing Secure Financial Freedom?

The main idea of this book is to help individuals ensure a financially free state. So, having discussed and understood the discipline of dividend investing, how does this particular feature contribute to the attainment of financial freedom?

Dividends investing helps to grow and expand financial status. The extra income gotten from the profit of income invested by shareholders helps to establish an expansion of profits. When you subscribe to dividend investing, it helps to build an independent financial state due to substantial growth in profit or interest over time. Also, unlike stock that does not have a stable financial state in most situations and they do not guarantee a profit, the dividend stocks offer a partial profit on the capital invested.

Conclusively, apart from the idea of rental estates highlighted in the previous chapter, dividend investing is another stable way to achieve financial freedom and independence. It is most reliable because it gives participants an option to sell their shares if the dividend of a particular company reduces or if it loses sustainable profit in the investor's opinion.

CHAPTER FIVE

Stock Investments

At this point, you have become familiar with the topic of stock. However, if you have skipped the definition of stock in previous chapters, this is another opportunity to familiarize yourself with the issue of stock. Unlike the previous chapters, the topic, benefits, steps and strategy of stock investment to benefit a stable and significant profit would be discussed.

What Is Stock Investing?

Stock refers to the percentage of shares allocated to a particular individual who has invested a significant portion of money in becoming a shareholder or investor of a specific company. These investors purchase stocks or shares in a company that they believe would contribute to their financial status with an increase in the value of their product and stock. A stock is a sort of investment in the ownership of a company; giving you a percentage of the ownership rights of a company. In simple words for more understanding, stock investing is purchasing shares or a portion of a company to sustain a financial status or receive a substantial amount of profit in the case of companies that allocate dividends. Apart from an increase in the economic situation of the investor, what do companies gain from investment in stocks? Why would any company want to share their right of ownership with an individual by allowing them to invest in their business or company? There are a lot of factors attributed to this. However, the most suitable answer is their need to multiply profit of products and to raise capital for the establishment of their business or company and also ensure a constant level of funds to operate their venture. Any individual who owns a particular percentage of shares is referred to as an investor or shareholder, an individual who holds this position is entitled to a substantial share of the profits made from the products of such company. Take, for instance, an individual who purchases about 200 shares of a company which has 1000 shares in total, that person holds claim to the ownership of 20% of such company's profit. Therefore, a shareholder or investor cannot be regarded to be the sole owner of a company; they only own a percentage of the company that their shares covers. How then are the shares to be sold accessed? Companies of the public broadcast the message of their desire to sell through the stock markets and this sale is further confirmed on such platforms applied to, an example of a stock market platform is the New York Stock Exchange. Through, this chapter, there would be an elaboration of things that should be understood and considered as basics for anyone interested in stock investment. It is essential to understand the basics of stock investing as it would serve as a guide to assist in ensuring the success of an individual's experience in the stock exchange. As the general issue in finance, nothing is permanent, and there are constant fluctuation and decrease in any issue that may concern stock investment; hence, the importance of the basic principles of stock investment discussed through this chapter. They are dedicated to ensuring that you are equipped with the right ideas and opinions that would assist in managing any issue or subject of stock investment. Among the many principles presented in this chapter is the need to ensure your investment is well-spread. No rule restricts you or constrains you to a particular company for investment. Therefore, the increase and development of the number of companies invested in cushioning the effects and failures on your finance. For instance, if A invested all his money in company Z, and B invested all his money in company Y and some other companies, sharing the funds invested. B would not be as affected as A who has focused all his funds on a particular company, causing a breakdown if there is a decrease in the profit made by Company Z or if such a company becomes bankrupt. Having stated the importance and the need to invest in stocks, how then do you make money from stock investments?

How to Invest In Stocks

Although many individuals claim to be wildly interested in the topic of stock investment. They are not able to act upon these desires because they lack the knowledge to make necessary procedures to make these desires a reality; the desire being 'stock investing.' Therefore, it is important to highlight and define the right steps to ensure you are in alignment with the proper procedures to stock investing.

Identify your mode of purchase, in stock investing; you have the option to either purchase your shares or stocks through the company/brokerage or as an individual. Each of these options has unique features and opportunity; therefore, you would have to identify the option best suitable for your condition. Every company does not offer individual purchase; however, the companies that do offer it in some cases might insist on a minimum investment between $25 to $100. Therefore, it is advisable to register with a brokerage company; open a brokerage account. The process of opening a brokerage can be compared to the simplicity of opening a statement with the bank. The percentage charged on your profit or value by the brokerage company is not fixed, hence the importance to consider every option possible.

Basic Principles in Stock Investing

To ensure that your stock investment journey is a smooth sail towards financial freedom, it is essential to highlight and define some basic principles that guide the stock market. Also, you would be introduced to the dynamics of the stock market; its procedures and functions and how to manage some of the situations you might find yourself in as a stock market investor.

In stock investing, every shareholder needs to understand that they only own a percentage of the shares that make up the company, they do not have a right or entitlement to the assets that are held by the cooperation, company or firm. Therefore, you can not claim to own the totality of a company as an investor or shareholder. An investor or shareholder can not make decisions that may affect or concern the company by himself or subjectively. Therefore, a shareholder can not leave the company with confidential documents without the necessary authorization even with the claim or opinion to carry out an action that would benefit the company because the company owns the materials, not the shareholder; the document is in the company's name. This is known as the principle of separation of ownership and control.

Furthermore, the ownership of stocks in a particular company gives you the right and opportunity to vote on issues that concern the finance and welfare of the company during shareholder meetings. It gives you the right to receive a percentage of the company's profits; which are referred to as dividends if it is included to be a feature of the company in their stock quote. This principle also gives you the opportunity or liberty to sell personal shares at any time and to any individual of your choosing. The issue of not being able to make decisions for the company or cooperation is not regarded as a problem by most shareholders, as far as they are attributed to the right percentage of the company's profits. Therefore, if an investor desires an increased rate of profit compared to whatever is acquired, such an investor needs to increase the percentage of shares purchased in that company.

However, for individuals who own a higher percentage of stocks or shares than most people, they have a higher level of control and voting power in the company when compared to other shareholders who own less. The authority or power that your vote carries marginalizes based on the percentage of shares allocated to you. Also, for individuals who own a large portion of the company's stock, they are given the authority to choose individuals who make up the company's board of directors; this obligation is most evident in the case in which a company buys out another company. You do not buy only a percentage of shares in this situation; new management owns the entire company. Therefore, the new administration is given the liberty to choose a new league of the board of directors. The newly elected board is saddled with the responsibility of reelecting new executives or professionals that would ensure an increase in the value and profit of the cooperation. Managers and Chief Executive Officers (CEOs) are usually among the newly elected executives.

In stock investing, every individual is offered two significant types or options of stock to invest in; they are the common and preferred stock. Therefore, any intending investor has to choose the type of stock that would be invested. However, before this choice can be made, as it is one that should be made wisely and carefully, an individual has to understand the provisions of each type of stock. These divisions are subsequently discussed below:

- Common stock: generally, when the issue of stocks is being discussed, it usually refers to common stocks. This particular division of stock investing gives the investor or shareholder an entitlement or opportunity to vote on issues that concern the company during shareholders' meetings. Individuals who invested this kind of stocks are entitled to receive dividends of their investment if they have invested in a company which pays investors. Also, the investors in this category are entitled to elect the board of directors. However, in the hierarchy of priorities, and in the case whereby an unbalanced financial state of a company is present, the common stock investors are at the bottom. In the case of a liquidation, the common stock shareholders only have rights to the remaining assets or profits after the bondholders, or preferred stockholders have been issued their share of profit and assets, this particular principle of the common stock can be regarded as a risk on the investors

- Preferred stock: the division of preferred stock does not offer the entitlement to vote to individuals who have chosen to invest in this sort of stocks. However, these investors have an advantage in rights or claim to assets and profits of the company compared to the stockholders in the common stock category. They are allocated their dividends before any other group of shareholders and are given more priority than the common stockholders in a situation where the company becomes bankrupt. They have a supreme hold and right when it comes to the issuance of dividends. However, this particular set of people have limited powers when it comes to voting in a shareholders' meeting or in issues that may concern the welfare of the company. Their right to assets and profits of the company upon liquidation is second to the bondholders and higher than the common stockholders. However, a company is not regarded to be at default if it is unable to pay dividends to preferred stockholders as it is the case for bondholders. The purchase of preferred stock is usually made through the services of stockbrokers.

The significant difference between preferred and common shareholders is the mode of procedure that is adopted in the distribution of dividends in the case of a collapsed financial state or a company in distress. In the case of a liquidated company or a company in economic shambles, the preferred stockholders are paid the areas of their dividends before such payment can be made to the common stockholders.

Modes Of Attaining Profit In Stock

Stock investment has more investment risks than any other form of investment, hence, the necessity to familiarize you with the procedure and steps to ensure stock investment decisions and choices are carefully made to acquiring a suitable financial position, especially the status of financial freedom. After the entire process of investing, how then is money created? In what form is profit acquired from the money or time spent in the shares of a company? The earnings of shares invested by an investor are made though two primary forms; resale of stocks and dividends.

The resale of stocks: after a percentage of shares has been allocated to your name; for companies that do not pay dividends (dividends is the percentage of the earnings of your stocks that the management of the company chooses to pay to an investor.) It is not compulsorily held that you have ownership of that particular percentage of shares. If the company or business does not seem to appeal to you anymore, you could decide to sell your shares or stocks to another investor or an individual who has no connection or relation to the company in question. Therefore, the sale of stocks is a significant way to ensure that there is no loss of capital since you have the opportunity to sell your shares of a company in the case that you perceive a fluctuation in the finance or economy of the company.

The second reliable and significant form in which profit can be made is through dividends. Dividends refer to the payment or allowances received by shareholders based on their percentage of shares from the company or business they have a percentage of ownership. This should be regarded as regular payment of a shareholder or investor of any company, but this is not the case in every company. As an investor, you are not entitled to any percentage of dividends unless a cooperation decides to give it; therefore, not all businesses pay the profit on stocks. However, if you have invested in a company that does not pay dividends, you have the opportunity to reinvest your earnings if you do not intend to sell your shares. You can reinvest the profits acquired into the company that provided such an advantage in the first instance.

Therefore, the first option to make a profit from stock investment is much reliable as the individual controls the profit. In the case of dividends paid by companies or business, any management could decide at any point in time to put a stop to the payment of dividends if it does not suit their financial position at the time. Also, they can decide to increase or decrease the dividends paid; there is no fixed percentage of profits for companies that choose to pay.

Benefits of Attaining Stock Investments

Having explained the different steps and procedures that are put into a stock investment, you might still have concern or doubt of the benefits that this particular investment has to offer. However, investing in the stock market provides a variety of advantageous reasons and benefits. The following are some beneficial reasons for every individual to invest in the stock market:

- Diversification of funds: the stock markets provides a variety of categories or options for investors. Therefore, it allows the diversification of funds into different accounts or companies, allowing each individual to make different earnings based on the company and the percentage invested. Also, it helps to avoid total loss of funds, due to the diversification available in the general stock market, every individual is allowed to prevent a total loss of capital by investing in different accounts or companies that the stock market provides. Apart from the diversification of funds, it also offers the opportunity of diversification of assets. Some companies issue their investors or shareholders assets, identifying as an investor of such company would give you access to such assets and ensure that your assets are not based or focused on a particular subject matter and area.

- Easy access: A large number of individuals are more interested in ideas that can be easily accessed than those which prove difficult. The most accessible mode of access in this time is technology, stock markets and stocks can be approached and gotten through the internet, this is due to the technological innovations that have been put in place through the years. The access to stocks is readily made available with the intervention or help of the brokerage accounts or firms. The process needed is to identify a brokerage firm and input the information required from you. With details adequately attributed, you are ready to be a shareholder or investor of any company that needs your services.

- Option to invest in smaller accounts: some individuals are not interested in the investment of funds because they believe their funds would be at a loss. Stock market investing gives you the option to invest a small number of funds and not your total funds. This is done through the establishment of the Systematic Investment Plan (SIP).

- Inter-continental investment: it is essential to mention that stock investment is not restricted to a particular country. You are given the opportunity and option to invest in businesses and companies within and outside your country. The prospect of inter-continental investments is closely associated with the diversification benefit. Therefore, you make profits in funds or accounts that are different from the country inhabited by you. Also, it helps to attain assets in these countries.

- Partnership: in some situations, individuals are not allowed or permitted to participate in the task or jobs that they truly desire because of various reasons. The option of stock investing allows investing or partner with companies whose vision is closely related to yours. This may not be the case in some situations. In some cases, the partnership is needed because you do not have the right funds to establish a business idea.

- Attainment of dividends: for companies or businesses that issue profits to their investors, this is a standard benefit of stock investment. Majorly, it is you attaining more money from a company or business than what you invested; doubling your money or capital. Therefore, for an individual interested in passive income, the stock investment option is a pleasant way to earn while doing nothing, especially when you have a substantial percentage of funds.

Stock markets and investing is an essential aspect of financial freedom to be considered. It helps to grow not only an individual economy but also the national economy of the country or state an individual belongs. Therefore, with stock investing, you are enabled to increase with the growth of the nation's economy.

This is possible because as the economy of any society is strengthened, there is an increase in jobs provided and income; this allows the products of every company to get more audience. Therefore, the growth of the economy of a nation is vital to the growth of a company, as a result of this, paramount to your attainment of financial freedom.

CHAPTER SIX

Exchange-Traded Fund (ETF) Investing

For individuals who are interested in the profit of investment but the available options in stock investment does not favour or satisfy them. The topic of exchange-traded fund brings a change in your situation of finance as it offers investment in stock, bonds and other assets. Individuals interested that are interested in the provided investment options available would find the knowledge and understanding of exchange-traded fund needful. The establishment of the ETF plan is rooted in the Index Participation Shares of 1989 which had trade ties with the American Stock Exchange (ASE) and also, the Philadelphia Stock Exchange. These firms or institutions can be considered as the genesis of this particular investment option.

- Mutual Fund: this refers to a combination of funds or money collected from shareholders or investors to be invested in securities, these securities include stocks, bonds and some other assets. These funds or capital invested are usually monitored or managed by certified or qualified financial advisors, who ensure that the funds are appropriately managed and allocated to ensure profitable gain for the investors. Mutual funds are similar to exchange-traded funds because they both include a combination of assets and offers investors an opportunity to diversify.

- Underlying Asset or Index: an underlying asset is used to identify the main object that gives value, meaning or helps to identify the main subject of the contract.

What Is an Exchange Traded Fund (ETF)?

Having been familiarized with the history and establishment of the exchange-traded fund, the question "what is an ETF?" then arises. It is important to regard this particular question because it is the base which every other point or idea of ETF attains meaning and understanding for potential investors. To simplify the topic discussed in this chapter; it is crucial to define the term briefly- mutual funds, which would be referred to during your course of the exchange-traded fund. This term is subsequently discussed briefly;

Therefore, an exchange-traded fund (ETF) is a fund; as implied by the name. It allows its participants a variety of securities in trade in different investment options of exchange. The securities of the exchange-traded fund offer many investment options individually. However, these options are often combined in some cases, such as commodities, bonds and stocks. The principles of the exchange-traded fund may be compared to mutual funds because of the variety of investment options like stocks and bonds to be traded. It is also similar to an ordinary stock, in the case that it allows shares to be sold throughout the day, unlike the mutual funds which only trades once per day and this opportunity is only available after the market has closed. The exchange-traded funds have the attribute of fluctuation similar to ordinary stock; hence, the reason for the increase and decrease in prices of exchange-traded funds for both sellers and buyers.

The option or idea of exchange-traded funds is attractive primarily to individuals who are interested in diversification, both diversification of assets and funds. It does not offer a solid choice in assets, unlike stocks, the reason it may attract more investors than the regular stock.

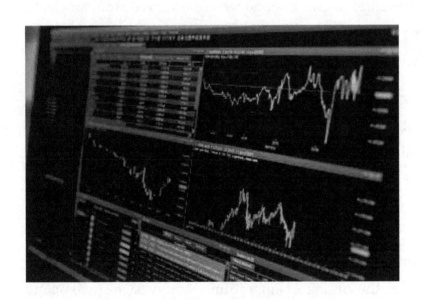

Types Of Exchange Traded Fund

It is essential to attune or familiarize every individual or potential participant of the exchange-traded funds with the different types available, and to highlight the advantageous each option would provide. The various types of exchange-traded funds are used to generate profit and other beneficial provisions. The following are the types of exchange-traded funds:

- Bond Exchange Traded Fund: this refers to exchange-traded funds that invests in bonds. This particular kind is common in the fixed income category, mainly because the new and old prices are available to all shareholders or investors as they are traded on stock. However, this specific category of exchange-traded funds usually thrives when the economy is in a recession because money is often moved from stocks to bonds by investors. This is a significant indicator of the situation of an economy.

- Sector Exchange Traded Funds: it tracks a particular industry or market or sector rather than the whole or available general market. The sector exchange-traded funds invest in the assets or securities of a precisely defined sector. Take, for instance, the sector exchange-traded fund may only track the index for financial stocks, energy stocks or technology stocks; it depends solely on the area specified. It provides the option or opportunity to invest in a company without the stress of combining the individual stocks provided in that specific sector. This particular exchange-traded fund is commonly based on the United States-based stocks. This does not limit an individual who seeks to invest globally as some individuals are participants of this; the global investment option is explicitly done to gain from the sector's performance worldwide. However, in choosing to invest in a particular sector, it is important to identify or research if the sector is indeed a classification. This is the point of the establishment of the Global Industry Classification Standard (GICS). There are many sectors available in the world, and each sector has a sub-sector that is attributed. Hence, the role of the GICS in highlighting and defining the classification of sectors.

- Inverse/Short/Bear Exchange Traded Fund: this involves the use of various derivatives to gain from the loss or decline in the value of the underlying assets. The inverse exchange-traded funds entail holding minimal positions, and it also allows the opportunity of lending some securities and selling them; however, with the desire to repurchase them at a lower price.

- Commodity Exchange Traded Fund: this is an investment in physical or common commodities and natural resources. Usually, this type of ETF is focused on a particular kind of merchandise or on investments that would be made based on the conclusion of the contract. It is important to note that an individual who purchases a commodity exchange-traded fund has ownership rights to the set of deals that are backed up by a commodity, not a physical asset. The most recognized and popular products usually invested in are oil and gas, gold, silver. The investment in the gold commodity is so popular that it was among the first commodities invested; it was officially identified as an ETF commodity by Benchmark Asset Management Company Private Ltd in India in May 2002. Also, the popularity of the gold commodity can be attributed to the recognition of the SPDR Gold Shares as of the second-largest exchange-traded fund in November 2010. Unlike every other exchange-traded fund that has been discussed, this kind of exchange-traded fund does not track indexes because it does not invest in securities.

- Currency Exchange Traded Funds: these exchange-traded funds have the sole purpose of providing foreign currencies with investment options and exposure. This particular exchange-traded fund is the largest in the world due to the currency investment exposure option it offers.

Exchange Traded Funds Strategy

The exchange-traded funds are a suitable way to financial freedom, and it is also an ideal start for beginner investors because of the many benefits it provides, benefits such as cost-effectiveness, diversification and tax benefits. However, these exchange-traded funds can only be used to its full effectiveness with the understanding and strategic choices in the process. Therefore, it is of fundamental importance to familiarize you with the features that make ETF one of the most efficient strategies to attaining a financially free status. The following are some of the most critical features and plans that must be applied to make the most of the exchange-traded fund.

1. Fixed dollar amount: this involves the purchase of an asset in the amount of a specific fixed dollar, notwithstanding, the change that is attributed to the cost or price of such asset; it remains the fixed dollar amount. Majority of the percentage of investors are individuals who have a stable salary source and would be able to save or contribute some rate of their basic pay. If you are capable of doing this, then you should invest or contribute a portion of your basic pay to an exchange-traded fund or a group of them. This particular principle of contribution or investment would help to teach and establish the policy of saving, which is essential to the attainment of financial freedom. To become indeed financially free, you must have grown familiar with the

discipline of saving as it helps control expenses. Also, this helps to secure your funds and lower the risks on the money invested. The situation of a fixed amount accumulated a more significant percentage of interest or profit when the exchange-traded fund is law, and a lower percentage while high which helps to secure your finance in a financial state and sometimes above.

2. Allocation of assets: as the title illustrates, this involves the distribution of a portion of a whole to different categories of assets; stocks, bonds and commodities. This is most effective for individuals interested in the diversification advantage of exchange-traded funds. The exchange-traded fund has a low investment tolerance which allows participants to set an asset allocation strategy depending on their tolerance of risk and investment time.

3. Rotation of sectors: exchange-traded funds allows participants and investors to participate in different sectors depending on the current situation of the economy.

4. Invest in markets that provide ETFs: exchange-traded funds are available in the stock markets. There are exchange-transfer funds for different sectors. Therefore, you only have to identify the ETF specifies in your particular area of interest.

5. Identify a sector of investment: after the interest to be part of the exchange-traded fund has been recognized. The most important thing is to identify the area you would like to invest as the exchange-traded fund offers investment options to individuals who show interest.

Benefits of Exchange Traded Funds

Over time, many individuals have identified as participants of the mutual funds due to the securities provided. However, the establishment of the exchange-traded fund offers a different approach to the benefits that were only peculiar to mutual funds. Therefore, it is essential to be aware of the advantages of every investment option to ensure that your interest in a particular field or sector of investment does not collapse. It is for this reason that some of the advantages of the exchange-traded funds over other investment options are being discussed.

- Availability of diversification: an investor in finance may have an interest in the discussions or profits provided by different other sectors but might be limited because of inexperience or ineffectiveness in such an area. However, this does not seem to be a significant issue with the provisions of ETF, which allows an investor to gain exposure in a specific sector. The exchange-traded fund is now available under every recognized sector or aspect in the world. Exchange-transfer funds are traded in assets, commodity and class. Through the purchase of one particular fund, the exchange-traded fund can help to identify other securities, such as stocks and bonds. It also helps to reduce the risk of loss due to the spread of funds or capital across various markets and assets, as a result of this, offering a more significant income rate than the regular investment options. The most common example of this diversification option available being put to good use and portraying effectiveness is the Vanguard Stock Market Exchange, Traded Fund. They are participants in investing over three thousand five hundred (3,500) United States stocks. The feature of diversification is evident as their investment involves companies in various, if not all the sectors that are tied to the economy of the United States.

● Cost-effective: in stock investing and mutual funds, active management requires the payment of funds and other expenses which vary depending on requirement demanded by the level of management. The costs that may be incurred through the process of management may include administrative expenses, marketing costs and distribution costs. However, the exchange-traded funds are of low cost compared to the mutual funds, and they are recognized for this particular feature. They are identified and known for the low expense ratio that it offers investors, and this specific ratio is usually within the range of 0.10% and 0.25%. The exchange-traded funds do not require any actual work or participation, hence the reason for the drastic difference between it and the managed mutual funds. It usually does not require significant management, and it is even regarded as a passively- managed fund because it does not require research or analysis.

Also, the exchange-traded funds are low in cost in the aspect of notifications, statements and transfers that are required, unlike the traditional funds which give investors the right or entitlement to get notifications and reports regularly. In ETFs, sponsors are expected only to provide the information to direct participants and capital owners of specific creation units.

Lastly, another cost-effective feature of the exchange-traded fund is that it does not require redemption fees like mutual funds. The investors or shareholders that are participants of the exchange-traded fund can avoid the short-term fees of redemption needed by the mutual funds.

● Tax benefits: comparing the structure of the mutual funds and the exchange-traded funds, the former incurs a higher capital profit taxes than the former. In the case that the exchange-traded fund would even incur tax on the capital gains, it is only taxed at the time or moment the exchange-traded the investor sells the fund. In this same subject, the mutual funds are taxed on capital gains throughout the investment time rather than the time sold. However, in considering the payment of dividends, the payment of dividends to the exchange-traded fund investors is less advantageous compared to the traditional mutual funds. The exchange transfer funds issues two significant categories of dividends (profits of a particular investment), which are qualified and unqualified dividends. Each of these categories has a set requirement that confirms it to be a qualified or unqualified dividend. An exchange-traded fund is approved to attain qualified dividends when the particular exchange-traded a recognized or specific investor has owned fund for at least sixty (60) days before the fixed or expected date for dividends to be paid out. The qualified dividends offer tax rate depends on the rate of income by the investor or shareholder. However, the rate available is between the range 5% to 15% while unqualified dividends are taxed based on the investor's profit tax rate. However, the income of investment (dividends) gotten from companies in the exchange-traded fund is reinvested immediately, unlike the mutual funds whose reinvestment time may vary.

- Flexibility in Trade: The ordinary trade in a mutual fund is allowed only once during the day, this time is secluded to the end of the market when the market closes. Investors are required to wait until the Net Asset Value (NAV) is asserted for them to know the price of the new shares and the profit made from the shares sold. This does not seem to be an obstacle for some people, although it can be obstructive for individuals who belong to the category of short-term investors and those who require flexibility in their finances. However, the exchange-traded funds shares the similarity of stock investments which allows investors or shareholders to buy and sell shares or assets during the day, and the exchange-traded funds also permit this.

This allows investors to place specific orders in place to avoid certain risks or loss. An example of such a request is a stop-loss order, and this particular market order allows investors to sell some of their assets or sell out entirely of the exchange-traded fund, at a specific price. The flexibility of the exchange-traded funds also allows investors the benefit of placing orders in different ways.

- Niche Trading: This particular benefit is most identifiable with the sector exchange-traded fund. The exchange-traded fund allows investors or individuals to invest in some areas that the regular mutual funds do not provide. Due to the classification of the GCIS, exchange-traded funds may cover more than the ordinary sectors, and it encompasses the sub-sectors also.

CHAPTER SEVEN

Options Trading, Rental Properties, and Flipping Houses

The previous chapters have explored various options that could aid or increase the possibility of financial freedom for each individual. There are three basic options or categories of tasks or opportunities that do not require the investment of capital in a company or business by buying stocks or shares. The options that would be discussed in the course of this chapter also do not require you to be a retailer or an employee, and these options offer participants or individuals the opportunity to be identified with the "self-made" financially free status. The possibilities that belong to this category are options trading, rental property, and flipping houses. The effects of these financial income decisions on a current economic state would be discussed; also, the effectiveness of these options will be one of the subject issues in this particular section of the book. These options (options trading, rental property, and flipping houses) are categorized in the same chapter because they have similar requirements. They can be referred to as sub-sectors under the general sector of finance, basic pay, or salary received from the issuance of passive income (salary received from tasks that do not demand extensive activities from an individual. This brings us to the junction where it is vital to understand the meaning and content of these options.

An Introduction to Options Trading

As the name or title of this particular option implies, this is a trade. Therefore, options refer to a contract or agreement that allows individuals to trade for a specific subject of interest or any underlying asset. The business in options is not a compulsion for investors. However, it is allowed for any investor who presents or showcases interest in the sale or purchase of securities, exchange-traded funds, and also underlying assets. An option is a recognized or qualified agreement that allows an investor to buy and sell underlying assets or securities within a specific time range within a particular time. The purchase, that is, the buying and selling of options which include underlying assets and securities, can be done through the normal process of purchasing various other assets or stocks. Therefore, options are purchased through the services of a broker when an individual has created or activated a brokerage account. Although it might be presented or understood that options are overly efficient, they are not void of the risks present in other investment options. Therefore, an investor that is in the business or interest of options trading has to be aware of the risks that are present in this particular trade. This is the primary reason for the warning that every brokerage service offers participants before the contract is fully enforced. This warning usually includes the fact that options trading consists of a significant risk of losing profits. Two major terms are significant in the purchase and engagement of options trading, and these are "call option" and "put option." The call option refers to the situation where an individual or investor buys a particular percentage of options that allow him to purchase shares at a different time, while the put option will enable you to buy an option that allows you to sell shares at a later or different time. Furthermore, in considering the role of options trading and comparing it to stock investment, this particular option does not equal the entitlement or right to claim ownership of a specific company. However, options to a significant extent is considered at a more substantial advantage because it puts participants at lower risk by giving them the right or entitlement to withdraw or rescind an options contract at any time it seems favorable.

In finance and investment generally, these options are commonly referred to by most businesses or companies and even individuals as derivatives because they are a sub-sector of securities. They are called derivatives because their price or cost is dependent on the price of something else. That is, the value of a derivative or options, in this case, is derived from the cost of a different product. Therefore, in the modern-day, many products are derivatives of other things. Take, for instance; the paper is a derivative of wood, coffee is a derivative of cocoa, and also a stock option is derived from a stock. Therefore, the price of options is derived from the value that is attached to a different asset.

There are two basic types of options, and these are the American options and European Options. The names do not imply that these options are different based on the geographical location; the only difference is the terms of period or time of exercise. The American options refer to options that are exercised at any time within the date of expiration and purchase, while the European options can only be applied on the date it expires.

Advantages of Options Trading

After the definition and explanation of the options, it is essential to clearly state the benefits that are available to individuals who plan to participate in this particular category. Therefore, the reasons for every individual to use options trading is discussed in subsequent paragraphs. These reasons are also the essential benefits that are feasible for the participants or investors of options trading.

- The benefit of speculation: this is a chance or a review on the wager of the price of assets and the position it would take later, that is, the possibility that it could increase or reduce. Individuals who are effective in the use of this particular advantage are referred to as speculators. Therefore, based on the analysis made by a speculator, he might believe that the price attached to a specific stock might increase, based on this thought, the speculator might purchase a stock or put the call option in place to purchase the stock. Therefore, the purchase of a call option protects individuals from risks and provides an acceptable level of leverage than buying the stock itself without the certainty that the price would be increase or decrease.

- The benefit of a hedge: hedging refers to something that provides security from risks or losses. The basic function of options recognized by individuals is its hedging function.

Therefore, under options, investments have the opportunity to be insured by their investors. You are given a similar benefit or relief that is available to your other belongings, this benefit is an insurance policy which helps to ensure that your investments are covered by insurance in the case of liquidation.

An Introduction to Rental Property

Most individuals have friends or family members that are tenants or inhabitants of a home that does not legitimately belong to them. However, these people are not the subject of discussion in this section. Instead, this section is dedicated to the actual owners of the houses or individuals interested in this particular trade.

Rental property refers to properties that are purchased by an individual who is usually referred to as an investor. Other individuals or tenants usually rent this purchased property or home, this agreement or relationship between these individuals is contained in a contract known as a rental agreement or a lease. Most of these rental properties are invested in with the primary intention of profiting when leased or through the resale of the property at a later time. In a few situations, it is done to earn through both of the stated options. In a rental property, there is a significant requirement to qualify as a property investor, and a property investor could refer to a single individual or a group of people. A registered company or business could also decide to invest in rental property. However, there are two primary classifications of rental properties; these are the residential rental property and thee commercial rental property.

The residential rental property refers to a category or group of homes that are restricted to be inhabited by individuals a living and dwelling space. This particular category consists of various structures of homes, and it includes apartment units and duplexes and bungalows as long as it is beneficial for the individual dwelling in such space. This particular investment is quite attractive and attainable by most investors because every individual can relate on this level due to their prior experience as tenants. Also, this particular section of investment is capable of offering a stable income source monthly or annually, and its tax advantages are more attractive than other investment options.

The commercial rental property refers to the category of properties that are used solely for business and commercial activities. It encompasses both buildings and land that provide profit for a particular institution. However, if a building is registered as a commercial rental property, it has different laws that apply to it, and the percentage and process of taxation are different compared to the residential rental property.

Steps to Ensuring a Profitable Investment In Rental Property

Having defined the term "rental property," it is important to elaborate on the essential measures that would ensure investing in rental property is profitable to you as it has been for other individuals.

- Identification: it is vital to identify and understand the principle of rental property. The sector of rental property or real estate investment has helped to establish some of the wealthiest people in the world. As this is one of your many goals, to reach financial freedom, it is no surprise that you would seek the benefits of this principle to identify with the same economic status. However, this might be a beneficial investment decision for them, but it is not always the case for every individual. The position of a property owner is infused with a lot of responsibilities and quite demanding. Therefore, you must believe that you can deliver on all grounds that pertain to your duties as a property owner.

- Acquisition of skills: most new or developing property owners do not have the funds to hire a maintenance specialist after the investment of money into the rental property. Hence, the need for them to acquire some primary skills to attend to damages that might occur in the house. However, this does not signify that they would be in charge of repairs for a long time, this might only be needed until the profits of their investments, that is, the payment of rent by the tenants is acquired. In the case that the property owner decides to remain the handyman for such an apartment or building, he saves the cash or funds that would have been required for professional workmanship.

- Settle debts: this particular requirement has been emphasized throughout this book. For any investment option to yield profits for investors, such an investor is required to have paid debt, or else the interest of such debt would continue to affect his savings. However, in real estate or rental property, it is not necessary to pay the debt before embarking on your real estate quest if the rental property would provide profit that is higher than the debt. Even in this situation, ensure that your income or amount of salary is higher than the mortgage.

- Avoid flipping: as a beginner in the business of rental property, it is very attractive to bargain a fixer-upper to renovate and turn into a rental property. There are several detriments to your finance when you choose a fixer-upper to be flipped. Such houses are expensive to renovate, although, at the time bought, you might be of the opinion that you are saving a large percentage of money. While in reality, you would spend more than the original budget if you had purchased a house that does not need to be flipped.

Therefore, it is more reasonable to buy a house that needs minor or no repairs at all. This particular opinion is upheld by Matt Holmes, Chief Executive Officer of Holmes Real Estate Group.

- Calculate your profits: although a lot of individuals are familiar with the popular term, "do not count your hens before they hatch." In this particular case, the determination of profit is important as it keeps you in tune with the primary goal or reason for the rental property. This specific idea also helps to keep track of your profits and expenses; this also helps to determine if the rental property provides a valuable return compared to other investment options. Cash-on-cash performance in stocks offers as high as 7.5% in profit in some situations while the bonds offer 4.5% in some cases. However, the rental property may offer a 6% gain in some circumstances, compared to the other investment options, the percentage of profit from this particular option is favorable. Also, there is a probability that this profit could increase over time.

- Location: it is essential to get a low-cost home of the right location as this would determine the level of availability of tenants. Therefore, the percentage of expenses obtained from a particular home is based on the total amount of the house when purchased. In choosing the location of a rental property, some key features are to be considered; these features are the tax rate of the properties, low crime rate, a reasonable school area.

How Effective is Rental Property to Attaining Freedom?

Rental property is an option of passive income, and it is even one of the primary ways of attaining passive income. Therefore, the ownership of a real estate or rental property alongside a regular job or no job at all is a definite way to attaining a financially free status. This is a primary option of investing to attain financial freedom, especially for individuals or investors who are averse to stock market investments. The rental property provides the opportunity to earn passive income, for property owners who do not intend to fix damages in the house themselves, this is a suitable suggestion for passive income. The process of becoming the owner of a rental property does not require any active participation or management, apart from the initial capital invested in the purchase and general upkeep cost. Therefore, you can be interested and invest in a rental property without it damaging your daily job, routine, or schedule.

There is an enormous growth in income available to real estate owners. As a property owner, after the investment of funds to earn such title, there is a growth in the percentage of income. The profit or revenue gotten from the real estate or rental property does not remain static; it is so beneficial that the benefit of your investment grows with an increase in real estate value. Also, comparing the stability in the amount of both the stock market and rental properties, the latter is more stable in value, providing a hedge compared to stock investing.

The other investment options provide the opportunity to invest in assets such as stock and shares, and these are all assets that may not be visible; that is, they are not physical. However, the option of investing in rental property is a tangible and more dependable asset because it is something you can monitor closely compared to stocks and shares.

Conclusively, in the course of investing in rental property, it is essential to have realistic and reasonable expectations concerning profits. It is important to note that although rental property would provide a large salary or paycheck at some point, this is not done from the beginning stage, and it may take a little more than the expected duration in a situation where the wrong property was selected. Therefore, the choice of property is a critical factor to be considered in rental property investments. Also, an individual with little or no experience in the field could partner with a corporation to have a professional understanding of the workings of rental properties.

An Introduction to Flipping Houses

Through the course of initiating you with the concept, idea, or principle of rental houses, the term "flipping" or "flipping houses" was mentioned a couple of times. Hence, the necessity to initiate you with this particular option in this section.

"Flipping" as a general term is the purchase of an asset or assets to be sold for profit rather than withholding the position or status of ownership. This term is usually affiliated with real estate or houses, and this is the focal point of the discussion in this section; the flipping of houses and not flipping as a general idea.

Therefore, flipping in this context usually refers to the purchase of a house or real estate property and selling it within the time frame of a year for a quick profit. In some cases, it refers to refurbishing or repairing the house before it is put up for sale. This is a common source of income for people, especially in the United States, where it was reported that 207,088 houses were flipped in the year 2017. There are two significant types of flipping. Firstly, there is one where investors buy properties that are in a primarily appreciating market, and these identified houses are immediately resold without the investors rehabbing the physical condition of the property. This procedure or particular type is carried out based on the status of the market and not the terms of property. The second type is referred to as the reno flip. The reno flip constitutes the renovation of the targeted property to be flipped, these renovations or fixings are done based on the knowledge of the investor on what potential buyers would like to improve. The idea of flipping is so lucrative that it provides the option or opportunity of wholesale. In the business of wholesaling of houses or properties, an individual who has been recognized or noticed to be exceptionally productive in identifying undervalued houses establishes an agreement or a contract to purchase a particular property. However, the purchase of such property is subject to a period of inspection, after the concluded period, the wholesale contractor is allowed to sell the rights of the approved property to an investor who pays him a percentage. The property sold by the wholesale investor does not necessarily have to be flipped by the buyer; he is allowed to settle for the property as home after renovations and repairs.

The business or idea of real estate also consists of some risks that can be detrimental to the financial state of the individual. For instance, if an investor has decided to invest in a recognized zone, such an individual cannot identify the time the value of such a market could decrease. Therefore, the value attached to an exchange could fall at any time; the investor is disadvantaged as the assets would continue to depreciation, which is a loss for him.

How to Flip Houses Efficiently?

A lot of individuals might be interested in flipping houses, and many more might have experienced this line of income. They might even believe that flipping houses are not a reasonable or reliable investment option because of the risks that are present in this particular field. However, this does not have to be the case for every individual, because, with the basic knowledge of flipping houses, profit can be efficiently made. Therefore, this section will consist of the requirements of house flipping and the necessary steps to ensure maximum effectiveness in the flipping of houses.

Ensure that you have enough capital or credit. The option of house flipping can not be useful for you if you do not have a substantial percentage of money as capital or excellent credit. These are basic requirements in the renovation and purchase of the property or house that would be eventually flipped. Therefore, it essential to have an excellent credit score. If this is not the case, then you should endeavor to create one now. The credit score is vital as it determines the interest that would be gotten or given on a home loan once flipping starts. Flipping of houses requires plenty of cash as a significant amount of money is needed to purchase the property and to carry out necessary renovations.

To What Extent is Flipping Houses A Success?

In ensuring that flipping houses do not become detrimental to an individual's finance, it is important to understand the following steps before the flipping of houses.

- Understand the targeted market: before you purchase a property to be flipped, you need to know the interest of the targeted people at that particular period. In house flipping, to ensure that profit is made, an individual can not make speculation on the desire of targets.

- Identify the available financial options: there are various financing options available in real estate property projects. Ensure that you consider each one to choose a specific one that assists your particular situation. This specific idea would help you in making the right decisions for your homes.

- Analysis: ensure that the expenses and profit that can be made from a particular project is appropriately analyzed. The 70% rule is the basic guideline adopted by most flippers, and this is used in their analysis before a house is purchased. The 70% rule provides that investors should not pay higher than 70% of the ARV (After Repair Value.)

- Negotiation: this is a crucial requirement in house flipping as it determines the percentage of expenses in a particular deal or on a specific property. Therefore, negotiation in renovations or repairs would help save a tremendous amount of money.

- Knowledge of average projects: agreed, not every property or house would require the same renovation, however, the experience of what an average repair on a regular day would help determine if a particular property is a good deal, especially for individuals who plan to renovate.

- Networking: it is important to network with potential buyers. The act of networking does not require a house that needs to be flipped; you can talk and discuss with them to understand the renovations and kind of houses that would interest them. Also, it saves you the need or stress to search for buyers when a property is ready to be flipped, and it gives you profit when the market is still of high value.

- Offer: once an investor has identified a potential property that would be of profit to him, it is necessary to make an offer to purchase. However, before the offer is presented, ensure that you have recognized the highest amount you can pay for such property without affecting your profit.

- Contracting: some individuals might not be interested in the contracting business because they believe that they can handle the repairs themselves. This is a fair opinion;

however, you need to be able to distinguish between repairs that can be handled by you and those that need professional attention.

- Resell or re-list: in flipping houses, there are two available options, you can choose to sell your house by yourself, or you could list it to a realtor who lists the house to be sold in the Multiple Listing Service database. Although many individuals may not show interest in the services of a realtor due to costs attached to services. As a beginner, it is advisable to employ their services irrespective of the fees because the resale of a property by yourself might take time, and there is a probability the property might have reduced in value if it is eventually sold.

To ensure that flipping houses is a success, the above procedures or steps should be strictly adhered to as they are the determinants of the success of this trade or investment option.

CHAPTER EIGHT

Retire Early

Retirement in plain terms refers to an end or the withdrawal from an individual's daily occupation or life, and it also signifies the close on an active job or working lifestyle. Closely related to this term is the position of a semi-retirement. Semi-retirement refers to a reduction in the working hours of an individual. Most individuals who choose to retire before the suggested time of retirement do so because of their eligibility status for pensions. However, some individuals retire because of unfavorable situations. Situations like illnesses or incapacity to function efficiently in a particular position might demand retirement in some cases.

It should be noted that retirement has not always been a principle that existed in most countries or institutions due to the life expectancy rate and the absence of retirement plans, this directly meant that employed individuals had to work till death. However, in the later 19th century and early 20th century, the concept of retirement was established. This principle was first introduced in Germany in 1889. The historical antecedence of retirement is not the focal topic of this chapter; this section is expected to specialize in the role of early retirement and financial freedom.

However, the option of early retirement in attaining financial freedom might seem ironical as it is a means to generate funds and income through the basic pay. However, this position can assist in achieving financial freedom and has gained recognition over the years. This principle or terminology is commonly referred to as the FIRE, that is, the Financial Independence and Retire Early movement. An individual is considered to have retired early if withdrawal from a job or current occupation is made before the tenure approved by the government or law that concerns such a corporation. Not every individual that claims to have retired early has applied for it, some individuals in such a situation because their employment contract was terminated before the usual time. Still, they would instead employ the euphemistic term of early retirement.

What Is The FIRE Movement?

Financial Independence and Retire Early (FIRE) movement was established based on the content of the 1992 book by Vicki Robin and Joe Dominguez, titled "Your Money or Your Life." involves the attainment of financial freedom and independence through early retirement. The main principle or idea in the book that launched the FIRE movement is the belief that individuals usually trade their life energy for money through their dedication to their jobs or their involvement in the workforce. It is a retirement movement that allows participants or individuals to retire earlier than the expected traditional time or plan. However, for the provision of financial independence and retire early movement to work for you, potential participants should have begun contributing at least 70% of their salary or basic pay to a retirement savings plan, plans like the 401(k)s and the thrift savings plan. Individuals who adhere strictly to the guidance of the FIRE movement might eventually be allowed to quit their jobs and survive on the contributions made to their retirement savings. However, the withdrawal from the retirement savings has to be done minimally to ensure an individual does not exhaust the entirety of the savings. The contents and movement of financial independence and early retirement is usually adopted by individuals whose lifestyles consist of extreme or maximum saving of their salary, and these individuals ensure to save up to 70% of their income during their years of working with a traditional corporation. However, once they have attained a reasonable goal, in some situations, 1 million, they quit their current job or occupation, some even go as far as quitting the traditional workforce. These people survive on the discipline of spending their savings wisely and not elaborately; the main participants of this movement make small withdrawals from their savings through the years. This usually falls between withdrawing 3% to 4% of the savings annually. However, this range of withdrawal is not a compulsion for every individual, as the percentage of annual or yearly withdrawals would be determined by the total amount available in such an account. The survival of the FIRE movement depends on the withdrawal percentage, diligence in monitoring expenses, extreme maintenance of the available funds and reallocation of investments by each individual. However, this plan also provides its risks, the failure or decrease in the value of the stock market or the interest rate might lead to a defect or failure of the financial independence and early retirement plan. However, the FIRE movement has a variety of types to fit specific situations of each individual, and these variations provide a guideline for devotees of each to live by, this assists the success of the movement in individual lifestyles. These variations are subsequently discussed:

- Fat Financial Independence, Retire Early: this category refers to an individual who has more advantage than the traditional retirement investor, that is, their savings percentage might be higher than the regular savings. Individuals who belong to this category have a normal lifestyle and are individuals who save a percentage higher than that which is expected from an ordinary retirement investor. These people spend more money on ensuring they have their chosen lifestyle compared to other variants, and their expenses are usually between a million dollars and more.

- Lean Financial Independence, Retire Early: individuals in this category save to the extremes. Their savings usually affects or dictates their lifestyle. It is the strict adherence to substantial investment savings for retirement and a minimal lifestyle. This particular category refers to people whose lifestyle are based or controlled with less than $25,000 (twenty-five thousand dollars) per year.

- Barista Financial Independence, Retire Early: some individuals have quit their regular day to day jobs. However, they still have income from being an employee of some sort. This category of people is explicitly categorized under the barista variation. This variation refers to individuals who have quit the regular jobs that pay them their normal salary but are still employees of minimal jobs which pay them to cover their current expenses. This is usually done to ensure their retirement savings funds is not squandered and are kept until they are compulsorily needed.

- Coast/Side Financial Independence, Retire Early: this particular variable is closely related to the barista. Precisely like the barista FIRE, these individuals have quit their jobs and are employees of a part-time job to cover their current expenses. However, the variation between these two is that the coast FIRE proponents can afford their current daily costs with their retirement funds without an adverse effect on their retirement savings.

Steps to an Effective FIRE Plan

Financial independence and early retirement is more than quitting a job or writing a retirement plan. The idea or principle might seem simple in theory, but the execution? Not so simple, there are some specific guidelines and options that must be considered, confirmed and put in motion determine if an individual is ready to be a participant of the financial independence and early retirement movement. Hence, the need to highlight some of the basic requirements and steps of the FIRE movement.

- Step 1: identify the kind of lifestyle that would benefit you. The first step to ensuring that the FIRE movement is effective for you is to identify the type of lifestyle that resonates with your personality. The biggest problem that is faced in many financial decisions and institution is the fact that individuals show interest-based on the profit or money offered by such a decision. Based on the opinions from the book "Your Money or Your Life," individuals are made aware that you can always make money through whatever means you decide, however, the time of your life that is lost can never be retrieved. Therefore, before you consider the monetary benefits of a decision, consider the effect it would have on your lifestyle. If you have decided on the kind of lifestyle you want, then you can determine whether the principle of FIRE would work for you, and also determine the percentage of money that would be reasonable for you to save.

- Step 2: calculate your expenses and budget. Every financial journey decision demands a correctly laid down budget. Therefore, after the proper identification of the kind of lifestyle that would benefit you, it is essential to make a budget for the cost of sustenance. Thus, the process of calculating your dream lifestyle would define and highlight the percentage of money that needs to be saved annually; supposedly you have a specific age you would like to retire. Also, in calculating money, it is not only the cost of lifestyle that should be considered. The tax that would be demanded on such savings should also be considered, the allowances of inflation or deflation in whatever market should also be considered in whatever calculation made.

- Step 3: Prioritize. After, the budget or the rate of money that should be saved annually has been decided. It is essential to prioritize your expenses to ensure that you are living comfortably and wisely. Therefore, an individual interested in the provisions of FIRE should be interested in spending on necessities and valuable things rather than items that are desired, wanted but not needed. Therefore, all the extra money that could have been spent on desires can be committed or contributed to a savings account because, in most situations, the height of your savings rate would determine the suitable time of retirement. The height of your savings rate is dependent on consistent contribution, to ensure that saving does not become a burden or chore to you, ensure that you view it as a means to live the lifestyle you desire. Savings is simply a means to a goal. The only procedure that would determine your participation in the Financial Independence and Retire Early movement is saving and investing in a retirement savings plan. To fast track your journey to financial freedom, it is vital to create a balance between the basic pay or salary, the money spent, and that which is contributed to your retirement savings. Conclusively, saving faster or quick attainment of financial independence demands a reduction in expenses which would lead to an increase in contributions.

- Step 4: Pay off your debts (good debts and bad debts). Surprisingly, debt is being referred to in the positive here as the only type of debt we are familiar with is the negative one. The concept of the good debt relates to debts that you can use to generate profit, and an example is the mortgage debt which is used for real estate investments and student loans when it helps to get a highly profitable job. However, the bad debt, as you may have guessed is the debt that is detrimental to your finances. Money is lost when it comes to bad debt. A generally or commonly known example of the bad debt is the credit card debt with an interest rate of up to

20%. In the case of FIRE, it is essential to pay up all existing debt as it is a loss of money on your terms. However, if you are an individual that has both the good and bad debt, the advisable strategy in paying them off is one that demands you to pay the debt with the highest interest rate, which in most cases is the credit card debt. This procedure of payment can be made based on the hierarchical order of interest rates.

- Step5: Participate in your current job to get a promotion and skills acquisition. Most of the money that would be contributed to your retirement savings plan would be procured from your full-time or regular job, hence, the need to ensure that you function to your fullest capacity to earn a raise. However, in most situations, specific individuals deserve a raise or a promotion, but they have been denied this advantage. It is necessary to demand a promotion if you belong to this category because the increase in salary or basic pay would increase the percentage of funds contributed to retirement savings, thereby causing a reduction in the number of years an individual has to endure before retirement.

- Step 6: Passive income. If you are unfamiliar with this term or unaware of it, this refers to side hustles or a regular job that allows you to earn without an active role. This is where the acquisition of skills in the previous step comes to play, and skill could hasten the amount of money contributed to your plan. However, your passive income does not necessarily have to be a skill. In this case, it is merely something you can do to acquire funds or money apart from your regular or full-time job; although the best passive income options are those jobs that determine or demands you to participate in activities that you generally enjoy.

- Step 7: Invest. Investment is fundamental in the Financial Independence and Retire Early plan. Investment has been discussed in various sections of this book and investing is not limited to only stocks. What does the investment option have to do with FIRE? If you intend to retire early, but all your funds and salary are locked up in a savings account without gaining profit from it, it could be a bit tiresome before an individual attains financial independence. However, when an individual can invest savings into an investment account, it fast tracks the entire saving process as the profit of investment or dividends can be reinvested and later moved to the retirement savings account when profit has been made from the initial capital. This is an essential procedure in attaining financial freedom with the early retirement plan. Basically, you are making a profit from your initial money, and both the profit made and the capital invested can be later contributed to the account. However, it is advisable to invest in the most dependable assets which are stocks, bonds and real estate. There are other available investment options, but these are the most dependable and effective ones. Also, it is necessary to ensure that a company, business or corporation is willing to pay dividends or profit of investment before the entire investment procedure is carried out. Therefore, an individual interested in investing in a company's stock is expected to have read or familiarized himself with the company's stock quote.

- Step 8: Build daily habits. Having followed the required steps to attaining financial independence as well as early retirement, you have to build habits of consistency in savings and persistence in sticking to the budget of expenses. Therefore, you have to consistently stick to the steps to have a beneficial effect of the FIRE plan. You cannot follow the steps religiously for a few months and abandon it at some point because you believe your financial state is doing well. Strict adherence would enable you the ease to adjust to the change in any case or situation.

Sustaining Financial Freedom/Independence After Retirement

The steps and ideas that are expected to be followed to ensure that every individual is allowed to be financially free are available to every individual. The steps to the attainment of early retirement as well as financial freedom have been stated. However, there is still an issue for individuals when it comes to the sustenance and management of money after retirement. As many individuals believe that it is quite impossible because the main reason to have a job is to make money and attain freedom. Even assuming that you have a secure retirement plan, there are unplanned expenses that could arise, and what way do you plan to reinstate the funds that have been unceremoniously withdrawn? These are questions that have been laid down and designed to be answered in this section of the chapter. The inability to settle these questions would discourage individuals from the objectives of this chapter; hence, the primary reason this issue is being discussed. Some of the ways to sustain financial freedom or independence after retirement are, through investments, budgeting, proper maintenance, a financial advisor, etc.

At the point of retirement is essential to set new life goals. Retirement signifies a new stage in life, and it is essential to set the expectations that would define this particular cycle of life to ensure that your current financial situation is not affected adversely by it. Therefore, it is important to set out or write out the current amount that you have in your savings account, and the percentage of daily expenses that your new lifestyle would require.

It is important to make a budget after the life goals or expectations have been clearly stated out. Therefore, it is advisable to make a budget for every sphere of your new lifestyle as this is the only way to ensure that your expenses are on track and your savings are not overspent to a position that would render you uncomfortable. The budget would create an awareness of the funds that are available and will discourage any attempt to overspend on wants rather than necessities.

Ensure that you do not create any debts. At this point, loans should not even be an option for you as it would only eat into your savings. Therefore, it is important to ensure that all high-interest loans like credit cards are paid in full balance each point. This particular option was previously emphasized because of the high-interest rate credit cards embody.

Indulge the available various investment opportunities. Some individuals might have a large retirement savings plan that they begin to squander the money or funds, simply because they claim not to have expenses. Instead of this, such individuals could invest funds in a company, business, corporation to receive the profit of their investment, thereby creating a mode of income for themselves and doubling their savings.

Also, it would be beneficial to employ the services of a financial advisor if the entire process of retirement math plan does not appeal to you. In most cases, it is helpful for individuals to seek professional help in allocating funds to each section of their lifestyle. This allocation is to ensure that they do not go over budget or budget less and have to remove emergency funds which would destroy the main point of creating a budget.

Benefits of Early Retirement

What do you have to gain after retirement? As a young person, why would I want to retire early when there are more experiences and benefits for me in the workforce. Firstly, you cannot know how advantages and essential an opportunity or something is to you until you give it a try, and often it is better to understand the advantages of a particular decision in discussions with people who have experienced such situation. Therefore, in determining if early retirement would be beneficial to you, it is advisable to seek the opinion of those who have succeeded in the quest. The quest, in this case, being early retirement.

- Early retirement and financial independence would make it easier to explore the world. Many individuals are interested in viewing more than the state, country or continent they are born. However, most people are unable to do this with complaints of time and funds. The FIRE plan is a significant way to live this lifestyle. However, some individuals might insist that this particular "benefit" is a disadvantage to their savings, they are not wrong about this, but there is a way to make this work. This can be done by balancing expensive countries or places with the inexpensive ones, and this technique has been tested by its proponents who had travelled the world for four years with the total cost of $30,879. The individuals with this testimony are Kristy Shen and Bryce Leung. They claim to spend less now that they are travelling the world compared to the expenses they had living in a major city.

- Early retirement would put you in a situation where you would not have to worry about money. For some individuals, their biggest challenge is the thought of their salary as they are living on paycheck to paycheck, however, individuals who have been able to sustain and adhere to a retirement plan can forfeit this concern. With strict adherence to a maintenance plan, their retirement savings might be enough to last them a lifetime

In conclusion, to ensure that you are contributing the most to your attainment of the financial independence and retirement plan, it is vital to have a consistent savings plan. The 401(k)s and the Thrift Savings Plan (TSP) are some ways to ensure consistency in retirement savings as they both offer automatic saving contributions which involve the withdrawal of a particular percentage from your account to your personal savings account. It also helps to receive contributions from the institution or corporation that might have employed you.

CONCLUSION

This entire book is sectioned in a way that each chapter gives a fresh and new option to the attainment of financial freedom. It helps that every chapter provides a new investment option or financial plan for individuals, therefore, it gives individuals a new idea of financial freedom. The fact that these investment plans and subjects have been suggested creates a state of realism that financial freedom or independence is a reasonable approach. The role of financial freedom for each individual is dependent on the strategy and decisions of each individual. The effectiveness of financial freedom or each of the options can not be generalized, although an estimate for the extent of effectiveness can be made.

However, many people desire the benefits of attaining the financially independence status but the truth in most situations is that they are not ready to sacrifice and dedicate the diligence and discipline required by financial freedom. Therefore, they find themselves in a situation where they have been able to adhere to the guidelines of financial freedom but once they perceive a small amount of independence in their finances, they abandon the laid down regimen that has gotten them to that particular stage. This is the primary reason for the majority of losses gotten by individuals in their quest to attaining financial freedom. This is not usually the fault of some individuals as some blogs or websites provide a ridiculous principle of living before the attainment of financial freedom. Imagine being advised that the attainment of financial freedom and independence would require you to sell all your materials and move into a trailer with your family of five or you would not buy good food, instead you should depend on food from dumpsters or waste from restaurants. These principles are impossible for anyone to adhere to and it defeats the whole purpose of attainment of financial freedom. Individuals are not expected to starve and live unhealthily because they want an independent status, you are expected to live your specifically chosen lifestyle before and during your course to attaining a financially free status.

Individuals should be familiarized with the ideology that the attainment of financial freedom will not happen in one night, like every financial decision that can be made, it needs time to grow before benefits can be retrieved. Therefore, whatever choice or decision you make to attain financial freedom, it important that you are able to exercise the virtue of patience to ensure that your finances and investments grow and develop to their full capacity. To make the topic or idea of financial independence appear more realistic, there are some levels and stages of growth peculiar to financial freedom that should bereligiously observed.These stages are subsequently discussed.

Stage 1: Establishment of an emergency fund. Many individuals claim to be interested in achieving financial freedom, however, their life is still determined based on the next salary or pay received. They do not have an emergency savings or savings of any sort, all their funds and money is lavishly spent the moment their company or corporation pays. These category of people are commonly referred to as individuals who survive or live paycheck to paycheck. This also includes paying off any credit card debt as it carries a large percentage of interest. However, this is the reality of most average Americans, this same category of people are also the same individuals that claim to be interested in achieving financial freedom or independence, some even claim that the entire financial freedom principle is unattainable. How can you achieve financial freedom when your debt continues to grow in its percentage of interest? Therefore, it is important to have a savings account where you are able to religiously contribute a percentage of you salary for unexpected expenses and to avoid money squandering.

Level 2: Retirement. At this stage an individual might have been able to gather or save enough money or funds to quit his job for a while or the long-run. The entire idea of financial freedom is to reach a stage where working or employment becomes a choice and not a necessity. However, the thought of quitting your job for the long-run might seem ridiculous or unreasonable because you are unable to for-see future needs. If the idea of full retirement is unreasonable for you, the step of taking a break from your job for a while is a nudge and a step in the right direction because that creates a familiar atmosphere with the feeling of retirement. It can be considered a preparation in advance.

Level 3: At this stage, individuals are expected to be financially stable, that is, the ability to indulge your major desires and still save a substantial amount of money. There is a feeling of relaxation and confidence when you can claim to be financially free and still be able to contribute to your saving plan. Therefore, any individual at this stage should be able to have a satisfactory lifestyle and still have a substantial amount of money to save at the end.

Level 4: Time. If you are an individual who has been able to enforce the early retirement scheme, then, you would realize that you have a large percentage of time to yourself. To invest in things that actually interest you not because you need financial assistance or support. Therefore, at this stage in your course to financial freedom, your time and schedule would become flexible. The flexibility in time and schedule is closely related to financial freedom. An individual in this stage is given the freedom to choose the activities and events that make up his day, also they are able to pursue tasks because of passion rather than compulsion, also, an individual becomes his own boss. There is the personal decision and shift in the program and time and events to involve your personal development, therefore, you can move things around your schedule until it fits your personal goals at that time. Every individual is familiar with the fact that one of the basics of financial freedom and independence is to ensure you pursue your passions, have more time for yourself and the important people to you without running out of funds to support yourself and your family while doing it. Any individual who claims to belong to this stage should be able to do this.

Level 5: A stable retirement plan. Individuals in their course to financial freedom must have been able to secure a retirement plan that would be able to withhold all your future expenses. Assuming you are an individual who belongs to the regular financial class, you need to ensure that you have earned enough to stabilize your life after retirement. Therefore, it is important that you have enough funds to actualize the lifestyle you desire after retirement. This is done by saving or investing in assets to ensure a long-term stream of income or dividends. Also, individuals who have been able to accumulate stable streams of passive income are also on the right path for an individual who plans to retire early.

Level 6: Financial freedom and independence. This is the final stage that the entire course, discipline and suggestions this book is designated to reach. It involves not having to stress about the profit of your passive income or the next paycheck and even the retirement plan you have laid out. It simply involves a stress or fret free life. This is the exclusivity that the financially free status offers. The attainment of this level usually means that you have more money than you will need to spend, most financially free people do not reach this status, they often stop at the fifth stage which is also a percentage of achievement. However, this level is usually occupied with individuals whose wealth is gotten from lotteries or inheritance or individuals who establish their own independently successful companies. Common examples of this founders are Bill Gates and Warren Buffet who have successfully attained financial freedom. Their businesses or companies are successful to the extent that if any of them decides to purchase yachts, planes and other unnecessary things, they would not succeed in exhausting the funds or wealth gathered. That is the true meaning of financial freedom.

Therefore, having highlighted the different levels of financial freedom, identify the stage you belong to and reflect if you are truly satisfied with it, if not, then ensure that you identify the things that would improve your financial growth to assist in achieving the specific level desired. Therefore, the definition of these steps is to encourage individuals to continue growing their wealth and to create an awareness that there is always more to sustain.

In affirming that the idea or principle of financial freedom and independence is actually a realistic information, it is necessary to share some testimonies of the financial freedom movement. Why exactly is this important? Because for some or many individuals, seeing is believing and in this case, they would have to read actual situation where financial freedom has been attained to eliminate the ideology that it is only a myth that can never be manifested. Hence, the importance of the following testimonies.

The first testimony to be considered would be that of Christina Yumul, who was able to move from San Diego to a different location which was in actual fact more expensive to afford-Maui, Hawaii. Alongside, moving she was able to settle her debt of $30,000 which was gained due to student loans and some excessive spending. This particular individual was able to prioritize, which was is one of the suggestions in this book, instead of the expensive lifestyle of partying to gain herself emotional satisfaction. This was replaced with hiking and hours on the beach which provided a similar level of relaxation. With the extra funds that she was able to save from doing these things, she was able to make minimal payments of her debt consistently. Apart from prioritizing, another choice that aided her was her application to have her paychecks sent as contributions to pay off her loans.As a result of this, she was not tempted to spend the salary or basic pay since it never really got to her. Christina was able to manage the small percentage of salary that remained by spending on necessities and not wants, also she ensured that she did not indulge herself in credit card loans as this would only create another percentage of debt to be settled by her. Therefore, she has been able to establish financial independence by paying her debt, establishing her own company and maintaining a healthy spending habit.

Also, a couple was able to pay off a mortgage that was supposed to be for 30 years in 6 years. 23 years earlier than the original year expected. This particular testimony was accounted for by Paige Hunter. This particular couple shared that the most beneficial part of attaining financial freedom is that that they are able to contribute to causes that actually interest them, and they are able to explore the world beyond what they know. The most interesting part of this story is that the Hunters have remained subscribed to the notifications of their mortgage despite the fact that it has been paid. Therefore, they get reminders every month for the mortgage and Paige described that happy endorphins are conjured in her because of this particular knowledge.

You might be wondering at this point "do I have to take a loan or be in debt before financial freedom is a possibility?" because the previous examples have started from the position of debt. The answer is "no", in fact, this next testimony would inform you that financial freedom is possible for any individual of any age or status. This is the case of Jessica Jabbar, a 27 year old advertising executive in New York City who claims to have saved six figures due to adherence to a strict saving regimen. According to her, she was able to attain this landmark by creating a strict and detailed budget for every sector of her life and also creating limits for everything she was involved. This individual also believes that now that she has made her first million, the most reasonable thing for her is to invest this funds. She believes that this funds as investment capital would do more profit to her financial status compared to when abandoned in a bank account.

For Sara Woznicki, after graduating from college she as ale to secure a job as a marketing specialist in Richmond, because his particular job had a low salary range, she struggled to pay rent and furnish her apartment. However, with assistance from her

139

parents she was able to achieve some of her desires. However, after she attained a better payed job, her parents still rendered some assistance to, although it was minimal compared to the level they provided in her previous job. According to Sara, even after getting some percentage of responsibility due to the reduction of her parents' support, she was not exactly financially free until she was encouraged to get her own car insurance. The responsibility of the car insurance was solely on her and she could not testify or ascertain that she was financially until this point. With the newly established financial freedom and independence, she was able to save up and travel beyond her country for thee first time which is one of the benefits available or exclusive to a financially free status.

However, in some cases, you do not feel that you have attained financial freedom until some loans have been paid. In some cases, financial freedom creates the discipline that allows you to acquire only the necessities of life that would not have an adverse effect in your life. Therefore, financial freedom requires a discipline of wise budgeting, spending and saving. For Jill Bong and her husband, they were able to experience financial freedom when they admitted to the fact that some unnecessities had an adverse effect on their financial state. How did they dispose of these things? An example of the major expense which was unnecessary in their life was their high-loan payment house. They had a home in Colorado which was not contributing positively their finances, they decided to move to an affordable area and this had a remarkable effect on their finances. Due to this major change in their survival or living lifestyle, they were able to contribute better to other matters they had genuine interest and to invest in situations that would grow their finances. Because of this they have not been worried about their jobs since they have a reduced percentage of expenses and they are able to save more.

For individuals interested in the Financial Independence and Retire early movement, Dj Whiteside was able to testify on the effect of investment in stocks, cash and mutual funds on your early retirement plan. These particular couple had plans to retire early and had ensured they were consistent in their contribution to their retirement savings plan. At some point their decided to examine the worth of their retirement savings and identify if it would be sufficient for them in the long run. They realized that they had enough funds for their retirement years and even if they stopped contributing to their retirement savings, they would have a sufficientS amount of money due to heir investments and salary. According to them, financial freedom in relation to financial freedom or independence gives you confidence about your life post-retirement.

Therefore, based on the content and context of each of these individual stories, the concept of financial freedom is not one that can be generalized. Financial freedom has various individual meanings and interpretations for people in different situations. For Sara Woznicki, she did not regard herself as financially free until she was able to cut all financial ties with her parent. Therefore, different situations defineyour financial freedom. For some individuals, it is being able to buy gas or petrol for their vehicles without worry, others the ability to spend unlimited time with their family without feeling guilty for missing jobs. For most, it is simply being able to pursue the things they are passionate about.

Financial freedom is simply being the author of your own life by taking charge of your finances.

Retire Early with ETF Investing Strategy:

How to Retire Rich with ETF Stock Investing Passive Income

Nathan Bell

versions of the work, both physical, digital and audio unless express consent of the Publisher is provided beforehand. Any additional rights reserved.

Furthermore, the information that can be found within the pages described forthwith shall be considered both accurate and truthful when it comes to the recounting of facts. As such, any use, correct or incorrect, of the provided information will render the Publisher free of responsibility as to the actions taken outside of their direct purview. Regardless, there are zero scenarios where the original author or the Publisher can be deemed liable in any fashion for any damages or hardships that may result from any of the information discussed herein.

Additionally, the information in the following pages is intended only for informational purposes and should thus be thought of as universal. As befitting its nature, it is presented without assurance regarding its prolonged validity or interim quality. Trademarks that are mentioned are done without written consent and can in no way be considered an endorsement from the trademark holder.

Introduction

First, I would like to thank you for choosing *Retire Early with ETF Investing Strategy* and congratulate you for taking the first step to securing your future. Choosing an "out of the box" way to retire can be a scary step to take, but you are serious about your future and are willing to look at different options.

Choosing a retirement strategy that's not mainstream doesn't come without risk or worries. It's understandable since there isn't always a lot of easy information about it, but this book is here to help. Here you will find everything you need to know about planning for early retirement and investing in a little know thing called EFTs.

Together we will go through the information you need to know to successfully retire early, starting at the fact that you can retire sooner than you think. This will also help to convince you that retiring early can be a good thing. Then we'll move into the logical next step, and that's figuring out the money that you are going to need in retirement. There are a lot of people who get to retirement and discover they don't have enough money to live how they were before retirement. This is what scares a lot of people. But if you sit down and figure out what you are going to need, then you won't be hit by that unfortunate situation.

Then we'll move into looking at developing six income streams. That may sound like a lot of work, but not all of these are active income sources. Most will be passive income and things that you can continue even after retirement. This will ensure that you have the money you need to retire when you want, and the more money you have to invest, the more money you will have to live on.

Then we'll move into talking about investing, which is likely why you came here. We'll discuss what it means to be an income investor and how to figure out how much risk you are willing to take. Risk is a big player in investing and something that gets overlooked by inexperienced investors. If you risk more than you can afford, you are placing yourself in a bad situation that can't be easily undone. You have to know exactly what your risk is.

After that, we'll move into look at ETFs. ETFs aren't quite mainstream in the investing world. Most people choose the obvious investing choices, but those can get quite expensive, and some come with greater risk. This is why "thinking outside of the box" is a good idea with investing.

Once you understand ETFs, we'll come up with an accumulation plan for your ETFs and then the best ETFs to invest in. Ultimately, what you choose to invest in will be up to you and your risk, so you might do some more research and find other

ETFs that fit your profile better than the ones we discuss, and that is perfectly okay. It is your money and not mine.

Then we'll move into deciding if you want to live off of dividends or sell your investments when the time is right. You could also choose to do both, but will look at that later on. Then we'll wrap things up with how you get to enjoy the rest of your life as a rich person. This will discuss the best practices for investing and retirement, as well as some frequent questions about ETFs to help improve your decision-making process.

While you may learn a lot of new terms and such in this book, some of which may be intimidating, you can retire early with this plan. If you trust my information and you take the time to budget, you will find success in ETFs and early retirement.

Chapter 1:Can I Really Retire Sooner Than I Think?

Early retirement seems like a fantasy to many, but it is possible to retire earlier than most. Most people retire between age 66 and 70, but there are some who continue working. Then you have some people who have decided to take their lives into their own hands and retire before the age of 60. Early retirement has changed in meaning over the years.

Retiring early is no longer defined as the time when you choose to quit working forever. Instead, it is the moment when you don't have to actively work to earn money. But you are also free to continue working if you do something that you really enjoy. There is a huge difference in doing a job you love or job that you can easily leave once you are tired of it because you have the flexibility and freedom of a person who planned and saved money.

There is scientific proof that working is good for a person, and most people who completely stop working begin to lose their mental faculties. It is even possible people who quit working altogether at an early age could die sooner. That means it might be best to see early retirement as a time when you choose to work because you want to and not because you have to.

We no longer have to live by the old school idea of once you retire you are done working. You can choose to do whatever you want when you retire, as long as it makes you happy.

You may still be wondering if it is worth the risk to retire early. I mean, with the lowered mental function if you do stop working completely, to possibly running out of money, who wouldn't question it. Let's look at five reasons why retiring early is a smart decision, and isn't as risky as people like to make it out.

1. Putting retirement off could end up being risky.

The first thing to think about when it comes to retiring early is that we don't know how long we are going to live, or how long we'll stay active and healthy. A lot of people end up hitting early retirement, not because they want to, but because they didn't have any other choice. They were either laid off, had a serious health problem, or had to start caring for somebody else. For this reason, along, it is a good idea to be more aggressive in saving up for your retirement so that you can get there on your own terms.

2. You completely despise your job.

If you really don't like your job, it might just be worth it to retire earlier than you had planned. Hating your job has a lot of implications for your mental and physical health, so it's not good to stick with something you hate. According to various studies, 20 to 40 percent of workers aren't happy with their jobs.

When you don't like your job, you can end up suffering from sleep problems, weight gain, stress, and depression.

These same problems can also end up leading to irritability and fatigue. Not only that, but that unhappiness at work can spill over into your home life, causing you to be less happy in your marriage and create dysfunction within your family.

You should also know that retiring from the job that you hate doesn't mean that you have to give up work altogether. It could mean that you could go after a passion that you have always wanted to follow but weren't able to.

3. It is possible to be very productive during your retirement.

If you are worried that you are going to be unproductive and bored during your retirement, know that you can still do things even when retired. When you take a look at your retirement goals and savings, you may find that you can't quit working completely, but you could still be able to retire earlier than you thought and continue to work a bit, part-time.

If that's the case, you should look at finding something to do that is less stressful and more enjoyable. By generating some extra money this way will help your nest egg to last longer. If you like the job you currently have, you may be able to cut down to part-time can continue working there for a few more years. If you continue to work, if you only work 10 hours each week and make $12 an hour, you will still bring in an extra $500 each month. That little extra income each month will be able to cover some major expenses like food or utilities.

It's actually a good idea for a lot of people to continue to work some during retirement because jobs provide you with structure and gives you a chance to socialize.

If you don't want to continue working, you can be productive in other ways, as well. If you have made sure you will be financially secure, you can volunteer your time to organizations that you find important. If you are good at a trade or have a skill, you can offer lessons, such as language lessons or music. You could also start selling baked goods or crafts, or you can do some freelance work.

You can use all of your free time during retirement to improve your health as well. You won't be rushed anymore, so you can focus on fixing nutritious meals and take bike rides or long walks, or simply go to the gym on a regular basis. By getting healthier, you can enjoy your retirement years doing fun things.

You may even notice that your sleep has started to improve because you won't be faced with the stress of your job, and you also might not have to wake up as early.

4. You can easily prevent yourself from running out of money using annuities.

A lot of people steer clear of early retirement because they believe they have to have a stockpile of money to make sure they don't run out. There are several ways to prevent this, but one way is to spend some of your retirement money on some fixed annuities. This is like buying yourself a pension income that you can depend on. It gives you the ability to set yourself up to get a monthly check and even some that you adjusted for inflation.

5. It isn't worth delaying your Social Security.

Lastly, you could be putting off retiring because you know that each year past the full retirement age that you delay collecting your benefits, they will go up by around eight percent. You also may be aware that collecting early, which you can start at 62, creates a smaller check.

What you might not know is that delaying isn't that easy of a decision. Even the Social Security Administration explained this by stating that if a person were to live to the average life expectancy, you are still going to get the same about of money no matter if you start receiving at 62 or at the age of 70. While you may get smaller checks when you collect early, you will receive more of them. You can use that money to invest in stocks as well.

This means that retiring early could be more within your grasp than you may have thought. At the very least, you could retire a few years earlier than previously believed.

The best way to make sure you can retire early is to come up with a retirement strategy. Any good investment strategy should be a simple one that focuses on real estate, bonds, and stock, and to make sure it is executed consistently. You need to have short-term investments, which is money you will want to have within five years, and long-term investments, which last ten years or more.

While you are free to invest in whatever you want to, you should only invest in things that you understand and stick with assets that have done well historically. You also want to make sure that your money is working as hard as it can by making sure it is invested in a tax-efficient way. And all that means is that you invest in your accounts correctly. Throughout the rest of the book, you will learn about these things to ensure you get the most from your investments and retirement.

Chapter 2:Determine What You Want and Need Your Retirement Money For

You have made the decision to retire early, so the first thing you have to do is to plan for retirement. One part of that is figuring out how much money you are going to need. The road to retiring early takes discipline to invest, save, and earn all you can.

Early retirement is different for everybody, so what yours is going to look like is going to be determined by what you need. We will look at the general steps you are going to need to take to reach early retirement, and then you can change them up to make them work for you.

Take An Inventory

The first thing you need to do is to take an inventory of your finances right now. There are two things that you must figure out, and that is your net worth and your annual spending. Both can be figured out with a little math. For the annual spending, you can get a good guesstimate by looking at your credit card statements and all of your checking account habits. It would probably be in your best interest to start semi-automated tracking using an app to keep up with the amount of money that you spend each year.

To figure out what your net worth is, because everybody has one, all you have to do is subtract your liabilities, the things you owe, from your assets, the things you own. Don't confuse your net worth with your income. Your net worth is one figure that represents what your financial standing its. This figure could be positive or negative, big or small. While a lot of people love the sound a $1 million net worth, there isn't a right number. Most people will find that their net worth increases as they age.

More importantly, having a high income doesn't necessarily mean that you are going to have a high net worth. In 2016, it was found that the typical American family had a net worth of $97,290.

The first thing you need to do is list out all of your assets. Write down whatever you have that is of substantial value. While you do need to include intangible things, like investments, you do not put your salary here. Income is cash flow and not net worth. Assets you would include are the value of your home, vehicles, cash value of a life insurance policy, balance in retirement accounts, investment accounts, savings accounts, and checking accounts. You could also include cash value of things like expensive clothing, furniture, art, and jewelry, as well as business interests.

Then you will list out all of your debts. This is everything you own to lenders and creditors like mortgages, loans, credit cards, and tax liability. Then you will take your liabilities and subtract them from your assets. Now you have your net worth, but that is simply a snapshot. If you are making payments on your debts or adding to a savings account, this number is going to increase. It can also decrease as well, so be careful.

As far as annual spending is concerned, all you can do is looking through your bank statements to see how much money you spend each year. And it is a good idea to save up about 25 times your annual spending.

Figure Out Your Target Number

Once you have an outline of your early retirement, you have to figure out how much money you are going to need to make it happen. As mentioned above, most early retirees say it is a good idea to have 25 to 30 times your expected annual expenses invested or saved. Once you figure out your target number, you can then break it down into monthly, weekly, and daily savings goals.

This is part of the process that you might find a bit difficult to do on your own, especially when you are looking at multiple scenarios, such as a recession could affect investments. Finding a good financial planner to help you crunch your numbers and provide you with an actionable plant can help you to reach your goals. They can also keep you accountable if you want them to.

Hopefully, you will be close to paying off all of your debts by the time you do retire, so that would mean that you have more money to use just for living.

To start figuring out your target number, look at your current monthly spending and think about what numbers will lower, what might increase, and what you may add or eliminate. Once you have figured out your final monthly expense, multiply that number by 12, and now you have your annual retirement needs. To make that number even better, I would recommend increasing that number by 10 to 20 percent. This will ensure some wiggle room.

There are two things that people tend to overlook when coming up with this number, and that is health care and taxes. Both of these can end up bringing your early retirement to an early end. Health coverage will be covered later, so we get to talk about taxes. Your goal should always be to minimize them. In order for that to happen, you are going to want to strategize about how and when you pull income from investment accounts.

Alright, now you need to figure out your savings needs. Let's say that you figure out that you spend about $60,000 a year, and that's factoring is some wiggle room. To make sure you are well prepared, you will want to make sure you have at least $1,500,000 saved. That is 25 times your annual needs, which is what I mentioned earlier. This rule also assumes that your retirement nest egg has also been invested so that it will continue to grow. If it's not, then you will likely be out of money in 25 years.

That also brings us to a second rule. The four percent rule. This means that you are allowed to withdraw four percent of your invested savings the first year of your retirement. The following years, you will draw out that same amount once it has been adjusted for inflation.

The rule comes from research done in the 1990s that tested various withdrawal strategies against historical information. You may decide to take a more or less conservative approach, depending on the investments you make, risk tolerance, and the way the market is performing.

Change The Way You Are Spending Now

You will find it hard to build long-term wealth if you are constantly spending more money than you are making. If you want to retire early, it is very important that you start to live below your means as this is the best way to invest and save aggressively.

The main places you need to look when it comes to reducing your expenses are food, transportation, and housing. This can go quite a long way to increase your savings. Depending on the amount of money that you spend, you will want to aim for one of three types of early retirement: fatFIRE, leanFIRE, and FIRE. FIRE stands for financial independence, retire early, and it is a numbers game.

LeanFIRE would be a person who has saved 25 times their annual expenses, which means that they have lived off of a "lean" budget, and will spend less than average Americans. But, a person who reaches fatFIRE will spend more than most. Regular FIRE would be a person who is spending in line with the average of Americans.

According to Census data, the average American household spends around $61,000 each year. For the regular FIRE person, they will continue to spend that amount after retirement. LeanFIRE would spend less than that after retirement and fatFIRE, would spend more. If you don't plan on embracing frugality in retirement, then you are would fall under fatFIRE. But if you are a simple Midwestern couple, then you would likely be considered a leanFIRE. All of this will play a part in the previous step of figuring out your numbers.

Leverage The Income Your Make

It is very important that you keep all of your spending in check, but you will only be able to cut costs to a certain extent. A bigger difference can be made by increasing the income you are currently making. To cut your daily spending and expenses takes a constant and consistent effort, and is a short-term solution, but increasing your flow of cash is a long-term solution.

It is a good idea to start a side hustle to help diversify all of your income. The most lucrative ones tend to be passive incomes, like real estate. Coming up with a passive income source to cover your monthly expenses will provide you with more flexibility. We will discuss these sources in the next chapter.

Max Your Retirement Accounts

In nearly every story about financial independence, you will hear a common strategy: frequent and early savings. Typically, one of the best ways to improve your savings is to have retirement accounts.

IRAs and employer-sponsored retirement plans will provide you with unparalleled investment growth and tax advantages. Right now, you can add $6000 to a traditional IRA and $19000 pretax to a 401(k) that you can get a tax deduction.

There is a caveat to stuffing retirement accounts as full as you can when you are planning on retirement, and that is the restrictions on withdrawals. You aren't allowed to remove money from your 401(k) before the age of 59 and a half without a penalty. However, you are able to dip into your Roth IRA, which you fund with after-tax money and take out your contributions tax-free whenever you want.

Invest What You Have Left Over

Once you have maxed out your retirement accounts, you should move over to brokerage accounts. This money you will invest directly into the stock market, and then you can cash out whenever you need to. We'll talk about investing in ETFs later on.

Work To Pay Off Your Mortgage

When you are preparing to retire early, an obvious move is to eliminate high-interest consumer debts, but paying off a mortgage early isn't always so cut-and-dry. Some people see being liability-free is a good idea, but others see the money saved in interest payments pale to the possible investment returns.

Look At Your Health Insurance Options

When you leave your full-time employer, it means you are also saying goodbye to employer health insurance. If you plan on waiting for 65 to roll around to get Medicare, typically, the best option would be to join a working spouse's employer plan, if that option is available to you.

Otherwise, you should look at getting continued coverage through your former employer under COBRA, through possible subsidies with the Affordable Care Act, health-sharing plans, or having a part-time job.

Come Up With A Backup Plan

No matter how much planning you put into place or how foolproof the plan may be, you still need to think about what could go wrong. What if you discover that you don't like the unstructured days of retirement, would you decide to go back to work? What would happen if the economy tanked and it takes your net worth, would you be able to cut expenses? Going through some worst-case scenarios is a good way to make sure you are ready for anything.

Once you have your plan figured out, it is time to start putting that plan A into action. But as you are doing that, you have to make sure that you continue to enjoy your life right now. You need to make sure you save and invest, but you can't forget how to live in the present.

Chapter 3:Develop and Income Stream From 6 Sources, Not Just One

The next thing you need to do is to start diversifying your income. I know hearing the number six for how many income sources you should have sounds big, but I'm not asking you to have six jobs you have to split your time between. Instead, a lot of what diversifying your income involves are passive income sources, which are things you aren't actively working on each day. Some researchers have found that millionaires, on average, have seven income streams.

You may be wondering if the extra income streams are what made the millionaire or if it was the other way around. While seven may not be a magical number, it does seem that these two concepts on two sides of a coin. It could be that multiple income streams made the millionaire, but it is also true that millionaires simply understand how important it is to have multiple income streams.

The goal of coming up with several income streams is to maximize potential in the different categories you have available. Since you are just starting out, you can't really expect that you are going to generate a bunch of income. However, if you make sure that you are maximizing your income potential through your main salary, you will discover that you have excess income that you will be able to reinvest in other income streams so that you can earn even more money.

We looked at net worth earlier, and that is another goal of these income streams. You want to increase your net worth as much as you can while you are still actively working. The more your net worth is, the better your retirement is going to be.

I mentioned that most of these are passive income streams. I want to take a moment and explain what that means. Active income is the money you make from jobs you have to actively go to and work, such as your office job. If you don't do anything at that job, then you won't get paid.

Passive income is making money from something that isn't directly related to active work. Dividends and interests are two examples of passive income. Most of these passive income sources will require active work at first that you make a little bit of money for, while most of your income will come later.

You shouldn't think that passive income doesn't require any work. You will still have to do some work. It just means that the income you make isn't directly tied to hour many hours of work you put in.

We are going to look at some of the most common income streams that you can get started in. Of those, you simply need to pick at least five to start, since you already have your primary income source. While it may sound like a lot of work, having these extra income sources will allow you to save up more money faster than if you simply had your main source of income.

There are a few things you want your other streams of income to be. First, you want it to be flexible. Ideally, you want to be able to call the shots when it comes to time, especially if you a full-time job. Second, you want it to be scalable. You want to find income sources that have, at the very least, the chance of creating a lot of income. Third, you want it to be sustainable. You want your secondary money sources to be able to generate money for you even when you are aren't actively working. Lastly, you want them to be enjoyable and inexpensive. You don't want your secondary sources of income to cost you money or create more stress for you. The goal is to ease your financial woes and not to make them worse.

Primary Salary

Your primary salary is likely your main income stream. This is where everybody starts, and it is most likely your full-time job. The goal here is to try and maximize this salary so that you can start generating the free cash you need to invest it into other income streams.

How is this done? Well, you will want to try to get as high of a paying job as you are able to. Ask your boss for a raise. Use sites like glassdoor.com to see if your salary competes with the same job at other companies. There are some companies that force their workers to leave just to get a raise and then return for another raise. This is a very common strategy, and it just might work for you.

There is also another theory about this primary salary. You could try to generate enough to have a little bit of extra cash flow, but you work at a place that is stress-free and have some time to dabble in different projects. If you have the means to do so, having a startup is one way to do this.

Either way, the main perk of this primary salary is that it normally provides you with benefits like insurance, which can help to protect you as you are pursuing your other income streams.

- Secondary/Spouse Salary

I don't count this as another income stream for you. Instead, this is secondary to your primary. No matter what you plan on undertaking, it is important to have a team. Teamwork can help you in a variety of ways, even if it is simply bouncing new ideas off of somebody else. For most people, this is going to be your spouse. If you have a spouse, then the two of you should bring your primary incomes together and maximize them.

Investment

The first option you have, after employment, is to find diversification through investing, which is a logical step that most people take. It is very important that you look at the reasons why you want to invest because, at some point, you are going to be using that money for something. In this case, your reason is likely for early retirement. But when it comes to investing, it isn't all about storing money away for a rainy day, that's what having an emergency fund is for. Investing means you have the capital to generate income.

Look at it this way, when you're saving for retirement, you want to save enough in your investments to create enough income to replace your main salary. Let's say your primary salary makes you $50,000 each year. To be able to create $50,000, you are going to need nearly $1,700,000 saved up, and then be able to create three percent cash flow on that.

If needed, you can also draw down on your principal, but this is a return of the invested capital, and if you were to continue doing this over a long period of time, you could end up using up all of your resources.

Rental Property

Another very common way for a person to make extra money is to purchase a rental property. This is a lot like investing in that you will need a sum of money to purchase another piece of property, and then that property gives you money through rent.

There are expenses that you will have to take care of, which are different from investing, and these include things like taxes, utilities, mortgage, and so on. This will all have to be considered when you calculate the return on the rental property.

There are tax advantages to having rental properties that you don't get with investing. The main problem with having rental property is that that initial capital that you need to get started. Most people that are starting to diversify their income aren't going to have a 20% down payment in order to buy property. This is typically why this is done later on.

However, you have some options to doing this earlier, like looking into real estate crowdfunding. Real estate crowdfunding gives you the chance to become a limited owner in real estate, and you don't need as much money to start. This is a good option for getting started in real estate.

The site RealtyMogul gives you the chance to get started in real estate for as little as $5,000. You will have the option of commercial and multi-family properties to invest in. FundRise is another platform you can try. You only need $500 to get started, and they offer several different options.

If have a little more money than that, you could try Roofstock. They give you the chance to buy a single-family turnkey investment online.

Some people like to try out house flipping, but this can be very risky. You are going to not only need the money to buy the house, and the credit to do so, but you will need funds to fix the house before you can try to sell it. That's the thing with house flipping is that you sell the house once you are done, and don't rent it out.

House hacking is also another option. This is similar to owning rental properties. This is simply where you leverage the house you currently live in as a rental. This could mean renting a room or setting up an Airbnb listing.

Hobby or Online Business

Another common income stream is to create a side business. You could make this business offline or online, and I like to refer to them as a "hobby business" because it typically gets created from a person's hobby. For example, if you are a techie person or like working online, you could sell things on eBay or simply create your own website. You can also promote your own services online with sites like Fiverr.

If you would to work offline, you could start working with something like Partylite Candles, Avon, or any other various jewelry and clothing lines.

Some people will also choose to write an eBook since anybody can be an author on Amazon nowadays. Writing the book is the simple part, making actual sales in a different story and takes a lot of work.

If you are good at photography, you can also sell stock photos. There are a lot of different websites where you can do this. Fredigitalphotos.net and 123rf.com are a couple of options.

You can also choose to offer a service instead of an actual product. If you have a skill set that people could pay you for, then this a good option. Some common things people pay for are lessons in music or language, writing, social media management, babysitting, tutoring, consulting, coaching, and resume help. This is a great option because you get to set your own hours and price, but it can also take a while to create a client list.

Be A Micro-Entrepreneur

I think this is different than selling a service or product. This is a side hustle, but you have the freedom to choose when you want to do it, but you aren't faced with having to start your own business. The first option would be to start driving for Uber or Lyft.Ride-sharing is one of the side hustles that you are able to do, truly, 100% on your own. You get to choose when you drive. The only thing you will need is a new-ish car and some spare time.

Another option is to deliver for Uber Eats or DoorDash. If you don't like the thoughts of having strangers in your car, then you could simply deliver food to stranger's houses. Again, you are free to choose when you do this during the day.

Coming Up With Several Income Streams

The point is that you need to diversify your income in several different ways to help you retire early. You don't have to get all of your income streams up and going at once. Pick the first one you think you can start right now, and begin with that one. Then continue to add another income stream as you can.

There a some of these options that doesn't require you to have a bunch of money to start with. All of them will require some time to get started, though. You can simply continue to work, invest excess income, save up a bit to get a rental property or rent out a room in your house, and then start an online job without having to break a sweat.

When it comes to coming up with your passive streams, they aren't all created equal. The stock market is the only passive income stream where you bear all of the risks and get all of the rewards. In all other cases, you have more risk than the rewards you could possibly get because other people may be involved.

Chapter 4:Become An Income Investor

Income investing is a strategy to help you build wealth that involves coming up with an asset portfolio that will provide payouts that you can depend on. This means, for most, gathering a collection of high-quality bonds and dividend-paying stocks that they can count on as a cash source that requires little work from them. Having a well put together portfolio of various stocks and bonds is a rewarding and accessible route to creating a decent stream of "passive income."

There are some people who believe that income investing can only be done by retirees and older investors, and there are a lot of good reasons for this association. However, having investments that are income-generating is a valuable financial avenue for those of any age. Dividend-paying stocks often outperform those that aren't, and a safe choice is quality bonds because they can help your wealth preservation and they can prevent your purchase power from being eroded. This means that you should think narrowly when it comes to who should and should not become income investors.

The best makeup of your portfolio is going to depend on what you want to achieve and how much risk you are willing to take. Because of this, you should make sure that you understand all of the various forms of assets that can help you create an effective portfolio, some characteristics and metrics to be on the lookout for a while evaluating items, and an idea of what you goals are so that you can figure out the holdings and strategies that fit your needs.

Income investing was born from social unrest during the 20th century. Despite all of the nostalgia of the time, society was actually really messy. It was messy in the fact that Irish and Jewish people weren't able to get hired, and if you fell into the LGBTQ category, you were signed up for electroshock therapy. Black women and men were always faced with the threat of rape or a mob lynching. Everybody thought Catholics were being controlled by the pope. If you were female, you wouldn't get hired for anything other than typing, for which you only got paid a fraction of what men did for the same work. They also didn't have company pension plans or social security, which resulted in most elderly people to live in abject poverty.

But why did this cause income investing? These types of circumstances caused the rise in income investing simply in order to survive. Unless you were a well-connected white man, decent pay was out of the question. The main exception was if you owned stocks and bonds in Pepsi or Coca-Cola. These types of investments didn't care if you were young, old, white, black, male, female, or whatever. You were sent interest and dividends during the year, depending on your investment and the company's performance. This is the reason why it became a rule that as soon as you had earned some money, you need to save it and invest it. They didn't trade stocks during that time. They invested and forgot about it.

Now, let's move to look at different aspects of income investing.

Bonds

Bonds are a type of investment known as fixed-income, which means that they will give you a certain amount of money during a specified time period. When you buy a bond, the money you pay for is basically a loan to the company or government. Once you have reached the end of your agreed-upon loan period, which is called maturation, the bondholders will be able to cash in their bond and get its principal value. How much interested that your loan will generate will all depend on the length of its maturation and the risk of the default.

You have two main types of bonds you can invest in:

- Government:

These bonds are basically money that you loan a certain government that will provide you with a certain amount of interest every year. Bonds for the US are typically seen as the safest choice because the US government has, historically, been a stable government. There are some government bonds that provide you with special tax advantages, like a tax-free municipal bond.

You can also choose a foreign bond. However, depending on which country it is for, there can be a bigger risk of not receiving the principle once you reach maturation, or never getting your principal value back. If the foreign government decides not to make good on the bond, it is often very hard to get restitution since you probably won't have access to their court systems.

- Corporate:

These bonds have pretty much the same setup as a government bond, but there are some differences that you should be aware of. As you would guess by the name, these bonds are simply loans given to a company at a specified amount over a certain period of time. Much like with government bonds, depending on the risk, the interest will be higher or lower. As opposed to government bonds, corporate bonds normally have to be bought in 1000-bond lot.

A lot of people think bonds are safer than dividend stocks, but this might not always be true. If you choose a bond with a high-interest rate, that will normally be because there is a higher risk that the company or country won't pay back your loan. Those who provide a high yield but also have a really high risk of defaulting will often be called "junk bonds." Investors have the option of using the bond rating from a third-party site to assess how likely it is that your principal will be repaid.

Dividend Stocks

When it comes to stocks, you are basically buying a part of a company. The shares that you buy will generate a part of the free cash flow and earnings of the company. Not every company will send money straight to those who hold stock, but the ones that choose to do so are called "dividend stocks."

Dividends provide companies with a way to give their shareholders money. These are normally paid out of their free cash flow, which is figured out by subtracting the capital expenses from their operating cash. Companies can also choose to use their cash piles, or if they have to, take out debt to pay their dividends, but investors don't typically like these methods of funding.

Besides purchasing single stocks that pay dividends, investors can also buy mutual funds or ETFs. ETFs are basically securities that have been bundled together and then purchased on a trading exchange. Mutual funds are another type of security that bundle together bonds, stocks, and other assets, which are actively managed and purchased from a broker or fund manager.

Certificate of Deposit

CDs are another fixed-income type of investment that works a lot like a savings account or a bond. Your money isn't loaned to a company or government, and is, instead, given to a ban. Then longer of a term you choose, the better your interest rate will be.

Rates that you can get on these investments are often going to be lower than bonds that are held for a comparable time, but these to have a greater upside in that they are insured by the FDIC for a max of $250,000. This means that even if the bank goes belly up, you will still be able to get back your principal.

The low-yield, low-risk investment makes CDs perfect for retirees who are looking to preserve the money they have and allow it to grow and offset the effects of inflation. However, if you try to remove the money before the specified date, you will be faced with a penalty.

Payout Ratio

The payout ratio for a company is the percentage of its free cash flow or earnings that is put towards covering their dividend distribution. You can find these ratios by dividing the FCF and the complete amount of dividends that the company will distribute during a given year. If a company has a payout ratio over 100%, that means they are making less cash than what they have to payout on dividends, and that means they will likely have to take out debt or use cash assets in order to pay. This is normally an unsustainable dynamic and tends to signal that a suspension or dividend cut is getting close.

Companies with low ratios tend to have a bit more leeway with their dividends, but they could end up having other needs that can end up preventing them from giving a big payout.

Payout Growth

The payout growth is basically how much a company has been able to increase its payouts per share over a certain time period. The growth rate can be figured out by taking the dividend at the close of a certain period, subtracting the value of the dividend at the beginning of your comparison period, and dividing that number from the start of your comparison period.

If a company were to repurchase the stocks or retire some of the shares, it would reduce how many dividend-generating shares it has. This would mean that buybacks would give the company a chance to increase how much dividend they would pay per share over a specific time without having an increase in their total distribution because there won't be as many shares receiving payments.

Dividend Yield

This is a certain percentage of a company's yearly payout that is represented by a percentage of the price of their stock. You can find yield by dividing the annual dividend with the price of the stock.

If you bought a stock for $50 a share and it pays out a dollar each year, its yield would be 2%. That means if you bought 50 shares, you would get the equivalent to a value of a share in through the dividends in a given year. Depending on what payment option you choose, you could get $50 in income or get an additional share for your holding through a reinvestment (DRIP). Investors tend to end up owning fractional shares because of being a part of a DRIP program, and the fractional shares are still going to pay your dividends, and you can sell them just like full shares, provided that you are operating your stocks through a brokerage.

Dividends tend to be paid out according to the company's schedule. Most choose to pay on an annual, quarterly, or biannual basis, but there are some who will pay monthly. Some companies will provide a special dividend, which is a payment that is unscheduled and does not repeat.

Taxes and Dividends

Most of the time, your dividend payouts are going to be taxed at the rate of 15%, but this tax rate could go from zero percent to 20%, depending on various situations. If you have a DRIP account, you are still going to have to pay taxes. If you own 100 shares with a two percent yield, and you reinvest the $200 in the payouts through a DRIP, you are still going to be taxed on that $200 even though you reinvested it.

You can minimize this by shifting the timing of the taxation to work for you, which most people do through IRAs. The downside would be that you have to leave the money in them until the age of 59 and half, or you will have to face fees, but they still make helpful tools. You have two options for IRAs, Roth and traditional.

With traditional IRAs, the taxation of the funds you add to the account is deferred. When funds are added to the IRA, you will be able to take a deduction from your taxable income and is a great way to reduce the taxes you owe. However, your withdrawals will be taxed normally. Most people will often generate less income during retirement, so pushing the taxation until after you retire could mean that it is taxed at a lower rate.

When it comes to Roth IRAs, you have to pay taxes on the money that is added to the account during the year that you add it, but it won't be taxed again when it is withdrawn. This makes a Roth IRA useful for investors who are income-focused and still have several years before retirement because it gives dividend payments a chance to accumulate.

Dividend Growth Investing

Dividend growth investing will require you to select stocks that have rapidly growing payouts, even if they don't offer great yields. This is done with the understanding that you will be able to build to have a bigger yield with time. Some stocks could look like they have a small yield if you were to compare it to an S&P 500 index average yield. However, if that company raised its payout annual by 15% over five years, the yield will have doubled by the end of that time period.

Companies will huge dividend payouts often grow earnings at a slower rate when compared to the market, and it tends to deliver smaller payout increases. Meanwhile, companies that make earnings at a faster rate than older companies in industries such as industrials or telecommunications are able to provide you with fast growth in dividend. Dividend growth stocks are able to provide you with a better balance between a growing returned income and an increase in stock price than the ones who already have bigger yields.

How Important are Payout Growth Streaks?

You should always look at finding companies that, historically, has delivered a consistent payout growth each year. Companies that cut dividends often means that they are not doing well, and when they consistently have increases in dividends mean that there will be a continued growth in payouts.

After a company has been able to create a multi-decade streak of consistent payout growth, dividend growth will become an expected part of owning a stock. The company will be able to count on the backlash from their shareholders if it doesn't give them the increase in payouts, or if they cut their dividends. You want to look for companies that have proven their self to be sturdy and can thrive over a long period of time, but shareholder expectation is also able to encourage a company to continue to grow their dividends during slow periods or recessions.

185

Chapter 5:How Risky Can You Be? Come Up With The Right Mix of Stocks, Bonds, Real Estate and Cash

Investing isn't something that works the same for everybody. Everybody is in it for various reasons. All of your personal and retirement goals have a lot to do with the way you choose to manage your investments.

Depending on what you want to do in retirement or what you would like your investments to do for you, is going to change your decision-making process and your risk-management strategies. It is very important that you understand what your goals are. The more you understand them, the better your chances are to reach them.

Making sure that you consistently achieve your goals will make you a better and more successful investor. You can't make any stock purchase without there being some risk. Investors take risks because it gives them a chance to succeed. But with each stock, you have different types of risks, and those different risk levels can vary widely. So how much risk should you take? I can't answer that for you because, once again, everybody is different. It will all depend on how much risk you can afford.

Risk tolerance is basically how much exposure to loss you are okay with. It's basically how much money you are willing to lose trying to reach that big payoff, and long you may be willing to wait to get your money.

Another term you will hear is risk-reward. Risk-reward is the trade-off that lies under nearly anything that can generate a return. Whenever you invest money into something, there will be some sort of risk that you might not actually get your money back. For facing that risk, you can expect a return that compensates you for your possible losses. Basically, the bigger your risk, the more you should get back for holding that investment, and the smaller your risk, the less you will get.

How much risk you are willing to take will determine how fast you will reach your goals, or if you ever meet them. If the goals you have involve a short timeframe, it may not be a good idea to play it safe. For a person who has a modest goal and few decades to work that "slow and steady" approach, that may be the best option.

First thing you need to do is to start by looking over your investing goals. Are you going to be able to reach your goals by slowing growing your money over several years? Do you have very lofty goals that are going to need big gains?

Also, you need to remember that various portfolios will be able to handle various levels of risk. If you have a large and carefully diversified portfolio, then it will typically rebound from loss caused by a risky investment, but a smaller portfolio could completely fall apart by too many risks or simple a single big risk.

For example, let's say there are two portfolios. One of them has $25,000, and the other has $250,000. Now, if they both lost $1,000, it would cost them $25,000 portfolio four percent, but the other portfolio would lose only 0.4%. If they both lost $10,000, that would be 40% for the $25,000 portfolio and four percent for the other portfolio.

Losing as much as $5,000 in a $25,000 portfolio would be completely devastating. It would take a fifth of your savings. On the other hand, in a $250,000 portfolio, a $5,000 loss is only a two percent loss. While this may be a simple example, it highlights the importance of knowing your risk. This is also what makes position sizing important.

Levels of risk, from lowest to highest, are conservative, moderately conservative, moderately aggressive, aggressive, and very aggressive. This is by no means a scientific scale, but it does give you a guideline that you can follow when you are picking investments.

Determining Risk

With all of the different investment types out there, how can an investor figure how their risk they are able to handle? Everybody is different, and it is pretty hard to come up with an exact model that works for everybody, but there are two things that you need

189

to consider when you are deciding on how much risk you are willing to take.

First is the time horizon. Before you make your actual investment, you must figure out how much time you have to let your money stay invested. If you are going to invest $20,000 today but you need to have a down payment for a new house in a year, investing your money in high-risk stocks isn't the best choice. The riskier your investment is, the bigger its volatility will be. If you have a short time horizon, you may have to sell the securities and take a big loss. When you have a longer time for an investment, it gives you a long time to recoup any losses that you may incur, which makes you, theoretically, more tolerant to higher risks. The means if you are planning on growing that $20,000 for a lakeside cottage that you are going to buy in ten years time, you could choose to invest in higher-risk stocks.

Second is your bankroll. Figuring out how much money you can lose is the next thing you need to consider when it comes to figuring out your risk tolerance. While this may not be that optimistic, it is the most realistic. When you invest only the money that you can afford to lose, you won't be as pressured to sell the investments due to liquidity or panic. The more money that you have, the greater risk you can take. For example, a person with a $50,000 net worth and another with a $5 million net worth both invests $25,000; the person with the smaller net worth is going to be hit harder by a decline than the other person would.

Once you have looked that these two factors, you can use the risk pyramid approach to balance all of your assets. You can view the pyramid as an asset allocation tool that investors are able to use to diversify their investments according to what their risk profile is. There are three tiers to the pyramid.

1. The foundation of the pyramid is the strongest portion, which helps to support everything that is above it. You should make sure that this consists of low-risk investments and have good returns. This is the biggest area and is made up of the bulk of your assets.

2. The middle section should be made up of investments that are a medium risk and offer a stable return, and it still allows for capital appreciation. While they may be riskier than the assets in the base, these should still be fairly safe.

3. Then the top part is reserved for high-risk investments and should take up the smallest part of your pyramid. It should be made up of money you are able to lose without facing any serious repercussions. Also, the money that is in the top part needs to be disposable so that you don't end up selling prematurely when capital losses occur.

Position Sizing

Position sizing is the idea that you add the right amount of money to your investments when it comes to your total portfolio size. This tends to be a tough concept to grasp because you have to start thinking about things that a lot of people don't want to think about. That is, how much are you willing to lose on one investment?

A good number to follow is to not risk any more than four of five percent of your portfolio on one idea. If you risk four percent of a $25,000 portfolio, you will limit your possible loss to just $1,000 on your investment.

Trailing Stop

Trailing stop is one way to limit your losses. One common strategy is to follow the 25% rule. This means that you sell if your investment starts to drop 25% from its highs.

If you take the $25,000 portfolio, for example, you would be willing to lose $1,000 on each of your investments, and you decide to use a 25% trailing stop, how much money do you need to invest in your positions? You would invest $4,000. If that $4,000 falls 25%, then you will have lost $1,000. That is a lot less devastating than the example I gave earlier of a 20% lost.

Bonds, Stocks, Cash, and Real Estate

Once you know your risk, you need to make sure that your portfolio has the right mix of bonds, stocks, cash, and real estate. There are many different rules of thoughts on portfolio diversity. One rule of thumb states that you need to "own your age" in bonds. That would mean that a 30-year-old needs to have 30% of their portfolio made up of bonds, and the rest would be made up of stocks. There is a riskier version of this rule that says you need to have 110 or 120 minus your age in stocks. That would mean the 30-year-old would need to have 80 to 90 percent of their portfolio made up in stocks, and then they would slowly switch over to bonds as they get older.

These types of rules are based upon the idea that a young investor typically has a better chance to recover from any losses that the stock market takes, and so they are able to take advantage of higher returns that equities provide. There are "target-date" mutual funds that provide you with a premixed portfolio of bonds and stocks that will change up as you age.

While these age or time-based rules can be very helpful to get you started out, but these rules are no match for careful financial planning. Since we are talking about stocks and bonds right now, we will continue with them. We'll talk about cash and real estate later.

The best way to figure out your stock and bond allocation in your portfolio is to figure out your risk tolerance, and likely we have already talked about how to figure that out. So, are you risk-averse, moderate, or risk-loving? Your asset allocation is also going to depend on your market portfolio's importance. For example, people often view their IRA or 401k as very important parts of their retirement plan since they will take up the biggest part of their portfolio.

Meanwhile, you can have a different portfolio in an after-tax account that contains punt stocks and is smaller. If your online trading account were to get destroyed, you would still be able to survive. If you end up killing your 401k, you may find that you have to delay your retirement.

There are five different recommended asset allocation models that you can choose from or come up with your own. First up is the conventional asset model. The main recommendation is for you to subtract your age from 100 so that you know how much of your portfolio should be made up of stocks. The idea of this is that as you age, you become more risk-averse since you don't have the same ability to generate income. Starting at age 30, 70% would be stocks and 30% bonds. Then, every five years, the stock percentage decreases by five percent while the number of the bond increases by five percent.

The next model is the new life asset, allocation model. This is where you subtract your age from 120 to figure out the percentages. Studies have found that we are living longer because of scientific advancements and better awareness about our diets. Since stocks tend to do better than bonds over the longer run, we need to have more stocks in our portfolio so that we can take care of our longer lives. The increase and decrease

194

by five percent remains the same, but you will start out at 90% stocks and 10% bonds at the age of 30.

Then you have the survival asset, allocation model. This is great for people who are risk-averse. Here you have a 50/50 allocation, and it increases your chances that your portfolio will outperform when there is a stock market collapse since the bands will increase in value. Bonds are also able to rise when stocks rise.

Then next is the nothing-to-lose asset allocation model. Since stocks tend to outperform bonds, this model is great for people who want to go all-in when it comes to stocks. If your time horizon is long enough, this might be a good idea. Up until the age of 50, all of your assets will be in stocks. Then at age 50 to 60, it will be 90/10. From 60 to 70, the allocations would be 80/20, and then they move to 70/30 and stay there.

For the financial samurai asset allocation model, you will combine the new life model and the nothing to lose model. While stocks will continue to outperform bonds, there will still be volatility. This will help you to prepare for any changes in returns for your stocks and bonds. This is good for people who have several income streams and those who won't depend on their portfolio in retirement. You will begin with 100% in stocks, and then from 35 to 50, your breakdown will be 80/20. From 50 to 65, you will have 70/30. From 65 to 75, you will have 60/40. From 75 on, you will have a breakdown of 50/50.

The one you choose will all depend on what your risktolerance is. Ideally, you will want your asset allocation to be something that will allow you to sleep well each night and wake up every morning excited.

Now, as far as cash and real estate go, it works like stocks and bonds, and all depends on your goals and risk. Some people prefer to be invested more in real estate because it tends to be more stable than the stock market. Like with the stocks and bonds, you can change these percentages as you age, and you probably will want to.

Also, you don't have to have all four of these to make up your net worth. If you don't want to deal with real estate, you don't have to, but it is a good idea to think about. Real estate is definitely touched to beat with comes to stability and long-term returns. Stocks and bonds can give you back nothing in return, but homes don't typically end up being considered zero in value.

Real estate is also capable of have volatility and risk, so that always has to be considered. If you decided to have a few B class rentals in a decent neighborhood, you could be faced with similar volatility to a bond fund. If you decided to buy a rental in Silicon Valley or have an AirBnB in Vegas solely for its appreciation, they can be a lot riskier, which would be similar to investing in tech stock.

The main point to this is, you want to have a diversified portfolio, but you also want to make sure that it stays in line with your goals and your risk. You should never invest in anything just because somebody says you should. You should only decide to invest your hard-earned money into things you believe in and that you trust.

Chapter 6:ETF Explained

An ETF or exchange-traded fund is basically a basket of securities like commodities, bonds, stocks, or even a combination of these that you can purchase and sell through a broker. These get put together into one entity that will then offer shares to investors that are traded on the main stock exchange. Every share gives the owner one share in total assets of the ETF. ETFs can give you the best attributes of two of the most popular assets: They mimic how easy stocks are traded, plus they have the diversification of mutual funds.

These have become one of the most valuable and important products that were created for investors recently. They give you many benefits, and if you use them wisely, are a great way to achieve your investment goals.

ETFs are offered on every asset class from alternative assets such as currencies or commodities to traditional investments. The structure of an ETF lets investors stay away from short-term capital gains taxes, to gain leverage and too short markets.

After a few false starts, ETFs started in 1993 with a product known by the symbol SPY or as traders call them "spiders," which became the biggest volume ETF in history. There are about one trillion dollars that have been invested in ETFs and almost 1,000 ETF products that get traded on the stock exchange.

These funds have taken the world by storm, and investors have taken advantage of all the opportunities they give to you. Investors have put around $3.5 trillion into ETFs. There are hundreds if not thousands of various ETFs available to buy.

How popular ETFs have become is because of their unique features and characteristics. I will get more into the details below. ETFs have opened the door to various investments that most investors hadn't ever had access to before. Because of the broad focus, simplicity, diversification, and efficiency, ETFs offer you benefits that no other investment could match.

ETFs normally track different benchmarks. Every fund will invest with the objective of matching returns that the fund chose. There are some ETFs that have managers that seek out their own investments, but since the disclosure rules require these funds to let the investors know about their holdings daily. Most managers who like to manage money using strategies will choose other tools rather than ETFs.

Most ETFs are registered by investment companies for tax reasons. This means that they normally don't pay corporate taxes a the fund level. Any taxable income they give you has to be passed to their shareholders. Anybody who has invested in ETFs are entitled to get their proportional share that the ETF generates. Funds normally accumulate some dividends in a short amount of time, and then they distribute the total either monthly, quarterly, or annually.

One great aspect of the ETF is the way shares get made and redeemed. Instead of working with shareholders, most ETFs will use special markets to make the trades. These markets create new shares by buying the stocks or investments held by the fund and deliver them to the company, which will issue shares that the market can then sell. The market can deliver a huge block of ETF shares to the company and get securities back. This structure makes sure that the market for ETFs stays effective, and it contributes to some tax advantages.

The fund provider will own the assets. They design funds to track performances of stocks and then will sell their shares to investors. The shareholders will own a part of the ETF, but they don't actually own the assets in the fund. ETF investors that track the stock market will be given dividend payments, or they will reinvest.

Even though ETFs have been created to track the value of the asset, whether it is a basket of stocks or a commodity such as gold, they will trade at prices that the market determines that are usually different from the asset. Since there are things like expenses, longer-term returns are going to vary from those of the assets.

Stocks Vs. Mutual Funds Vs. ETFs

ETFs will have fewer fees than mutual funds. This is why they are so popular. The normal US equity mutual fund will charge 1.42 percent in yearly expenses. This is called an expense ratio. An ETF average fee is about 0.53 percent.

ETFs do offer tax advantages for its investors. There is normally more turnover with mutual funds as related to an ETF. Selling and purchasing can bring in capital gains. If an investor sells a mutual fund, the manager has to get the cash through selling securities. This is also able to provide capital gains. In both of these scenarios, investors will have to pay these taxes.

ETFs are very popular, but how many mutual funds available is still going to be higher. These two also have different management structures.

Just like stocks, you can trade ETFs on exchanges, and they are provided with their own symbols on the ticker that allows you to track what they are doing. This is where their similarities stopsince ETFs are a group of assets, where a stock is representative of a single company.

Closed-end Funds Vs. ETFs

Closed-end funds are as well known as ETFs or mutual funds. This small market mixes together some of the attributes of ETFs and mutual funds. They have a similar structure to mutual funds, and they have been around longer than ETFs. They makea trade on the stock exchanges, and this gives you the same advantages of trading that ETFs give you.

The largest difference between these two is the amount of outstanding shares. ETFs have mechanisms where market participants can redeem or create a large block of ETF shares with the broker that manages the ETF. Because of this, if there is a high demand for a specific share, these participants can go to the manager and purchase some shares that they can sell to other investors on the exchange.

In contrast, there are just a certain number of shared that will be available at any given time. Whatever the company manages, the closed-end fund isn't able to issue new shares whenever they want to. They have to go through the same procedures as when they are trading any other stock on the market.

Since these companies don't like doing that, the supply and demand with investors looking for a fund play huge roles in pricing closed-end shares. If everybody is interested in a certain fund, then they might trade at well above what the normal value of that fund's assets suggest is the right number. If a fund loses its favor, then its shares can be traded cheaper than the actual value that is held within the fund. Since investors can't demand for a fund to turn over its underlying investment, these discounts might last for several years.

Closed-end funds aren't favored anymore since they have to be actively managed and have fees that are extremely high. There are some areas within the market where these closed-end funds still prosper. Investors in ETFs can normally find a better deal by looking for ETFs that have the same objectives.

Cons and Pros of ETFs

Investors have flocked to ETFs due to their access to diversified products, cheapness, and simplicity.

Pros

- Tax benefits: Investors get taxed only if they sell the investment, but mutual funds incur taxes over the life of your investment.

- Transparency: Anybody who has access to the internet can look for an ETF's price. The holding is open to the public. Mutual funds only get disclosed quarterly or monthly.

- Diversification: It is easy to think about diversification when talking about broad market verticals. For example, commodities, bonds, or stocks allow investors to diversify across horizontals such as industries. It takes effort and money to purchase all the components in one basket. With one click of your mouse, an ETF can bring your portfolio these benefits.

Cons

- Risk of the ETF closing: The main reason that this could happen is if a fund has not brought in enough money to cover the cost of administration. The largest inconvenience that a shuttered ETF is investors must sell faster than they would regularly want to, and it could cause a loss. You are also faced with having to reinvest and also the problem of taxes.

- Finding buyers for the ETF: Just like with all securities, you are going to be at the market's mercy when you want to sell. Any ETF that isn't traded a lot is going to be harder to sell.

- Trading costs: The cost of an ETF might not end after you pay the expense ratio. You could be faced with commission fees from brokers since ETFs are exchange-traded. There are some brokers who have dropped their commissions for ETFs, but not all of them have done so.

How to Shop for ETFs

You need to know that, while costs for ETFs are normally lower, they tend to vary depending on the funds. It all depends on who issues it and its demand and complexity. The biggest brokers are Vanguard, SPDR, and iShares. ETFs that track on the same index are going to come at different costs.

A trend for shoppers has been that some brokerages have dropped their commissions to zero.

Most ETFs get managed passively. They just track an index. There some who prefer a hands-on approach that mutual funds give. These get run by professional managers. Their goal is to outperform the market. Some ETFs get actively managed and tend to mimic mutual funds, but these will often have a lot of high fees. You need to think about how you want to invest before you decide to buy. Just because you can get an ETF cheap does not mean that is will fit into your portfolio.

How to Invest

There are many ways you can invest in ETFs; it basically comes down to your personal preference. For investors who like to be hands-on, the ETF world is only a couple of clicks away. There are all part of stander broker offerings, although how many they offer will change from broker to broker. Robo-advisors will build their portfolio out of ETFs, and this gives investors access to their assets.

ETFs have nuances that you need to understand. As long as you know the basics, you can choose if an ETF makes sense in your portfolio. What is stopping you from starting your journey of investing in ETFs?

Types of ETFs

- Alternative Investment ETFs: ETFs let investors trade volatility or get exposure to certain investment strategies like covered call writing or currency carry.

- Exchange-traded notes: Basically, debt securities that are backed by a creditworthy bank that was created to give access to liquid markets, and they have added in the benefit of generating no capital gains taxes.

- Actively managed ETFs: These were created to outperform an index. This is different from most ETFs that were created to track an index.

- Inverse ETFs: These were designed to profit if there is a decline in the index or market.

- Foreign market ETFs: These were designed to track markets that aren't in the United States like Hong Kong's Hang Seng or Japan's Nikkei Index.

- Style ETFs: These were designed to track market capitalization focus or investment style like small-cap growth or large-cap value.

- Commodity ETFs: These were designed to track a commodity's price like corn, oil, or gold.

- Industry and Sector ETFs: These were designed to give exposure to a certain industry like high technology, pharmaceuticals, or oil.

- Bond ETFs: These were designed to give exposure to every type of bond that is available like high-yield, international, municipal, corporate, U.S. Treasury, and many more.

- Market ETFs: These were designed to track on a certain index such as NASDAQ or S&P 500.

Disadvantages

Even though they are superior in many aspects, ETFs do have some drawbacks:

- Settlement dates: Sales of ETFs don't get settled for two days after the transaction. This means that when you sell one, the funds from that sale won't be available for you to reinvest for two days.

- Tracking error: Normally, ETFs track the index fairly well, but technical problems could cause some discrepancies.

- Illiquidity: Some ETFs that are thinly traded will have wide spreads, and this means that you will be purchasing on the high end of the spread and selling on the low end.

- Trading costs: If you frequently invest small amounts, there might be alternatives that cost less if you buy then straight from the company as a no-load fund.

Advantages

- Trading transactions: Since these get traded just like stocks, you can put in many types of orders that you can't do with mutual funds.

- Tax-efficient: You have more control over when you pay your capital gains tax.

- Lower fees: There isn't any sales load, but brokerage commissions will apply.

- Sell and buy at any time during the day: In contrast, mutual funds only settle at the close of the market.

The hallmark of the ETF industry has always been innovations since it started about 25 years ago. There will be more ETFs that get introduced in the future. Even though innovation is an investors' net, it is important that you realize that all ETFs don't get created equal. You have to do lots of research before you decide to invest in an ETF. You need to make sure you consider all the factors to make sure that the ETF is the best way for you to reach your investment goals.

Chapter 7: Accumulation Plan for Life in ETF

A simple definition of an accumulation plan is a financial strategy where investors try to build the value of their portfolio. When talking about mutual funds, this becomes a formal arrangement where investors contribute a certain amount of money into the fund periodically. By doing this, they are accumulating a larger investment in the fund through the increase of the value of the fund and their contributions.

Breaking It Down

In accounting and economics, capital accumulation is usually equal to the investment of savings or income, especially when dealing with capital goods. Capital accumulation refers to:

- Investing in nonproductive physical assets like works of art or residential real estate that might increase in value.

- Investing in assets represented on paper, capital gains, fees, royalties, rent, interest, or yielding profit.

- Investing in tangible means of production like development, research, and acquisitions that could increase your capital flow.

Why Do You Need An Accumulation Plan?

Having a good accumulation plan is necessary if you want to create a financial nest egg for your retirement. Most investors will do this by reinvesting in capital gains and dividends and with regular contributions. Basically, the main goal is to keep your funds invested, reinvest capital gains and income, and let these compound for as long as you can.

Accumulation plans could be useful for investors who want to build a position in mutual funds over an amount of time. It can also give you benefits of "dollar-cost averaging."

Voluntary Plan

This is a way of investing where an investor periodically invests small amounts of money into a mutual fund, which will create a large position for you over a period of time.

When you spread these contributions over an amount of time, you will reap the benefits of "dollar-cost averaging" since the contributions are going to purchase more shares of a specific fund when the price is low rather than when it is high. This is a great solution for anybody who wants to create a portfolio but isn't can't afford to invest huge amounts at one time.

In addition to having the advantage of building an investment over an amount of time, this plan gives you the benefit of investing in mutual funds that are very low risk. This plan also lets investors take advantage of "dollar-cost averaging."

Hire a Professional

It isn't that hard to find a financial advisor that will fit your needs. A quick search on Google, and you should be able to find a list of advisors in your area. Now, you might have to put in some research to find the best ones or the ones you can afford. Once you find your advisor, they can help you reach your financial goals.

Investing in ETFs

ETFs have become very popular, and they could play a huge role in your investment strategy. Investors have put over $5 trillion into ETFs. The last trillion didn't even take one year to accumulate.

This is why ETFs offer many advantages for investors, and they can be part of your investment strategy. It doesn't matter how complex or basic your strategy is.

ETFs are great for investors who are just starting out since they give you many benefits like low investment threshold, diversification, large investment choices, abundant liquidity, and low expense ratios.

These features make ETFs perfect for various investment and trading strategies that are used by new investors and traders. Here are the best strategies for anyone who wants to invest in ETFs.

- Dollar-Cost Averaging

We will start with the most basic strategy, which is dollar-cost averaging. Dollar-cost averaging is a technique of purchasing a specific dollar amount of an asset on a regular basis. It doesn't matter how much the cost of the asset changes. Investors who are just starting out are normally young people who have worked for some time and have a stable income. They make enough to be able to save a bit of money every month. These investors should be able to take a couple hundred each month, and rather than putting it into a savings account, they could invest it into an ETF or many ETFs.

There are some advantages to this type of investing for beginners. The first one is that it creates discipline to help you save. Most financial planners will tell you that you have to pay yourself first. This is what you get when you save regularly. The second one is when you invest the same amount of money in an ETF each month; you are going to accumulate more when the price of an ETF is low and less when the price of an ETF is high. This will average out how much you spend on your holdings. With time, this approach could pay off very well if you remain disciplined.

- Asset Allocation

This basically means that you allocate a part of your portfolio to different asset categories like cash, commodities, bonds, and stocks so you can diversify. This is a very powerful investing tool. Since most ETFs have a low investment threshold, it makes it easy for beginners to implement an asset allocation strategy. It all depends on your risk tolerance and investment time horizon. Young investors might be completely invested in their ETFs during their 20s since their high-risk tolerance and investment time horizons are higher. As they get into their 30s and start making lifestyle changes like buying a house, starting a family, they might change to a less aggressive mix like 40 percent in bond ETFs and 60 percent in equity ETFs.

- Swing Trading

These are trades that like taking advantages of large swings in commodities, currencies, or stocks. These could take anywhere from a couple of weeks to a couple of days to get them worked out. This isn't like day trades that are never left open overnight.

What makes ETFs suitable for swing trading are their tight bid spreads and diversification. Since ETFs are available for a wide range of sectors and various investment classes, any beginner could choose to trade their ETFs that are based on an asset class or sector where they have some knowledge or expertise. Somebody who has a background in technology might have a bit of advantage when trading technical ETFs. A beginning trader who tracks the markets might prefer to trade some of the commodity ETFs that are available. Since ETFs are normally baskets of assets and stocks, they might not show the same price movements as just one stock in a bull market. Because of their diversification, this makes them not as susceptible to large downward moves. This gives you some protection against erosion.

- Sector Rotation

ETFs make it easy for beginners to use sector rotation based on different stages of the economic cycle.

Let's say an investor has been investing in the biotechnology sector. With this stock up 137 percent over the past five years, this investor might want to take the profits from this ETF and put it into a different sector like consumer staples.

- Short Selling

This is a sale of a financial instrument or borrowed security. It is normally a risky endeavor for investors and shouldn't ever be attempted by beginners. Short selling an ETF is better to shorting single stocks since it has a lower risk of a short squeeze. A short squeeze is a trading secret where a commodity or security that was heavily shorted all of a sudden starts to spike higher.

Using ETFs to short sell helps a trader take advantage of broad investment themes. If a more advanced beginner is familiar with the risks of shorting, but they want to initiate a short position in the emerging market. Please note that beginners should stay away from double or triple-leveraged inverse ETFs that try to find results that are equal to two or three times the inverse of a one-day price change.

- Seasonal Trends

Another tool to help beginners capitalize on seasonal trends are ETFs. There are two seasonal trends that are very popular. One is known as the "sell in May and go away." This is referring to the fact that equities in the US normally underperform during the six month period from May until October as compared to the November to April time frame. The other trend is that gold will gain during the months of September to October. This is due to strong demands from India before the Diwali festival of lights and wedding season that normally falls between the middle of October to the middle of November. You could exploit the market's weakness by shorting the SPDR S&P 500 ETF near the end of April or the first of May or closing the short position at the end of October just after the market swoons. Any beginner could take advantage of the strength of gold by purchasing units in a gold ETF during late summer and then closing out after several months. Please note that seasonal trends don't happen as you think they will. Stop losses are normally recommended for trading positions to cap the large losses.

- Hedging

A beginning trader might need to protect or hedge against a downside risk if they have a large portfolio, maybe one that was acquired because of an inheritance. Let's say you inherited a large portfolio of blue chips and are worried about the risk of a huge decline inequities. One solution would be to purchase put options. Because most beginners aren't familiar with trading strategies, one alternate strategy is initiating a short position in broad market ETFs. If the market goes down as expected, your equity position gets hedged effectively because declines in your portfolio get offset by gains in the short position. Please note that your gains could be capped if the market goes up because gains get offset by losses in short ETF position. Basically, ETFs give beginners an effective and easy way of hedging.

Reinvesting Dividends from ETFs

A great way to grow your portfolio without having to get out your wallet is to reinvest the dividends that you earn from your investments. Even though mutual funds make dividend reinvestment easy, reinvesting those dividends can become complicated. You can make the reinvestments manual by buying more shares with the money you have earned, or you can do it automatically.

Not every ETF comes with an automatic reinvestment program. The longer the settlement time an ETF has, along with their trading, could make reinvesting ineffective

- Dividend Reinvestment Plans or DRIP

This is simply a program that is offered by brokerage firms, ETFs, or mutual funds that let investors automatically use their dividends to buy more shares of a security. Most people do this with mutual funds, but it can also be done with ETFs.

Even though DRIPs provide you with a handier and more convenient way to increase your investment, they can end up creating problems. Some firms will let you use DRIP buy only if you buy a complete share. If there is any money left over, it will beadded to your investor's account that you could forget about. Other firms will pool your dividends and then only reinvest them on a monthly or quarterly basis.

There are some who will reinvest as soon as the market opens up on payday, while others will wait until after the case has been deposited. This is normally later during the day. Since ETFs get traded like stocks, and their prices vary throughout the day, reinvesting at the beginning of the day might purchase a different number of shares that the trade that waited until later. This is just one drawback of automatically reinvesting your ETF dividends. You lose control of your trade and can't "time" the market to make it advantageous.

- Manual Reinvestment

If you don't have a DRIP option, or if your ETFs don't allow automatic reinvestments, you can reinvest your dividends

217

manually. This basically means you take the cash you have earned and execute another trade to purchase more ETF shares. This will depend on where you have your investment account. You could have to pay a commission. Some brokerage firms have commission-free dividend reinvestments.

Even though manual investing isn't as convenient as DRIP, it does give the investor more control. Instead of just paying the market price for a new share, you can choose to wait if you think the price might drop. It also gives you the option of holding your dividends in cash if you think the ETF isn't performing the way you want it to, and you would like to invest someplace else.

If you do end up manually reinvesting, make sure you know how settlement will delay your buying power. It can take payments longer to settle since ETFs rely on brokerages to track shareholders. ETF payments tend to take three or more days to settle. If the ETF is doing good, this long wait time could cause you to have to pay more for another share.

Reinvesting is an easy way to help your portfolio increase. Due to some of the practices with ETFs, they can be a bit more difficult to reinvest than mutual funds. Speak with your firm to see if you have a DRIP option. If you have to reinvest manually, keep track of the time to make sure you don't time the reinvestment poorly. Creating an order during the same time that the dividend is deposited may not provide you with the best price. You can use manual reinvestments to your advantage by actively managing your trades.

Chapter 8: The Best ETF

Mutual funds and retirement investing go hand in hand. Why shouldn't they? Mutual funds predate ETFs by more than 60 years. Most of the 401k plans don't hold anything but mutual funds. This is why most people link them together.

Don't look over ETFs. Most of the ETFs out there are great trading vehicles and tactical strategies. Some are extremely cheap that can give you what you need for retirement, which is income, protection, and diversification.

ETFs are very popular for anyone who wants to grow their money with long- and short-term horizons. ETFs, let you sell and purchase funds such as stock on the stock exchange. This is different than the normal mutual funds that just let you trade at the end of the business day. ETFs have a combination of quick liquidity and instant diversification. This is the best reason to think about them first when wanting to invest for the first time or as a part of your portfolio.

Most of the ETFs are just simple index funds. They will track just like bonds, stocks, or other investments. This is an inexpensive strategy since you won't be paying a manager to select and analyze your stocks. The good news is that it works.

If you like the strategy of buying and holding and allowing carefully researched investments accumulate returns with time,

ETFs just might be the right choice for you. Warren Buffett knows that it is hard to beat index funds. This is why he has place 90 percent of his money that he is bequeathing to his wife are invested in an S&P 500 ETF.

You don't need to be like Buffett and put all your cash into one of these funds. But these are a low-cost and attractive choice for small and large investors.

ETFs trade almost instantly if you enter a trade with your broker or online. Most ETFs will track just like any stock on the Dow Jones or S&P 500. ETFs can focus on anything that a normal fund can.

Just like any investment, ETFs do have risks. Normally a riskier investment will lead to larger returns. ETFs will follow this same pattern. Funds that focus on bonds and broad, diverse market funds normally offer the lowest risks. Narrower funds and commodity options normally bring more volatility and risk.

The decisions you make about your investments need to align with your financial goals. You need to know your risk tolerance. You have to know if you can afford to lose all or some of your investments and how the choices you make will fit into your financial plan.

You need to think about the underlying assets before you purchase an ETF, you aren't directly purchasing a company's bonds or stock. Rather, you are placing money into a fund that will then buy a "basket" of bonds and stocks for you. Be sure that the fund you are purchasing will invest in assets that you ultimately would choose for yourself.

You need to take into account the volatility and risks. Some people are fine taking risks and betting that these will pay off with large returns. Others want to stay away from large ups and downs. They are more concerned with making sure they have a steady income and preserving their capital. You will need to pick an ETF that will line up with your tolerance for risks.

Watch out for fees. There are some ETFs that are completely free of fees. These ETFs are a brand new concept. Before that, getting a competitive ETF from a company like Schwab, Fidelity, and Vanguard was on top of the competition, with fees as low as .1 percent. The most expensive ETF charged 9.2 percent. You need to compare all the ETFs you are interested in for hidden fees and specific features before you decide to purchase them.

You shouldn't ever purchase an investment if you don't totally know all the risks. If you any concerns, you need to consult with an expert or financial advisor before you enter your trade order.

Here are the best ETFs on the market today:

- "Vanguard S&P 500"

This is the best ETF, and it comes from that biggest mutual fund company. This ETF will track the S&P 500. Its expense ratio is only 0.04 percent. Warren Buffet has recommended this company by name.

Purchasing one of these funds will give you a piece of the 500 largest companies in the US. This gives you a lot of diversity along with a safety net since every investment is focused on the United States.

The S&P 500 is a proxy for the entire economy of the US. It brings a return of about ten percent each year. Even though the past performance isn't a guarantee of how the market will perform in the future as it could go down at any moment. This ETF would be a great choice.

- "Invesco QQQ Trust"

This company only owns Nasdaq stocks that aren't financial. This makes it a tech-heavy fund with some names that you are familiar with. Their ETF is the biggest one around and it is very liquid. It isn't expensive either. It only costs $20 per year for every $10,000 you have invested. It did have a bad performance during 2018. This just shows you how broad the market really is. This isn't saying anything negative about the ETF since it was up almost 33 percent the year before.

- "Fidelity ZERO Total Market Index Fund"

This ETF doesn't have much of a history; it doesn't have any minimums or fees. If you would like to invest for free, this is a great option. There isn't a minimum to invest. This makes it an option for new investors and people who need retirement accounts. The index will focus on the complete return based on the stock market in the US. This makes it more diversified than any S&P 500 fund.

This ETF offers an almost identical performance to the Dow Jones index. In the last ten years, it has outperformed large blends.

- "iShares Core S&P 500"

This ETF tracks the S&P 500. This gives it a broad-based, diversified portfolio in the largest company in America. This fund is backed by the company, Blackrock. The ETF is the biggest around. It has $160 billion in assets. This fund was created in 2000. It has an annual cost of only $4 for each $10,000 that you invest. The bad performance during 2018 shows the market's performance of -4.4%.

- "SPDF S&P 500"

You read that right S&P 500 does have more than one spot on the list. While the VOO from Vanguard is a great idea for long-term investors, this one is the most traded ETF out there.

Since this will track the S&P 500, active investors can use this to sell and purchase stocks in one trade. This launched back in 1993 as the very first ETF. Traders prefer this ETF because it is very liquid. It does charge a 0.095 percent ratio that is higher than Vanguard's. Because it is so popular and is traded frequently, most investors are happy to spend some money on this ETF.

- "ProShares VIX Short-Term Futures"

This is an unusual ETF since it lets investors profit on the market's volatility instead of a certain security. If the volatility goes higher, this ETF will increase in value. It is a great short-term trade since it needs to roll derivatives regularly. This can cost the ETF money with time. In spite of having only a few assets, the fund is liquid. Its expense ratio costs $87 each year for every $10,000 you invest.

- "iShares Russell 2000"

This tracks2,000 small stocks. It is comprised of the littlest 2,000 on the Russell 3000 index. This is a great way to track the stock market, but it focuses on the small companies within the public market rather than the largest.

This has an expense ratio of 0.19 percent. This is lower than most mutual funds but nowhere close to the bottom of the ETFs. If you compare it to any S&P 500 fund, iShare Russell 2000 managers will have four times the number of stocks to purchase and sell to keep the fund with the index.

There are a few investors who argue that small stocks have the room to grow more than the larger stocks, while others will argue that small stocks are more volatile and risky. If you want to purchase a huge batch of companies with one purchase, this is the best way to go.

- "Vanguard High Dividend Yield"

This ETF will track the "FTSE High Dividend Yield Index." This index includes American stocks that pay high yields. It has about $23 billion dollars to manage, and this makes it very liquid. It is sponsored by Vanguard, the most reputable name in the business. This ETF was created in 2006. It only charges $6 for each $10,000 that you have invested. It won't cut into the payout too much.

- "Schwab U.S. Dividend Equity"

Schwab brings us another low-cost ETF. This ETF is a great choice if you want to turn your portfolio into cash. This fund will focus on large companies that have stable dividends. Retirees who are looking to earn money from their portfolio without having to sell their stocks will use dividend stocks as an investment. This ETF is managed to track on the Dow Jones. It charges a competitive 0.07 percent expense ratio.

- "Vanguard Health Care Index Fund"

Another Vanguard fund makes an appearance. This fund charges ten dollars for each $10,000 that you have invested. This allows you to be exposed to more than 300 stocks on the sector. This can protect you from any negative performances in the industry. If a radical change affects healthcare in general, this fund stays protected. This fund was created in 2004 and has about $9.4 billion in assets.

- "SPDR Gold Trust"

If you would like to invest in gold without having to actually buy a bar of gold, this would be your best option. It charges 0.04 percent for its expense ratio. Gold is normally used a hedge fund against a decline in the market. If the economy or stocks fall, investors normally turn to gold as a safety net. This means that gold will usually trade inversely to the more popular index. Just remember that if you want to turn some of your hard-earned money into gold.

- "Vanguard FTSE Developed Markets"

If you want to add some international flair to your portfolio, companies in well-developed countries usually offer a good balance of return and risk. Funds that are as well developed might be more tempting, but be careful because these are riskier than the developed markets.

This ETF follows the "FTSE Developed All Cap ex US Index." This means that it will follow companies of any size in any developed country other than the US. This puts stocks in the developed Pacific nations, Europe, and Canada into your portfolio easily. It only charges an expense ratio of 0.07 percent.

- "iShares MSCI EAFE"

You have to make sure your portfolio is diversified because there isn't any investment that will work all the time. This ETF holds more than 900 stocks from over 12 countries, including France, United Kingdom, and Japan. Even though it is a blended fund most of these caps will yield a lot more than their American counterparts. This can lead to more money than the S&P 500.

- "Vanguard Total Stock Market"

If you aren't sure which index you should follow, or you want to invest in various market capitalization and sectors, this might be for you. This ETF covers the whole domestic stock market. This is a balanced fund that has a great mix of blue-chip, midcap, and small-cap stocks. This has a low expense ratio of 0.03 percent.

- "iShares Cohen & Steers REIT"

This is a real estate investment trust. They are a bit different than normal stocks. These were created by Congress back in the 60s to give investors access to real estate. It would be very hard for normal people to find a million dollars to buy or lease a strip mall or office building. Any investor can find a few hundred dollars for a couple of shares.

These are great for retirement investors for several reasons. These funds are obligated to pay out no less than 9 percent of their profits to their shareholders. This makes real estate a great source of income for retired people.

This ETF combines the expertise of Cohen and Steers with iShares to create a fund that protects you from market crashes. This ETF gives less than other REITs. It does have an emphasis on high quality and gives better price-performance. This makes it a winner.

- "Vanguard Total World Stock"

This is the best ETF for an investor who wants a whole world of stock without purchasing numerous funds. It might just be the only stock that you will ever need. It places over 8,000 stocks within your reach from all over the world. It has a yield of about 2.3 percent and only costs 0.9 percent. This is truly a one-stop-shop for equities. It is very cheap for everything you get. At this moment, it yields more than the US markets.

- "SPDR Bloomberg Barclays 1-3 Month T-Bill"

This is a money market ETF and is designed to protect you and your assets while you are earning money. These invest in short-term, high-quality debt like Treasury notes or CDs. They won't yield much, but they are a very low risk. This makes them ideal during turbulent markets.

There are other money market ETFs, but this one is an inexpensive and solid choice. You can't find many small ETFs out there. This one only holds 15 very short-term Treasury issues that range from one to three months. It has an average duration of only 29 days.

- "Vanguard Total Bond Market"

There is a place in most portfolios for bonds, especially retirement accounts. This is because they give out fixed distributions that retired people can use as income. It can help if you have other uncorrelated assets. Why are bond funds better than individual bonds? They are harder to research than other stocks. They normally don't get covered by the media. Bond funds take the responsibility off your place, and you get a bonus of spreading the risk across hundreds and possibly thousands of bonds. This has an expense ratio of 0.035 percent.

Chapter 9: Live On Income With Dividends in ETF, or Sell Everything and Make The Good Life

You might still be a bit confused as to how you make money from ETFs. Contrary to popular belief, ETFs aren't magic or lottery tickets. Just like most things, they do have their cons and pros that need to be weighed carefully. You have to seriously think about your personal resources, preferences, circumstances, and any other relevant factor. This chapter will give you an understanding of how profits get generated for ETF investors, so hopefully it will give you some questions to ask your financial advisor or help you make better choices about your portfolio.

How ETFs Make You Money

Getting money from ETFs is just like getting money from investing in mutual funds since they operate just about identically. How you make money on your ETFs all depends on the kind of investment it holds.

An ETF is kind of like a trust fund. It might invest in famous indexes like the S&P 500 or The Dow Jones, preferred stock, commodities like silver or gold, bonds, or stocks. So, what exactly does this mean for an investor? It basically comes down to one thing: The way you make money from your ETF all depends on the underlying investment of said ETF with time.

Basically, this is saying that if you own an ETF that focuses on stocks that pay high dividends, you hope to make money from dividends paid from the same stocks and capital gains.

If you own an ETF known as a bond fund, you are hoping to make money from interest. If you have an ETF in real estate, you are hoping to make money from the income generated by other real estate owned, office buildings, hotels, apartments, capital gains on property sales, and underlying rents.

Mutual Funds and ETFs Make Money Similarly

Just like mutual funds, there are three things that can help you increase the return on your ETF with time. These same things will hold true when you are trying to make money with an ETF:

- Stay Focused on the Long Term

ETFs normally perform in line with their holdings short of some type of structural problem or other event. This basically means that if you hold an ETF, you might have to suffer through some bad highs and lows in the market value during the year. You might see time like during 2007 and 2009 when your holdings are down between 20 and 50 percent or more. If you can't handle dealing with things like this, you don't have any business investing in these types of securities. There aren't any guarantees about what the future is going to look like, but historically, time has gotten rid of most of that volatility and investors will get rewarded well.

- Keep the Expenses Reasonable

Normally, this isn't a huge problem since ETFs have expenses that are affordable. This is the main reason that investors prefer them over individually managed accounts. Basically, this means that you, a financial advisor, or a financial planner can put together a portfolio of diversified holding and pick up things such as ETFs that will focus on industries or individual sectors for a ration like .50 percent annually.

- If You Don't Understand the ETF, Don't Invest In It

You will find some crazy ETFs out there. Some of these will utilize short stocks and super leverage, some that only invest in countries that are just above the third world, still others that will concentrate in certain industries or sectors. Warren Buffett likes saying that the first rule to making money is not to ever lose any. The next rule is to look at rule number one. You need to know exactly what the underlying holding of every ETF you own so that you know why you invested in it.

The main thing you need to remember is that ETFs are similar to other investments because they won't solve every problem. They are only a tool.

Dividends on ETFs

There are two types of dividends issued on ETFs. These are non-qualifies and qualified dividends.

If you own ETFs, you might receive money in the form of dividends. These could get pain monthly or other intervals. It all depends on the particular ETF. It's important to know that all dividends aren't treated equally when talking about taxes.

Let's look closer at the types of dividends.

- Nonqualified Dividends

These don't get designated by the ETF as qualifies since they may have been payable on stocks that were held by the ETF for two months or less. These get taxed at regular income rates. Nonqualified dividends are the total dividends less any portion of the total dividend that gets treated as qualified dividends.

- Qualified Dividends

These get designated by the ETF as being qualified. This means that they qualify to get taxed at the same rate as capital gains. It all depends on the investor's taxable income and MAGI or modified adjusted gross income. The dividends get pain on the stock that is held by the ETF. They have to own them for over two months during any 121 day period that starts two months before the ex-dividend date. Plus, the investor has to own shares in the ETF that is paying the dividend for over two months during the same 121-day time frame that starts two months before the ex-dividend date. This basically meant that if you actively trade ETFs, you won't meet these requirements.

Please note that qualified dividends get taxed at the same rats as capital gains, you can't use them to offset capital losses.

Other Distributions

It all depends on the kind of ETF; other distributions might not be qualified dividends. Here are a few examples of other kinds of distributions:

- REIT or real estate investment trust ETFs normally pay nonqualified dividends.

- Fixed-income ETFs will pay you interest and not dividends.

1. NII or Net Investment Income Tax

If you make a lot of money, your dividends might be subject to a Medicare tax of 3.8 percent plus any income tax on the dividends. This tax will apply to the net investment income.

2. Reporting Dividends

Wherever you hold your ETFs has to send a report to the IRS annually and they will send you any payments on your dividends that were over ten dollars. They will send you Form 1099-DIV.

3. Reinvesting Dividends

You could choose to either use your dividends to purchase more shares within the same ETF. There might be some commissions for reinvesting the dividends. You will need to check with the firm or financial institution that holds your ETFs.

4. Dividends ETFs

The dividend ETF is made up of stocks that pay dividends that you can track on an index. This ETF will pay dividends to all their investors that can be either non-qualified or qualified dividends.

If you get a fairly large amount of dividends from your ETFs, you might need to pay quarterly taxes. You might need to talk with your tax advisor to figure out your tax needs and make sure that you report your dividends on your yearly tax return.

A Guide to ETF Dividends

There are many great reasons to add dividend stocks to your portfolio. Other than the obvious reason for creating money, dividends usually hold up better than their counterparts during the rough times. They aren't as volatile on the market.

Owning dividend stocks won't be right for everybody. Most investors don't have time, desire, or knowledge to research and then construct a portfolio of stocks. If this sounds like you if you just want to make a solid portfolio before you add individual stocks, purchasing ETFs might be the best way to get some exposure.

- Individual Dividend Stocks Vs. ETFs

There are both drawbacks and benefits to both ETF investing and purchasing individual dividend stocks.

The phrase dividend stock refers to any stock that makes any cash payment to its shareholders regularly. These can be smart choices for investors who are looking for income since they can create a steady income but has more long-term growth than other investments such as bonds. Why would you use ETFs to purchase dividend stocks?

ETFs will simplify the process. ETFs allow you to purchase a portfolio of well-diversified stocks with one investment and without having to research or the risk that comes with purchasing stocks.

One drawback to ETF investing is you are going to pay continuous investment fees. These might be small and possible negligible sometimes, but portfolio managers never work for free. ETFs charge investors fees that cover expenses.

Individual stocks do have some benefits. The biggest one is individual stocks could beat the index with time, while most of the ETFs are passive investments that will track on an index. Passive ETFs will match the same performance as a stock on the index. A portfolio of individual stock could underperform on a specific index with time. An ETF will guarantees that you will match the index's performance after the fees.

- How Much Does It Cost to Invest in ETFs

I have mentioned the word fee a couple times now, so let's talk about the cost of investing in ETFs. There are two costs you should know: trading commissions and ongoing investment fees.

Expense ratios are a percentage of the assets and get paid out of the assets. You don't get billed directly. If you have an expense ratio of .3 percent meant that for every $2,000 you invested, you are going to pay $6 in annual fees.

Your broker might charge you a trading commission just like you would if you had purchased a stock. These could vary significantly depending on the brokerage you use. Some brokers have an ETF program where certain ETFs are commission-free but this selection is normally limited and changes a lot.

- Tax Implications

If you purchase your ETFs using your IRA, you don't have to worry about any tax implication regularly. If you invest in a standard brokerage account, there will be some tax implications.

There are capital gains taxes. These are taxes on any profit you get from your ETF shares. Capital gains don't get taxed until you sell the shared. At this point, they are called realized capital gains. If your ETF goes up from $$25 to $500 per share and you haven't sold it, it will still be an unrealized gain and won't be taxable.

When you sell it for a profit, there will be various capital gains tax rates that will apply depending on how long you have owned the shares. If you have owned them for over one year, you will get taxed at long-term capital gains rates. These are normally lower than the corresponding tax brackets for each level of income. If you have owned your share for less than one year, any realized gains are going to be taxed like any ordinary income, according to your tax bracket within the year that you decided to sell the shares.

The other tax issue you have to be aware of is dividend taxes. ETF dividends are taxable in the year that you bought them. Most dividends, meet the IRS definition of qualified dividends that get taxed at the same tax rate as long-term capital gains. There are exceptions. Some international stock ETFs won't qualify for preferential tax treatment.

Your broker will keep track of what dividends need to be classified in whatever manner. They will report that total to you and the IRS on a 1099-DIV at the end of the year.

- Passive Vs. Active ETFs

There are two types of mutual funds and ETFs; one is passively managed funds called index funds. The other one is actively managed funds.

Passively managed index funds will track an index along with the investment. Because you don't need any strategy to invest, index funds have a lower expense ratio.

Actively managed funds won't track a certain index. They will employ investment manages to create a portfolio of commodities, bonds, or stocks with the end goal of beating a certain index. Since they paid their active managers, actively managed funds usually have a high expense ratio.

- Should You Invest in ETFs

A good ETF dividend could be a great fit in any long-term investor's portfolio. ETFs make good sense for specific kinds of investors:

1. Older investors who use investments for their income. If you are older and need more income, but you would like to keep a significant allocation, ETFs dividends are a good choice. It doesn't matter how old an investor is, your portfolio needs to be age-appropriate with bonds and stocks along with dividend ETFs. This will let older investors do this while giving a steady stream of income.

2. Investors who would like to put money to work for them for a long period of time. If you would like to invest for five or more years, but you don't want to choose these individual stock, dividend ETFs are a great choice.

3. Risk-averse investors use reliable dividends to help make a "price floor" to sort stock prices and use this to boost them during the tough times. If the stock market crashes, dividend stocks normally outperform their counterparts.

If any of the above sounds like you, then an ETF dividend would be a smart choice for you.

The Risks

You won't find any stock investment that doesn't come with a risk.

Investing in dividend stocks by going through ETFs can help you navigate the company and certain risks of investing in stocks. If you have a broad dividend ETF, and a company had a bad quarter, this effect on this investment will be minimal.

But you are still going to need to worry about the risks that don't have anything to do with systematic risks. If the whole market crashes, as it did in 2008 and 2009, your dividend ETFs will probably go down in value.

Another risk is interest rates. In an interest rate goes up, it will put pressure on every investment that generates an income, and this includes dividend stocks.

So, in summary, investing in ETF dividends will have risks, especially with short time periods. But it is still a great way to generate a stream of income, and with longer periods of time, there will be better returns.

Chapter 10: Enjoying The Rest of Your Life As a Rich Man

The main reason that most people invest is to have a safe retirement plan in place. The majority of most people's assets can be found in accounts that are dedicated especially toward that purpose, but as hard as saving enough money to have a comfortable retirement is, learning to live off your investment when you finally retire is just as hard.

Making a living from your dividends once you retire is a dream many people have, but only a handful achieve. In this day and age will all the rising life expectancies like the longest bull market and very low yielding bonds, people who want to retire face challenges from every aspect of life to create a constant stream of income that will last over your lifetime.

Before you zero in on one investment vehicle or strategy, you have to know how much risk you are willing to take when talking about your whole portfolio and your rate of return that you can reach.

Even though everybody will reach their own conclusions, we are connected through a certain desire. We want to have a specific quality of life during our retirement that allows us to sleep well and not to outlive our savings.

We all think that investing in dividends could help us achieve all of these objectives, but if your nest egg isn't large enough to let you live off that income without having to touch the principal, it is necessary to keep some sources that can easily be diversified.

Most of the paychecks you get during retirement get funded by a combination of withdrawals from your principal and investment incomes. Income generators like systematic withdrawals or annuities usually give you a better income than having a dividend strategy.

Being able to withdraw money takes a combination of selling stocks or funds and spending interest income to take care of the rest. The four percent rule for personal finances thrives here. The four percent rule tries to give you a stream of income while keeping a balance that allows money to be withdrawn for many years to come. What if I told you there was a different way to get that four percent without having to reduce principal or selling shares?

A way you can enhance your income is by investing in mutual funds and stocks that pay dividends. With time, the cash that gets generated by those payments will be able to supplement your pension income and Social Security, and it could give you all the money you are going to need to keep up the lifestyle that you are used to. You can live by only using your dividends as long as you do some planning.

Dividend Growth

The main reason why stocks need to be part of your portfolio is that stock dividends will grow with time. That growth can outpace inflation. For investors that have a long timeline, this could be exploited to carte portfolios that could be used just for living off dividendincome.

The best strategy is to use those dividends to purchase more shares of a firm so you can get more dividends and purchase more shares.

Let's say you have invested $300,000 in Treasury bonds and another $500,000 in stocks that yield you three percent; this gives you $15,000 in dividend income every year. Once you have spent all of your dividends and you sell part of your bonds, you will finally reach the $40,000 you need for your annual income. After 21 years, your portfolio is going to be completely depleted.

Over that amount of time, your annual income could have gone up by another third to come to $20,000 a year, and this is after you have taken into consideration the amount of inflation. The most important thing here is that you still own all your stocks.

The mix of stocks and bonds are going to vary as based on how much of a nest egg you have, how tolerant you are of the market, and your objectives about returns, creating a portfolio with a couple dozen good dividend stocks that yield no less than three percent and they increase their dividend by 3.5 percent every year can be extremely attainable.

Some people who have retired with a systemic withdrawal plan could end up feeling pressured to reduce their spending whenever the stock market is going through a decline; you could still enjoy a decent pay raise if you have the right stocks.

You Have Already Retired

Compounding income is great as long as you have a timeline that is long term, but what if you are going into retirement now? For investors, dividend growth and a higher yield just might do the trick.

For investors who have retired and want to live off just, their dividends might want to up their yield. Securities and stocks that have a higher yield normally don't generate a lot of distribution growth. You can add these to your portfolio, and it would increase your yield. This will go a long way in helping you pay your bills.

Investors who have retired don't need to stay away from stocks such as Proctor and Gamble. Firms that have higher dividend growth will increase income near or greater than the rates of inflation. This can help up your income for your future. When you add these firms to your portfolio, investors will sacrifice some of their current yield for a bigger pay in the future.

An investor who has a small portfolio might have problems living completely off their dividends, but the steady and rising payment will help reduce their principal withdrawals.

Most withdrawal methods involve a combination of the interest income from bonds and asset sales. There are other ways to hit that four percent rule. If you can invest in quality dividend stocks that have payouts that will increase, both new and older investors could benefit from a stock's inflations beating, compounding, distribution growth. You just need to do some planning, and you might just be able to live off your payments.

Companies that Pay Dividends

In order to alleviate worrying about all the ups and downs of the stock market, find companies that will pay a safe a growing dividend. You should focus on growing your income through dividends instead of all that noise caused by volatile stock prices. This works better if you have created an investment strategy, and you have gotten rid of your emotional risk that comes along with investing.

While a portfolio of stocks can experience some variables in market value, that income from your portfolio can constantly grow with time. Even while going through a financial crisis, there are about 230 companies that will still increase their dividend.

This is in strict contrast with the systematic withdrawal system. Which one of these sounds a lot more stressful:

- A person who lives off of the cash that is distributed and produced by investment every month

- A person who has to choose which assets to sell just to get enough money to live through the year

Living on income from dividends gives you money without you having to stress over trying to figure out what to sell and especially when there is another crash in the market.

Your focus stays on finding safe dividend payments instead of being concerned about the market's volatility and how this will impact how much you can withdraw. If there isn't a reduction in the dividend, money will continue to roll in no matter the way the market might be.

Another good benefit of having stocks that offer dividends during retirement is most companies will increase their dividend rates with time, and this can help offset inflation.

Past performance of the stock market doesn't indicate future results. Those who need a decent size income will be able to protect their future with the correct stocks.

Having a strategy will grow and preserve your principal with time, which is very different than most withdrawal and annuity strategies. This gives you the chance to have something for your family. Investing in dividends will give you the flexibility to sell things if you were to need some money for something special or unexpected. Annuities don't have this kind of flexibility.

Dividend stocks have helped the market with time. They play an important role in capital growth and preservation. What exactly does this mean? Let's say you bought two $10,000 stocks on the S&P 500 in 1960. One of your investments didn't have any dividends. One's value was totally driven by the market.

The other investment had dividends that were paid by S&P companies. All payments were placed back into a stock once received. This helped them reach over $2.5 million by the close of 2017. The first investment only grew to $500,000. This shows that dividends do matter.

The importance of dividends will change with each decade. It all depends on how strong the market. During times when the stock market is stagnating, like during the 70s and 2000s, dividends had a larger part of the market's return.

Since the market is trading at a higher level today, which makes it harder to get capital gains,during the next decade, the market's return will be made up of dividends.

Stocks will always be more attractive than bonds, no matter the way you view it. The world of finance has undergone a lot of change during the past 40 years. You will no longer see double-digit yields on bonds. Most stocks will yield a lot more than bonds now.

Warren Buffett said back in May of 2018: "Long-term bonds are a terrible investment at current rates and anything close to current rates."

Why all the hatred for long-term bonds? Just like anything else, it is simple math. Long-term bonds will yield about a three percent rate today. This investment is taxable. This makes their after-tax yield around two and a half percent.

The Federal Reserve is getting about two percent annually for inflations. This makes the bonds after-tax return at only a half percent each year.

Bonds at this rate are completely ridiculous. When you think about the stock return at almost ten percent each year, dividends will increase their payments.

Other than fueling returns, investing in dividends has less volatility than other stocks, too.

Stocks that give dividend payments will have attributes that most conservative investors will like. They have a dividend that grows steadily,and that shows that the company is confident, stable, and durable.

To be able to pay out dividends, the company has to create a profit above and beyond the needs of the business. They are more careful in how they spend their money.

These qualities disqualify most of the lower quality businesses that have a lot of debt, weak cash flow, and volatile earnings. These characteristics could lead to huge losses and swings in the price of their shares.

Because these stocks have a lower volatility profile, they are more attractive to people who want to preserve more of their capital.

Hanging onto stocks instead of mutual funds or ETFs can protect all the money that you need to get while you remain in control of all your assets.

When you invest in securities on your own, it gets rid of the fees accumulated every year by most of the mutual funds and ETFs. This can save you thousands of dollars. All you will pay is a commission fee of about ten dollars for each trade if you go through a discount broker.

Managing your portfolio takes discipline and time. This is what makes it unacceptable for most people. Even though it doesn't guarantee that it will perform better, it will get rid a huge drag on your return, and that is the fees that most advisors and managers on Wall Street will charge you.

High fees equal lower dividend incomes. The fees that most fund managers charge are the main reason why Warren Buffett always advises a normal person that if they want the best long-term results, they need to put their money into low-cost funds.

You might have heard about low-cost ETF's that only have a fee of around 0.1 percent. If you don't have the stomach or time to purchase and hang on to these stocks, it would be in your best interest to look at these for your portfolio.

The downside is you lose a wonderful benefit, which is control.

Most ETFs will own dozens, and possibly thousands of stocks. Some of these might be great businesses,and their dividends are safe, but others might be a lower quality and decide to get rid of them. Some might give you extremely high yields while others won't generate any income at all.

Basically, this is saying that an ETF is many companies that might or might not match your income needs and will risk their tolerance extremely well.

Some ETFs found problems in the middle of the financial crisis since they weren't focused on the safety of their dividends. Their dividend income dropped by about 25 percent, and it took them several years to completely recover.

Choosing your own stocks while remaining focused on the safety of your income could deliver a faster-growing, higher income that is predictableas compared to the majority of the ETFs that are low cost. This helps you understand your investments and this will help you handle the dips in the market with better confidence.

Owning dividend stocks for your retirement has many benefits. You will preserve your principal. Your income will stay steady no matter where the stock prices go. You will be able to protect how much you purchase with your dividend growth. The initial investment fee is going to be lower. You are going to know exactly what you have to pay.

But there are some risks that you should be aware of when you want to live off of the income from your dividends.

The Risks

The correct diversification is the best part of constructing your portfolio. If someone only buys dividend stocks for their retirement, they are only concentrating on one investment style and class. Most people will advise you to keep 20 and 75 percent exposurefor your portfolio with cash and bonds, making up the remaining.

Allocating assets will depend upon your situation and what your risk tolerance is. The main objective for retirement is making sure that you keep your standard of living so that you don't end up outliving your money.

Some people will be able to meet this income amount through guaranteed interest from CDs, Social Security, and pension income. For these people, some investors might allow between 80 and 100 percent of their portfolio to be stocks that pay dividends in order to increase their income and to reach a stronger income growth capital appreciation. The mixture of your assets of cash, stocks, and bonds will be driven by how tolerant you are for risks and the income you need to live on.

Even though this goes against normal asset allocation, this calls for holding a balance of bonds and stocks. Most retired people look at their pension and Social Security as their "guaranteed" income. This makes them comfortable to invest in heavier stocks.

High-quality stocks can up the volatility of your portfolio as compared to having a mixture of stocks and treasuries. This allows you to generate more income. This income will then increase faster. This allows your portfolio to have a larger potential for appreciating capital.

The short term returns are going to be less predictable. This can end up being an issue if you have to sell part of your portfolio at times just to make ends meet once you are retired. A zero return on bonds will be more attractive if your portfolio drops by just 25 percent.

You could also get into trouble if you only have high-yielding stocks that are concentrated in a few sectors, such as utilities and real estate. You could also be affected by hindsight bias. People who are constantly wanting to own dividends that grow have caused stock groups to become hugely popular with investors.

These stocks get more attention from investors since they can outperform the market, and people like assuming many will continue to grow and pay their dividends, which isn't a guarantee. Look at AIG or GE before the financial crisis to get an example.

These two companies aren't alone. Companies who are a part of the S&P 500 lowered their dividends by about 24 percent between 2008 and 2010. The index fell about 22 percent. They outperformed the market, but they still took a huge hit as compared to bonds.

It is important to diversify your holding and own stocks rather than bonds. If a company can't pay its debts, it will file for bankruptcy. If things were to get rough for a company, it would get rid of the dividends first in order to stay afloat. Basically, this is saying that their dividend income and stocks are riskier than bonds. You won't ever find a free lunch.

Only focusing on the return of income is another trap that some investors fall into. If a company can pay its dividend doesn't automatically make them a better investment. It doesn't matter if your money comes from selling parts of your portfolio, bonds, or dividend income.

A lot of people prefer to keep their principals untouched and live off only the income our dividends generate every month, even if this does give less of a return. This is irrational and can cause you to chase higher-yielding stocks. It would be a huge mistake to buy stocks that match your objective.

Most stocks that have a yield higher than five percent are showing you that something might be wrong with a business, or they could end up cutting the dividend in order to help the company survive. With problems like this, the principal will face the biggest risk of facing long-term erosion.

You need to figure out why the company offers large payouts. We think that investors should find low-risk stocks that give five percent or less. These usually have better chances of growing and maintaining principal and earnings with time.

It doesn't matter because the reality is that most people who retire can't live off of the dividends every year without using some of their capital. These people need to try to create a portfolio for a complete return instead of income alone.

After you have figured out your portfolio, you can find out the amount of cash flow you will get from it, whether it is through selling assets, dividends, payments from interest, or other things. Payments from dividends are just one way to create a constant cash flow, but this should not be seen as a vacuum. You should always keep an open mind and make sure you stay aware of different income sources that could be a better fit.

Some other downsides with investing is the time it can take to remain current in holdings and the knowledge that is needed to get you started. Investing isn't rocket science; you do need a stomach for risk, and enough literacy to know the basics of a company, common sense, and a commitment to remain current with your holdings.

If you were to look at the savings you receive from being a do-it-yourself investor versus an investor who handles your money for a fee, you could save thousands of dollars if you are willing to make a commitment. This could end up helping you in the long run with retirement, and it beats having to work if investing is something you like better.

This also assumes that an investor is able to find stocks that are safe and will perform well and ETFs that are available.

Dealing with your assets and getting ready to retire is an overwhelming process. There are a lot of different decisions that must be made based on risk, life expectations, and objectives. These differences can drive decisions you make, but you can rush them.

For every decision you make, you have to review all of the fine print, flexibility, and fees of the stock. You need to remember that you need a constant cash flow, and you have tied yourself down to one source like dividend income, annuity payments, or bond interest.

Quality stocks can give you a foundation of income and complete return for most portfolios. Most investors don't have a huge nest egg that they need to live off of during retirement, but having a properly created portfolio of stocks could give you long-term capital appreciation, income growth, and a safe income to help you make a larger portfolio last the rest of your life.

FAQs

- Are there tax advantages for owning ETFs?

Just like conventional mutual index funds, the majority of ETFs try to stay on track with an index like the S&P 500. An ETF will only sell and buy stocks when the benchmark index does. Large investment moves, such as if a company gets taken away from the index, occurs rarely.

Plus, ETF managers will use the losses to help offset their gains. This will reduce or get rid of the taxable gains that the shareholders get at the end of every year.

- Do ETFs have dividend distributions and capital gains? If they do, can these be reinvested?

ETFs, distribute capital gains just like mutual funds do. This normally happens in December. The dividends get paid quarterly or monthly. It all depends on the EFT. It's rare for index ETFs to have capital gains, and you might face taxes even if you didn't sell any shares.

You might be able to reinvest your dividends, and capital gains it all depends on who you have your ETFs with.

- Why is an ETFs market price different from their net asset value?

The market price of ETFs is controlled by supply and demand. It all depends on market forces. The price might be below or above the NAV, which is called the discount or premium.

If you want to find out information on a certain ETFs closing price, look for the tab called "Price and Performance" on your ETFs profile page.

- How does an ETFs market price get determined?

An ETF's market price gets determined by the bonds and stocks' prices that are owned by the ETF along with the supply and demand of the market.

A market price can end up changing during the day and could end up being below or above the full price of what is in the ETF. These differences are normally quite small; it might be significant if the market is volatile.

- Are there certain kinds of ETFs that I can place?

You have the ability to place any kind of trade just like you do with stocks, and these include:

  o Stop-limit orders: these have multiple steps. This will require a trigger price. If the price moves past the price you picked, the order will be created automatically.

  o Stop orders: these also have multiple steps. You have to set a trigger price, and if that price moves past that trigger price, the market order automatically gets created.

  o Market orders: these will usually go right away at the best price available, but you won't have as much control over the price you will get or pay.

  o Limit orders: this ensures that you will get the price in the range that you have set. This will be the minimum you will accept or the max you will pay.

- What is the difference between a mutual fund and an ETF?

There are a lot more similarities than differences between mutual funds and ETFs. The largest differences are:

1. ETFs pricing is more transparent. They give you real-time pricing so that you will be able to see the change in prices during the day. Mutual funds aren't priced until after the close of the day. This means you aren't going to know the price until after the trade has been placed.

2. ETFs will have lower minimums. The minimum of an ETF is the price of one share. This might be as low as $50. It all depends on the ETF. Mutual funds might require you to pay anything from $1,000 to $3,000 or even higher.

Conclusion

Thank you for making it through to the end of *Retire Early with ETF Investing Strategy*, let's hope it was informative and able to provide you with all of the tools you need to achieve your goals whatever they may be.

The next step is to start looking at your current financial situation and figure out what your goals are for the future. As you have heard time and time again, investing and retirement won't look the same for two people. It is ultimately up to you how you decide to use your money and what to do to make sure you are able to retire as early as you want to. Once you have figured out your goals and you know where you stand financially, you can start to take some active steps towards making more money and saving more for your retirement. I would suggest getting into investing before you try to branch out into bigger things like real estate and the like. It also wouldn't hurt to check to see if you could be making more at your job and if you are using your time and money wisely there. In the end, find what works best for you and feels right. It's your life and your retirement.

Finally, if you found this book useful in anyway, a review on Amazon is always appreciated!

Description

If you are looking for a way to retire early and live the big life, then keep reading.

Investing may not be the first thing that pops into your head when thinking of retiring early, but it is one of the best options. If you have looked into investing, you have probably heard things like stocks, bonds, day trading, and so on, but what you may not have heard of is ETFs. They aren't the biggest player in the investing world, but people are discovering their possibilities. And ETFs come with a lot of choices as well, so that you can keep your risk right where you want it to be.

While investing in ETFs aren't the only thing you should do to retire early, they are a great place to start. I understand, though, if you're still skeptical about the whole retiring early thing. That's a touchy subject because there is mixed information out there. Some people say it isn't possible to retire early, some don't even think people can retire on time, but then you have the small group of people that tell you that, yes, you can retire early. That's what this book is here to teach you. You will learn:

- The best income streams to start

- The top ETFs to invest in to get the most return

- Dividends or selling, which is better?

- How to figure out how much money you need to have to retire

- What risk is, and how to figure our yours

... And much more.

Now, I understand that people are little leery of investing, and especially the thoughts of living off of investments in their golden years. There are a lot of unknowns in the world of investing, but with the right knowledge and planning, you can avoid a lot of the problems people face with investing. Also, you may worry that you could run out of money, but that's where the planning comes into play. We'll discuss everything you need to know to make sure that doesn't happen.

While it may not sound pretty or fun, planning is the key to make sure you can retire when you want and live the rest of your life doing whatever you want. It is possible to retire early, and if you trust me, I will teach you exactly how it can be done. All you have to is take a chance and buy this book. If the larger view of things, purchasing this book is just a drop in the ocean of the things you have bought to help your future. Take that chance right now and scroll back up and click "buy now."

Millionaire Habits

How Any Person Can Become a Millionaire Through Success Habits

Nathan Bell

Introduction

There is nothing wrong with desiring to be rich. The motive for riches is the desire for a richer and more abundant life. And this desire is worthy to praise. A person who doesn't wish to live more abundantly is abnormal, and so the man who does not dream to have more money enough to purchase all he wants is abnormal.

There are three reasons for which we live; we live for the mind, we live for the body and the soul. No one of this is holier than the other. It is not right to live only for the soul and deny the body or mind. And it is wrong to live for the intellect and deny the soul or body.

It is perfectly okay that you should dream of being rich. If you are a normal man or woman, you cannot afford to do so. It is perfectly right that you should offer your best focus to the science of becoming a millionaire. This book is going to reveal millionaire success habits that you can adapt and become successful like other millionaires. Keep reading if you want to become rich.

Chapter 1: Change Your Habits, No Procrastination

Have you ever wondered why some people are more successful than others? Or why you don't make a lot of money despite having performed well in school? To some, this question can be the focal point of a lifelong search. However, the answer is short. You are who you are because of yourself. You are in control of who you want to be. Your current life is the total of the choices you make in life, decisions, and actions you make in life. In other words, you can build your future by altering your behaviors. You can make new decisions and choices that ate more in line with the person you want to be and the things you want to achieve with your life.

Reflect on this, everything that you are or ever wanted to be is up to you. And the only real obstacle on what you can be, do and possess is the limit you plant on your own imagination. You can have complete control of your destiny by taking charge of your thoughts, actions, and words from this day going forward.

The Power of Habit

Almost 95% of what you do and achieve is the result of habit. Right from childhood, you have a series of conditioned responses that cause you to react automatically and unthinkingly in almost every situation. This means, people who succeed have learned successful habits and unsuccessful people don't have.

Successful people automatically do the right things at the correct time. Therefore, they achieve ten and twenty times as much as average people who haven't mastered these traits and practiced these habits.

Definition of Success

We can define success as the ability to live your life the way you want. This involves what you like most and interacting with people who you like and respect.

In a larger percentage, we can define success as the ability to accomplish your dreams, goals, and wishes in each of the critical parts of your life.

While everybody is unique and different from all other human beings who have ever lived, we all have four desires in common. On that note, you can perform a quick evaluation of your life by ranking each of these four categories on a scale of one to four.

- **Healthy and fit**
- **Excellent relationships**
- **Do what you love**
- **Accomplish financial independence**

Establish "Million Dollar Habits"

It's important to learn how to think more effectively and make the right decisions. Also, you must learn how to act correctly. This book will teach you how to plan for your financial life in such a manner that you accomplish all your financial goals quicker than you imagine.

One of the most vital goals you must accomplish to remain successful in life is the development of your own character. You want to become a great person in every sector. You want to be that person who everyone admires. You want to become a great

275

leader in your community and a role model for personal success to all individuals around you.

In every situation, the decisive elements in the achievement of each of these goals that we all share in common is the creation of the specific habits that automatically trigger the results you want to attain.

Habits Are Learned

The best thing about habits is that all are learned through practice and repetition. You can learn any habit that you consider desirable or necessary. By following your willpower and discipline, you can polish your personality and character in almost any manner you wish. You can write the script of your own life, and in case you don't like the current script, you can remove it and write a fresh one.

The same way your good habits are the reason for most of your success and happiness, your bad habits are the cause of most of your problems and frustrations. However, because bad habits are learned as well, they can be eliminated and replaced with good habits using the same process of practice and repetition.

You Have Total Control

The fact is that it's not easy to form good habits, but it's easy to live with. On the other hand, bad habits are easy to form but difficult to live with. In both cases, you form good or bad habits because of the choices you make and the behavior you portray.

One of your biggest goals in life should be to form the habit that results in health, true prosperity, and happiness. Your goal should be to develop the habits of character that allow you to become the very best person that you can imagine yourself becoming. The main purpose of your life should be to incorporate within yourself the habits that allow you to achieve your full potential.

In the coming sections, you will discover how your habits patterns are created and how you can positively change them. You will discover how to become the type of person who relentlessly like the waves of the ocean, aims to achieve every goal that you set for yourself.

The Origin of Your Habits

Tryon Edwards once said that any act that is constantly repeated eventually grows into a habit and that habit slowly develops strength.

Remember that you are unique. When you came into this world, you already had great abilities and talents to use.

Your intelligent brain has over 20 billion cells, each of which is interconnected to over 20 thousand other cells. The potential combinations and permutations of ideas, insights, and thoughts that you can create are equal to number one, followed by eight pages of zeros. Therefore, whatever you have achieved in life to this date is only a small percentage of what you are truly capable of realizing.

The average individual settles for far less than he or she can achieve. Compared to what you can be, everything you have done so far is only a small fraction of what is truly possible for you.

The problem is that you step into this world with the most powerful brain, surrounded by unlimited chances for success, achievement, and happiness, but you get started without an instructional manual. For that reason, you need to determine everything for yourself. And most people don't do. They experience life doing the best they can, but they never come close to doing, and being all that is possible for them.

Habits of Self-Made Millionaires

Most millionaires pushed themselves to those levels. They sacrificed a lot and persisted in their work before they accrued wealth. They also formed habits that allowed them to accumulate wealth. Don't forget that your habits are the reason why you are rich or poor. According to the author of Rich Habits, it's always two or three habits that distinguish the wealthy from those who are financially struggling.

Here are several habits discovered from self-made millionaires.

1. They love to read

How often do you spend time reading a book, a magazine, or even an article online? If you haven't been spending some time to read, then you're shy away from what self-made millionaires do. If you want to become wealthy, then you must make it a habit to read.

The key to success in life is expanding your knowledge base and skills. Set aside 30 minutes or more every day to learning by reading books. If you do, it gives you an edge in the competition, as most people don't read.

2. They have a mentor

Do you have a mentor? Approximately 93% of self-made millionaires attribute their wealth to having mentors.

Having a success mentor in life is one of the steps to become rich. A mentor can help push you to success fast.

There are five types of success mentors:

- Parents. Parenting is critical when it comes to becoming a millionaire. Your first mentors will be your parents. If your parent teaches you good daily success habits, you will struggle less in life.

- Career mentors. Getting a mentor at work you enjoy, trust, and respect can result in success in life. Find someone who is at least two levels above your rank.

- Book mentors. It is not a must to have a real relationship with a mentor. In certain cases, the best source of mentors is in books, especially books about great people.

- Yourself. Did you know you can mentor yourself by learning from your mistakes? This is the most difficult part of success because those mistakes and failures carry a certain cost in both time and money. But this is another powerful type of mentoring you can get because the lessons you learn are rooted in deep emotion and never forgotten.

3. They have a TO-DO Lists

Goals only become goals when there is 100% achievability and physical activity. Millionaires subdivide goals into physical action steps that form a to-do-list, and many have lists that follow a given habit.

Millionaires create success. When you develop processes, you don't need to think, which requires energy and contributes to decision fatigue. Habits are important because they generate a fuel that can be used to achieve something else.

4. They develop numerous streams of income

Self-made millionaires don't have only a single source of income. Instead, they create multiple streams, and most have at least three.

Having multiple sources of income enables you to conquer the economic downturns that always happen in life.

Revenue streams comprise real estate rentals, private equity investments, stock market investments, and royalties.

5. They use dreams to set goals

Before millionaires define goals, first they dream. They write down what their ideal life will appear, and then use this script to develop a bullet-point list of dreams. Eventually, goals are built around each dream.

Let dreams be a ladder, and the rungs represent your goals. Now, ask yourself, "What should I do for every wish or dream to become true? Are you ready to perform those activities? And do you have the right skills and knowledge? Then take action?

6. Pursue things that interest you

People always join careers because of the stability aspect, but wealthy people seek their interests. They erect their ladder on their wall. When you like what you are doing, you work harder.

Techniques for Eliminating the Habit of Procrastination

If you know you are overwhelmed with the habit of procrastination, then you need to remove that habit. As a habit, procrastination is costing you a lot of time. You are probably getting less done, and less of the critical stuff accomplished. Additionally, it might cause you stress, which has a wide range of effects for your health and; it is likely to harm your relationships. Procrastination is a dangerous habit.

The good thing is that procrastination is not permanent; you can eliminate the habit from your life. If you always procrastinate, first, you must determine the source of this procrastination and implement one of the following strategies.

1. When things get difficult, don't stop

One of the main reasons why people decide to procrastinate is a failure to handle discomfort. When things get difficult, you may not want to be reminded about it. However, if you want to change your life, you must be ready to do things which you have never done before and that which demands you explore a new world.

The same way procrastination is a habit; learning how to overcome discomfort is also a habit. When things get difficult, keep pushing. This will allow you to build the mental muscles of perseverance.

Lastly, you will reject the idea of giving up when things get hard. Think about what you will manage to achieve.

Each aspect of our lives has been affected by inventions meant to make our lives more comfortable. A lot is available to us at the click of a button that we don't know what discomfort is.

If you want to achieve your greatest potential and grow, you must learn to cope with discomfort. When you learn to do so, the habit of procrastination becomes much difficult to handle.

2. Think about your lifestyle

Your lifestyle must boost your work. If you are always tired and worn out, you are more likely to procrastinate. Monitor your sleeping habits, what you eat, and exercise. If you take care of your mind and body, they will help you get more done.

Also, remember to control your energy levels during your working day because energy is important to productivity and breaking the habit of procrastination. If you don't have any energy, you are likely to procrastinate.

It is equally critical to control your energy levels by taking care of your lifestyle. When you do so, you ensure that you have sufficient energy to bring to your work in the first place. By controlling your lifestyle beyond work, you really can boost your work performance.

3. Be realistic

If you always go to the gym, you should have noticed a large number of people who come in January. These people have made New Year's Resolutions to get in shape, and they are ready to get it done. But regardless of the best advice of the trainer, they believe that 3 days per week is not enough for them. They report 5 or more days and go flat out each day.

The next thing that happens is that their body fails to cope with this new level of pressure and intensity. They burn out within a few weeks, and that is the last time you see them.

Don't be like these people. Become realistic about how much work you can complete in a day and focus your plans on that. Completing that work every day will improve your confidence and motivation while preventing stress and burnout. And the more confident you feel, the less likely you are to procrastinate.

4. Try and do something, regardless of how small it might be

A time comes when it is not important what you do, as long as you are taking some action and get going. If you have been procrastinating a task, select one task on that job and get it done. It doesn't matter what that job is or how small it is, just get going.

If you repeat this step several times, you will begin to break down your resistance and establish some momentum.

Momentum is a powerful way to overcome the barrier of procrastination, especially where procrastination has become a habit. In these situations, it can be useful first to break the habit of procrastination and get used to getting work done.

Once you are accustomed to the habit of working again, you can concentrate on making sure that the work you are doing is the most critical work that you could be doing.

5. Become organized

You are organized when you know what needs to be done when it needs to be done and how you are going to get it done. Additionally, your life and working environment are organized in a way that boosts your productivity. This will allow you to avoid overthinking each job and jump straight into taking action.

Just as important as it is, when you are organized, you easily identify all projects which don't add value to your work. You can then remove these projects, hence reducing the overwhelm and pressure you experience. This limits the probability of procrastination.

There is also a middle ground between tasks that add value and those that don't. Some projects add value, but you are not the one who should be finishing them. You can outsource this work and create more time and attention in your schedule.

The tendency to be organized is one of the best tools for fixing the habit of procrastination.

6. Remove what you can

If there are items in your life which you do not want to do, then why are they in your life? Sometimes, the best thing to do is to eliminate something from your life completely.

Yes, there are occasions in your life where you have established the habit of procrastination because you don't want to be in the position that you are in. You may have to make some changes in your life to get back on track.

If you are genuinely unimpressed with the way things are going in your life, you will have to make some changes because it is not okay being unhappy. When you make drastic changes, you may find that you no longer have any desire to procrastinate.

Also, when you eliminate what you don't want from your life, you create enough space for the things you do want.

7. Look for help

There is enough help available for those who suffer from chronic procrastination. Don't suffer in silence; reach out for support. With some help and some clever techniques, it is possible to turn your life around.

Like many problems, sometimes you may fail to create enough space between you and your procrastination habit to examine it objectively. If you cannot be objective, you are going to find it difficult to address the true cause because you are unlikely to analyze all the possible reasons properly.

By getting the help of an experienced professional or a trusted colleague, you will manage to look objectively. Additionally, they are likely to have some important observations. In general, the more you understand your problem, the easier it will be for you to identify a workable solution.

8. Create a plan

One way to overcome overwhelm is to create a list of everything you want to finish to complete the job successfully. Set approximations for how long every task is going to take and organize the tasks according to how they need to get done.

Once it's complete, you don't need to experience overwhelm. You can focus on what needs to get done every day and; get it done. If you keep doing that, you will eventually finish the job.

One word of caution here; don't use planning as a way to procrastinate. Some people do this and keep planning without taking any action. The objective of planning is to give yourself an overview of what you need to do to get the job done.

Once you have this picture, there is no need to tense. Take action — no need to have every detail in the plan. Once you have a good idea of the pathways forwards, get moving, and the rest will follow.

9. Organize your day well

Most people want to complete one big task in a single sitting. But this is not right, and you must learn to identify when you work best. Master your energy levels and concentration span. This way, you will organize your jobs according to how you optimize your energy and time.

Think of a time in a day when you had enough energy. During this time, each task that you did felt so easy. You finished work earlier than you normally do.

Now, recall a time when you felt tired. Every job that you tried to do lasted forever, and you could not imagine that you will ever complete it. During this period, your confidence level was low, that you thought you could not complete the demands of your job.

While it is not possible to have high energy levels all the time, but you can concentrate on your energy levels. You note that time when you experienced high energy and schedule most of your jobs to be completed during those periods. Next, you can schedule other tasks that don't require a lot of energy during periods which you felt low.

In conclusion, the tendency to procrastinate is quite common. In case you have tasks that you need to be doing, but you keep procrastinating, then you need to stop this habit now and take action.

If you want to be wealthy, you should never settle for anything less than the best life you can create for yourself. Procrastination is a way to delay your success. Stop it today, and start working hard to fulfill your potential.

Chapter 2: The Secrets of All Success

One of the biggest problems that we experience in modern life is that there are many alternatives to do so many great things. There are many things around our lives struggling for our attention. And if we fail to control modern life, it will probably control us. Part of taking control of it is just choosing that this is what I feel, this is important to my life, and then concentrating on your feeling.

In life, most people struggle to explain where they are going. If you want to see how people struggle, ask five random people to tell you what they don't want out of life. For sure, they will all have a sizeable list. You will hear things like:

- I don't want to remain at my job now.

- I don't want to continue living in this crappy house for another year.

- I don't want my partner to keep asking me for money and time spent at home.

The "I don't want" always features quite easily. So easily that you might think they have been practicing it. It's like people are constantly thinking about them. And why does it happen like that? No one knows, maybe because they are.

So after you have asked these people to say what they don't want out of life, and they are mentioning their fifth or sixth item. Stop them suddenly, wait for a second, and say, "Well, I understand what you don't want out of life. Now, could you tell me what you want out of life?" This is the point where things get interesting. Watch out their facial expressions. You will see their puzzlement followed by a creased eyebrow. Now, they are starting to reflect on what you asked. Their reactions will be completely different from when you had asked them what they don't want out of life. Most people will respond, "Well, that's an excellent question," or "Let me think about that one."

It seems like they're saying, "I'm in a fast-moving car, and I know for sure I don't want to go to Las Vegas or California. But I'm not sure where I do want to go." What next then? You don't go anywhere. You run out of fuel and unable to reach your destination because you only know where you don't want to go. That looks pretty simple, right? Or you could be saying, "Oh man, is that the grand wisdom you have kept for me?" It's a big part of it. But you need to cover your head around what the wisdom really is. Once you fathom it, you will begin to see why this might be the biggest reason you are holding yourself back from breaking through to the next level.

Well, let me ask you a question. Do you know anyone who this description applies? Somebody who's quick to say what they don't want out of life than saying what they want out of life? This can be a friend, a spouse, or a relative who experiences life this way? Maybe someone who's closer to you, that person whom you see when you stare in the mirror after waking up each morning? You see, the current society is crazy.

And the unfortunate truth about this kind of society is that it doesn't matter how fast you can achieve, it doesn't matter how much ambition you have, and it doesn't matter how much energy you commit to something. If you don't have a clear vision and clarity on the destination you want to arrive, you will probably never reach there. Think about this: You can buy the most expensive vehicle in the world and drive as fast as you can, but if you don't know where you're going, you'll get nowhere fast.

Here are some things that you will come across often. "I need more time in a day. I wish I could find good help. I never have enough time to do my own business or expand my business to the next level, or get more money." Many people think they need 36 hours per day when the truth is that they don't have a clear vision of what they want out of their personal lives. Did Bill Gates, Tesla, or Mark Zuckerberg have 36 hours in a day in their race to success?

If you're overwhelmed daily because of insufficient time, distractions, or your own procrastination, then for sure, it's because you don't clearly know where you want to go in life. When you don't have a crystal plan about where you're heading, you tend to spend your time doing things that are restricting you from generating more money, receiving promotions, and enjoying your life at an optimal level. While you're doing these things that are in no way improving your future, you're forced to say no to doing things that could grow your business, your income, and happiness.

Alternatively, when you have a clear vision for your life, you will avoid wasting time on things, not enhancing your goals, dreams, or aspirations. Your actions will have objective and your hours will be committed to accomplishing those goals. Your procrastination will stop because you'll have 100% certainty what you cannot put off anything until the following day. So, let's see how you can get your vision shaped with the help of several habits from successful people. Once you create a vision for yourself, things will become clear, and it will be like you got a new pair of glasses and discovered your old prescription was outdated.

You know that setting goals is an important step in success. Benjamin Franklin was among the first people who outlined his goals and knew where he wanted to reach in life. However, what you are about to read in this chapter surpasses the normal "goal setting" process. Sometimes setting goals is difficult when so much around you is busy, noisy, and even scary. But soon you are going, to be honest about where you are in life right now. You are going to discover a secret tool that will help you to look into the future and see your path. After that, we will focus on where you want to go with your true "why." Then the only thing left is learning how to accomplish it. This whole book is written to provide you with the tools, steps, and, of course, the habits to achieve the "how."

What is Your Current Status? Don't Lie

Before you give a review of your life, let me urge you to be honest. In this book, you will come across tough questions. Don't attempt to answer what you think will make you feel good. This is what most people do without giving it a thought, and while I know the reflex, you need to consider the benefit of being honest. It is only once you are honest with yourself that you can move forward to accomplish your dreams, desires, and goals. So with that said, let's get started with where you are in your life at this moment. First, what does that question mean exactly? What this question means is what situations or situations are you currently going through in your life? Why are you reading this book?

It could be you are struggling with the notion of having untapped potential, or you worry you're just living a normal life instead of the life of your dreams. Maybe you are trying to get something that can secure your finances because your back is against the wall, and your mortgage is pulling your backside. Or maybe you want to begin something new to change your life for the better if your current status can relate to any of these situations, great.

Maybe you're just finishing your college studies, or going through college, and you don't know about your future. Maybe you believe it's time to rediscover yourself completely. Maybe you're just tired of listening to someone commanding you at the same boring job you've had for a decade if that is the case, congratulations! Maybe you are an entrepreneur who is ready for more profits, ready for the next level, or ready to hear the secrets that can push you to the next level. If so, congratulations on being here too.

These examples should help you reflect on your own current status and reaffirm to you that wherever you're at in your life, you're not alone. So dive deep and just be honest with yourself. Sometimes, human beings love to pretend that everything is okay. But we forget what really matters. You must try to remove that everything-is-fine mindset and outline what truly is in your heart.

So, stop reading right now and take a notebook, or your computer, or phone, and write down, "Where am I in life?" You can extend beyond your finances and list down where you are in the various parts of your life that are important. That can include health, family, intimacy, and your career. Continue to break down these areas on a piece of paper, and next to each one, put a small description of your current status. Don't write what other people consider you. Instead, when you stand before the mirror and you're honest with yourself, where do you lie? Before you can create your ideal destination, you must be aware of your starting point.

Be Clear on Where You Want to Go

Keep in mind that when you start to focus on what you do want rather than what you don't want, it turns into a success habit that can completely change the result of so many things in your life.

When the lesson of this chapter is ingrained in you, you might look at the jagged rocks for a second when something goes wrong, but then you'll instantly look for that clearing, the "positive point." And the more you practice this, the more likely you will focus on the clearing when life subjects you in a spin. Always remember that when you concentrate on the result rather than the obstacle, your life will never be the same.

Have you ever asked yourself how the richest men and women in the world became so successful? The answer is that they had a clear vision of where they wanted to reach and then taking action toward achieving it. Many of us want more out of life, but we are not specific to our goals, so we don't know how to arrive there. That could be the reason why you might be sidetracked by e-mails and phone calls. It's the reason why you may feel stressed, disorganized, and overwhelmed. It's why you may have the thoughts that the country is not the same as it used to be, and there is no chance for you to jump to the next level. This is completely false. There is a lot of opportunities now than ever. This might be the greatest period in history to stay ahead of the curve. But first, you must know your destination and build a map to help you get to that next level of your life. Once you have a truly crystal-clear vision, things that once pulled you behind will no longer have any power to stop you from realizing your goal.

Think About Choosing From the Future

The truth is that goal-setting is one of the most critical steps to success. But let's be honest a bit: setting goals using the old-fashioned style by just expecting a year, two, or even five years is hard. We have crazy, busy lives, and we can be slowed down by things we can't look up and see the future. With your family, work, and so many other things moving so fast, it's hard to concentrate on the road ahead. You spend a lot of time dealing with what you can see that staring into the future may be difficult.

So here's how you can overcome the daily obstacles. Assume it's one year from today, and when you reflect on the past year, you discover that it was the best year of your life. What does that sound like to you? What should happen to you to wake up every day on fire, free of distraction, and convinced you were not wasting your potential? As I write this paragraph, I'm reflecting on my future year and experiencing goosebumps because of what I'm seeing. I want you to experience that same feeling of excitement. Imagine what the best year of your life would look like and be emotional, be engulfed, and envision specific details about what made it so great.

To be specific, ask yourself the following questions when you reflect this year:

- How much money are you earning? What amount have you saved for your family's security? Is there anyone you're taking care of financially?

- Where do you work daily? Do you work from home, or you drive daily to a new location?

- How does your spouse look at you in the morning or after a long day?

- Are you pushing your current company to the next level?

- Are you beginning your own company? Are you evolving through the ranks at your job?

- Do you have a good relationship with your boss?

- How does your life look like when it's a year in the future, and you reflect, and it was the greatest year ever?

- What is your relationship with your family or kids look now?

Experience those feelings without any restrictions and nothing preventing you from these emotions. Don't console yourself, "Well, I could be in shape, but I'm too busy to work out" or "I could launch my own company, but I have to stick with this job just to pay the rent." That's envisioning the future with current demands holding you back like an anchor.

If you're yet to do so, stop and write down your responses. Be specific about each area. As you write, allow it to flow.

You see, when you know where you are right at the moment, you have a true starting point. Then, when you spend time to reflect on establishing where you want to reach over the next year, you've done more than most people who are stuck in place do. These people usually ignore this habit and practice. However, successful people don't ignore it. Therefore, when you know where you want to go, you will start to say no to certain friends, refuse certain obligations, reject certain opportunities, and reject certain e-mails. You will understand that deep down those things aren't supporting your vision. Once you are sure where you want to go, you can begin to implement action steps to realize the best year of your life, which will result in the best ten years of your life, and eventually into the rest of your life.

By exercising, you will stop being overwhelmed. You will find the additional time, and your stress will disappear. Ask all successful people you know or meet, and you will discover that they know where they're going in life and what their biggest goals are. They possess an inner vision that they stand by, and it's time to get yours or drive yours to the next level. Once you understand your current state and where you want to be, you will also find it easier to practice other successful habits.

Identify Your "Why"

Let's jump to the next important component. This is the part that makes your vision become your reality. This is the action step you must complete to make it real: determine your "why." Below are vital "why" questions you need to answer:

- Why do you want to increase your income to the next level?

- Why do you want your company to evolve, or to rise through the ranks?

- Why do you want to launch your own business?

- Why do you want your parents to retire?

- Why do you want to lose weight, have more passion in your actions, experience more joy daily, and live a life with more smiles than frowns?

The reasons why you want these things are deeper than you think, and you will learn how to identify those reasons out. And once you do, be ready to be unstoppable. Maybe, you will cry a bit as well.

The challenge with most people is that they don't dive deep into their hearts and souls to identify the truth about why they want what they want. Unfortunately, our brains can prevent what's in our hearts and souls. When you ask people to mention their "why," many will say, "I want more money to experience financial freedom," or "I want more money to solve my debt problems," or even say something like, "I want to lose weight, so I look beautiful." Well, these are all good responses, but they're not sufficiently deep reasons. Without a deep purpose, you cannot push through your most difficult moments. Ask yourself whether "I want a new house" is a strong emotion that you will forget the storm to get what you want? Ask yourself whether I want abs is a strong "why" to get you to the gym after a long day at work? I doubt that. However, when you can associate a deeper meaning to "why," it all changes.

One question we don't ask ourselves is, "What is the purpose behind our actions?" It looks crazy because it's a question we need to ask ourselves daily. When you can unearth your true "why," the exact driving purpose in life, and transform that into actions, you acquire the drive you need to move forward, faster than ever.

Why Is Your "Why" so Critical

Even if you teach a group of people how to sell $20 bills for 10 dollars, some of them will allow what's in between their ears to prevent them from succeeding. Even with something so simple, they will still deviate from success and not even realize they're killing themselves. In most cases, fear is the killer of our momentum, slowing us down that we finally come to a complete stop.

A Deeper Why

Do you want to have total freedom of your life and make the choices you want? Of course, this something you would. However, when you experience a tough day when things don't go your way when everything goes wrong in your relationship when your new business fails, what drives you to keep moving forward? Is it financial freedom? That's not deep enough. You need to identify the root of your "why." Why do you want to become a millionaire? Why do you want to accumulate wealth? Why are you reading this book? Of course, there is a much deeper level of purpose that pushing you.'

And when you discover it, you find the driving force that will never allow you to stop.

Chapter 3: The Power of Your Story

Every one of us has a story to tell or many stories that have shaped our lives. At its center, your story is where you live mentally, emotional, and sometimes even physically. Your story can be the drive behind your success or the anchor that is weighing you down.

What you need to do is to identify what stories you should be telling yourself. These are stories that are aligned with your new vision you have for your life.

The tendency to align your story with your vision takes some time. But is your wealth, happiness, and future success worth a little effort now for a better tomorrow? Of course, they are. So wake up, roll your sleeves, and let's do the work together. In this chapter, you will learn the stories that you tell yourself and how even the ones that are harmless tend to hold you back and reduce your maximum potential. And the first step is to understand why you narrate to yourself and other people certain stories. Once you understand this, you will learn how to change that story from a limiting one that is denying you of your confidence to one that can take you to the moon and far beyond.

Unearthing Your Story

To improve the stories and filter out the self-limiting beliefs in your life, you need to push some of them to the forefront of your mind. To achieve this, think about the areas in your life, you want to experience the biggest breakthrough. Because you're reading this book, the probability is that generating more money, expanding your own business, or finding work you like represent achievements for you. So stop for a second and ask yourself why these things you wish have not yet happened. Make sure you don't create excuses, filter your responses, or provide rationalizations, or even deny. Just be honest and write down the reasons you haven't accomplished what you desire.

To help you in the following exercise, consider which of the following factors could be preventing you from succeeding:

- Lack of time

- Your health

- Your relationships

- The economy

- Your education

- Your employees

- Your boss

- Your lack of capital

- Your unsupportive partner

Many other reasons exist; these are just to help you start to think about the obstacles in the way of your dreams.

Concentrate on what pops to your mind instantly when you think of why you haven't fulfilled the desires of your life? What is the story you have to tell? Often, when you want to grow in any of these areas, but you fail, it means there is a wall between you and your next level. And this wall is a story.

Now reflect on the stories that popped into your head and write the obstacles down. Think about how your story became a part of you. Maybe the negative news reports you received every day supported your negative story? Maybe the message that you need to improve on your weaknesses builds the story? Or maybe bad advice from your friends pushed your negative story until it became your truth and your belief?

Did Some Stories Pop Into Mind?

If yes, write them down. If not, stop reading for some seconds and think of what you are holding back. Probably, you're refusing this exercise, saying to yourself, " Well, I have no story; this is the truth." If that's what you believe, great; write what you think is your reality.

Now let's dive deeper and identify the limiting beliefs that shrouded this deeply embedded story. Remember, these stories may have been with you for quite some time. They date back to early childhood. The crazy fact is that the stories that disempower us have been ingrained in us by the people we have interacted with in life. These stories stir the excuses our subconscious sends us for not living up to our maximum potential. By the end of the following chapter, you should be able to stand up against your limiting beliefs and stories and throw them away for good. So let me describe here a scenario that hopefully can help you dive deeper and accomplish this mission.

If your grandparents experienced the Great Depression, perhaps they have extremely conservative opinions about saving money. They might say, "You have to play it safe. You have to get a job, whether you like it or not. Taking a risk can be very dangerous." And here's the truth: people went through hard times during the Depression. Many in that period couldn't even provide food for their families. At that time in history, there was no big margin for error. The focus on survival. A big part of the population did any job they could find, if they had not saved every penny, they could have lost everything.

If that is what your grandparents experienced, they probably raised your parents with a cautious mindset. They might have instilled their "Depression-era" beliefs in your parents, and they applied it to you. Those beliefs could be preventing you, and you don't even know. Maybe you want to expand your business or even take a new position, but fear has captured you and you don't even know why. In the following situation, I know why. It's a generational limiting story that was narrated to you from your parents and their parents before them. You are living with the ideas of a person from the Great Depression even if you are not living in that period. It is an invisible fight, or a villain within that is causing you to stagnate.

These beliefs can obstruct all sectors of your life right from the religion you believe to the political party you lean toward, as well as the kind of person you choose in a relationship. Your limiting beliefs are devious and dictate so much of what you do and who you want to become. Wouldn't you think it is crazy if someone said that someone else is controlling your mind? Well, in most cases, this is exactly what is taking place in your life.

So center on the stories and beliefs that are limiting you in various ways. When you think about doing something new or difficult like starting a business or trying to generate more money or get in the right shape, what do you say out loud to yourself? Write down the stories that pop up in mind and what you want to change. This entails extracting the beliefs that control your life.

Next, note where these beliefs originate. If you're like many people, you will analyze your stories and beliefs and say, "Wow, that's my college professor's belief, or that's my dad's belief." Although they may have come from these people, if they remain within you for long, they will become your reality. So you need to identify them and determine how artificial they are in most cases. You must see that they are not your beliefs but instead, beliefs provided to you by others.

Once you have identified them, I want to lead you on a path to not only prove your story isn't true, but also indicate how to reverse it and set a new, limitless, inspiring story that drives you toward all different categories of life success.

How Has It Impacted Your Life?

There is a possibility that you don't know how bad the effect of your story has been. Spend some time and examine its impact by answering these questions:

- Has it vanished or damaged your confidence and reduced your self-esteem?

- Has it made you live in confusion, doubt, or even going to therapy?

- Has it cost you your health, your peace of mind, career, or your joy?

- Has it made you scared of attempting to begin your business or create enough wealth with your ideas?

The odds are that you said yes to one or more of these questions. If that is true, examine and write the cost. What have you been denied, what kind of loss have you suffered, and what challenges have arisen because of the story you tell yourself? Don't fear about writing complete sentences. Just get it written down on paper, so you have something tangible at hand. The point is that you need to see the missed opportunities a bad story or negative belief can cause and thus generate more resentment toward it and more urgency to change it. But let's go even further.

Reflect on the future and think about what these stories will continue to cost you if you don't change them. On your path on where you want to reach in life, how can these stories get in your way? Imagine your life in 5 years, ten years, or even 20 years. What did you fail to achieve or do because of these stories and beliefs? Close your eyes and think about the missed opportunities in the future. Allow yourself to experience the pain of that missed opportunity. Are you going to give these stories enough power? Know what they have cost you and what they will continue to cost you.

Holding on to one bad story or one bad belief can have a ripple effect in many areas of your life. So let's flip it to an empowering, limitless story.

Show That It's Not True

To forget your old story for good, search for proof to show that's garbage. Are there people with no money and bad childhoods who proceeded to do big things, enjoy good relationships, have great friends, and be successful financially? Of course, yes. The odds are that the old story you have been believing is wrong; you need to find a prove that's a bunch of crap. It's pointless to think you are the only one with specific issues holding you back. Find proof that those limiting stories and beliefs are crap.

Create a Conversation With God

The following exercise will trigger true disgust for your old stories. Assume that you're conversing with God, or whomever you believe is your creator. Imagine God telling you, "Why are you not living to the maximum potential that I instilled in you? I brought you into this world and gave you limitless abilities in your life. What is preventing you from being your best, you?" Sit somewhere in silence and reflect on that question. Now, imagine yourself responding to God with the story you might have uncovered recently.

Now think about offering these rationalizations and excuses to a person who experienced cruelty, or a concentration camp. Probably you have gone through a tragic life, but the chances are, your story is more tragic. You went through a lot of divorces, or you have had a lot of expenses, or you always felt shy and had low self-esteem. We are not rejecting your difficulties, only asking you to reflect on them. Even if you've experienced the worst, people have endured epic battles and still arise to accomplish the impossible. And most of them defeated their past because they refused to allow the tragedy and difficult to define them. They defined a different story for their lives. So when say to God about how you never accomplished your career goals because your parents were very critical of you, doesn't it cause you to resent this story?

Say It out Loud

Because of the process we have discussed and the way we have narrated "your story," another method to rid yourself of your old story is to say it out loud and listen to how silly it appears. Say it various times, and listen to yourself articulating it repeatedly.

Say it out loud, "I don't have a good life because ......" Your story might have been traumatizing, but when you say it out loud, you start to hear how misguided it looks. Again, your life could be worse than anything I can fathom and am not in any way trying to limit your experiences. But regardless of what it was, regardless of how bad it was, you must be disgusted enough with the old limiting story to take the steps that allow you to replace it with a new story.

Identify the Good in Every Story

Now let's begin the process of transforming that limiting story to an inspiring, limitless one. When you change aspects of the story, your narrative starts to improve. Ask yourself, what is something good that featured in your story? What is something that you once believed was an obstacle in your life, but acquired skills that have made you who you are today? It could be you got fired from a job once, and it made you feel like you were not good enough, but it was that event that helped you spend more time on yourself and get in the best shape of your life physically and mentally.

Identify the good from your story and begin converting it into an inspiring story. Remember the words of Tony Robbins: suppose life happens for us, not to us. Reflect your story with this "identify the good" perspective, and those old stories begin losing their power fast.

Time to Change Your Story

Let's say you're living in a house full of old memories from your life, and some are great memories, but others are those negative ones that remind you of bad things that happened in the past. Now imagine that the house starts to burn, and you have a small suitcase in your hands and only a minute to save some of those memories. For you to arrive at that level of success in life, you must decide to compile only the memories, and that helps you move forward. If it's a negative memory that drags your mind, allow it to burn in the fire. Only move forward with those things that will allow you to make the best life possible. Keep in mind, and the past only lives inside you. You need to consider the past as research and development. It is there to learn from and become a better self. In case the past haunts you, or doesn't serve your grander future, then let that memory burn up in the fire.

Remember, yesterday is the past, and we cannot change it. Tomorrow is a movie in our head that is not yet filmed. And we only have this moment. So let that weight of the past disappear forever.

It's time to modify your story. Now that you know of what the old story has cost you, why it's not even true, how small outside factors push it, and most of all, how you should be embarrassed by it, you should be motivated to remake it.

Regardless of how your old circumstances were, you can leave them behind. In case you were cheated on, your lover stole your money, or your parents didn't love you, forget those stories and create a better version of your story and replace it.

Write Your New Story

While you create this story, make sure you do the opposite of what we did earlier and find proof that your new story is true. Search the internet for evidence, seek out a mentor, or speak to a trained coach. Do whatever it's possible to find proof that what you are now saying is possible. Most millionaires went through hell once or many times in their lives. Identify their stories and use them as leverage to develop your own. The evidence is everywhere, so look for it.

Write it down, revise it, but have it crafted. When you feel like you have perfected it, send it to your phone and copy and paste it inside the notes app so you can read it daily. Start repeating it to yourself and try to memorize it. And when the old story resurfaces in your mind, be aware of your thoughts. If you wake up at night and discover that you are telling yourself that same old garbage story again, say to yourself, "that's a horrible story! It's nonsense" And replace it with the new one.

Now Say Your New Story out Loud

When you have the new stories, then it's time to memorize it in your subconscious. Remember, you might have been thinking about those old limiting believes for 10, 20, or 30 years, or more. The same way it takes many sessions in the gym to get in shape, you also need to memorize your new story into your life many times. So make sure you say it loud for the next 30 days, every night before you sleep. Let it be the last thing you think about while you nod off, and ensure it is the first thing you think about when you wake up in the morning. Try to make this a daily routine for at least the following month.

Additionally, identify a person in your life that you can narrate your new story who would appreciate it. Let this person know how you have changed and share the process of exchanging old stories for new with this person.

Request someone to be your accountability friend or coach who can help direct you or at least keep you on track. If you know someone who can mentor you and guide you, get hold of him or her and don't let go.

Compare Your Two Stories

Finally, once you finish writing your new story, compare it to the old story. See how different the result of your life will be by not only changing one story or one belief but by converting all the stories that don't serve your higher purpose or your true "why." You have spent a lot of years with the old story that it might take some time to remove it from your consciousness. And that's fine. So don't lose patience, but remain persistent. But remember to repeat every night and every morning your new crafted story. It might require around 10 minutes every day, but meditate on it and try to feel that new story.

You can learn a lot about yourself and your future success by transforming the past stories and killing the villain within. Once you kill the villain within and change your story, you've embarked on the path to unleashing the hero that lives inside you and finally accomplishing the happiness and wealth you deserve.

Chapter 4: Attraction and Persuasion

Human beings want things to happen right away, and they may not. Often, we're just planting a seed that we don't know the result. It's difficult for us to understand that what we see in front of us might not be the end of the story.

Both the energy and the foundational building blocks of our matter are all interconnected. Our atoms join with the atoms in the air, which then connect to other organic matter, animals, humans, trees, and everything else.

Although the complexities of life after billions of years of evolution have developed a diverse set of organisms here on earth, we still all originate from the same source, which can be traced back not only to the very beginnings of the earth's existence, but also to the beginning of the universe itself, and time as it is today.

It's that one source of energy and the random mutations after multiple repetitions in the tree of evolution that have developed the unique beings that we are today. We are all unique in small ways. Yet, some of us are unique in very big ways. Not just in the physical appearances, but in our emotional, mental, and spiritual states.

With all of this uniqueness comes different techniques to one common subject that unite us all: money. Money is just a story. It is the greatest story that human beings ever created.

The thoughts in our minds, which travels as energy across synapses in our neurons, enable us to move towards or away from anyone's outcome. What we think is what we become. Money, in effect, is just a thought. It acquires life from the energy within our minds.

Law of Attraction for Money

1. Visualize your wealth as you've already achieved it

The law of attraction states that the things you believe inwardly and project outwardly will be the things you bring into your life.

If you want to attract money, then you need to visualize it as if you already have it.

Visualizing a life where you have all of the money that you wish not only develops a mindset that is more receptive to financial gain, it also allows you to imagine what your life will look like once you accomplish your goals.

This can act as a strong source of motivation that will continue to push you forward when things get hard.

Visualizing money like you already have, it can also develop an abundance mindset, unlike a mindset of scarcity.

One of the major reasons why the rich have no problem getting wealthy is that they see the money they don't have as something is both abundant and acquirable. Similarly, they see the money they possess as a tool that can be used to generate more money instead of something that needs to be saved or protected.

This type of abundance mindset happens naturally when you have a lot of money, but it can also be created by visualizing money as something that you already have in abundance.

If you want to establish a physical point of anchor for your visualizations, carry a hundred-dollar bill in your pocket.

By doing this can make you feel wealthier and prevent you from ever being able to say you are broke-and hence prevent the limiting thoughts that go along with being broke.

2. Determine your limiting beliefs about money

For you to activate the Law of Attraction in your life, you must determine and change your limiting beliefs about money. In the whole of our lives, since childhood, we've developed limiting beliefs about money that we have memorized over time and accepted to be true.

These are things like money doesn't grow on trees and is very difficult to acquire, or the idea that money cannot buy happiness, or the limiting belief that you cannot be rich and be a good person at the same time.

Before you can start to leverage on the Law of Attraction, it's important first to address any limiting beliefs about money that you may have.

When you see money for what it really is-an accessible, unlimited supply of a resource you can use it in any way you want, it's easier to develop the habits and mindset needed to acquire wealth.

One powerful way you can deal with any limiting beliefs about money is through the application of positive affirmations.

What you say to yourself is what you believe and what you actually believe becomes the truth. By applying positive affirmations to fight limiting beliefs about money, you can create a mindset about money that allows you to leverage the Law of Attraction.

3. The Universe will provide you with more

Remember that the universe will provide you with more of what you're grateful for. Therefore, you should not underestimate the power of gratitude.

Overall, the things that you're thankful for will be the things that you want to pursue with great ambition. Being grateful for something also eliminates any negative beliefs you have, and will make you more receptive to new opportunities.

As you continue adopting a positive money mindset that allows you to leverage the Law of Attraction, don't ignore the value of gratitude.

Acknowledge the money that you have. Appreciate for every opportunity you get to generate more money and be thankful when those opportunities pay off.

Regardless of how much or little money you are currently making, an attitude of gratitude is important if you want to become a millionaire.

4. Focus on abundance

The more you concentrate on a subject, the more it's rooted in your life. Make it a habit to focus on the abundance you already have. Show appreciation for the money you already have, your car, and all the other comforts you use in your everyday life. Feel that you are abundant and growing richer with every passing day.

5. Stop overthinking

The one thing that can affect the law of attraction is overthinking what you want. This can trigger feelings of resistance and tension. It is more important to manage your emotional state and realize that what you want is already coming your way.

Final Thoughts

You can apply the law of attraction for everything you want. Just keep in mind that the journey should be smooth and does not require hardship.

Chapter 5: Wealth Principles

We live in a world of duality, hot and cold, right and left, in and out. These are just some of the examples of the thousands of opposite poles. For one side to exist, the other side must also exist. Is it possible to have a left side without the right side? Not really.

In the same way that there are outer laws regarding money, there must be "inner" laws. The outer laws comprise of things such as business knowledge, investment strategies, and money management. These are important. But the inner game is just as critical. There is a saying that goes, "It's not enough to be in the right place at the correct time. You have to be the right person in the right place at the right time."

So you must ask yourself who are you. How do you always think? What are some of your beliefs? What are your traits and habits? How do you really feel about yourself? How confident are you in yourself? What is your relationship with others? How much do you trust others?

Do you truly think that you deserve to be rich? What are your odds to act in spite of fear, in spite of discomfort, in spite of worry and inconvenience? Can you do something when you're not in the mood?

The truth is that your character, your beliefs, and your thinking are an important part of what determines the level of your success?

The key to success is to increase your energy, and when you do, people will naturally be attracted to you.

Wealth Principle: Your Income Can Grow Only to the Level You Do

You probably have heard stories of people who have lost everything financially, haven't you? Have you seen people who initially had a lot of money and then after some time they lose it? I hope you know the cause. It is important that when you start to handle big money, you must be ready for it. If not, your wealth will be short-lived.

You must have the internal capacity to create and retain large amounts of money. Additionally, you must be able to handle the challenges that come with possessing a lot of money.

When self-made millionaires blow up financially, they still recover because they don't lose the formulae for creating wealth. Unlike most lottery winners who when they lose all the money, they get stuck in the original state they were.

The Roots Create the Fruits

When it comes to life, our fruits are represented by our results. So when we look at the results, and we don't like them, what do we do?

Most people continue to focus on fruits-our results. But what exactly creates those results? It is the roots and seeds that create those fruits?

It's whatever that it's under the ground that creates what is above. So if when we don't like the fruits, we need to start by watering the roots of the tree, weed the tree, and apply fertilizer to improve the fruits. But do we do that? Of course not. In short, if you want to change the visible, you must first begin by changing the invisible.

Wealth Principle 2: Money is a Result; Your Weight is a Result; Illness is a Result. We Are in a World of Cause and Effect.

Have you ever heard someone complain that a lack of money was a problem? The fact is that a lack of money is never, ever a problem. A lack of money is just a symptom of what is happening underneath.

Lack of money is the effect, but what is the main cause? It narrows down to this. The only means to change your "outer" world is first to convert your "inner" world.

No matter the results you're ripping, whether rich or poor, positive or negative, always keep in mind that your outer world is a reflection of your inner world. Suppose things aren't moving on well in your outer life, it's because things are going wrong in your inner life.

Declarations Are a Powerful Ingredient for Change

Declarations are a valuable tool for change. Each declaration you make has its own vibrational frequency. When you say a declaration aloud, its energy travels throughout the cells of your body, and by holding your body at the same time, you can experience its unique resonance. Declarations both send a powerful signal to the universe and your subconscious mind.

I urge you to state your declarations aloud every morning and evening. Performing your declarations while looking into a mirror will enhance the process even more.

That said, I request you to place your hand on your heart and say the following aloud:

"My inner world defines my outer world."

"I have a millionaire mind."

Wealth Principle 3: Between Deeply Rooted Emotions and Logic, the Subconscious Mind Will Select Emotions.

Remember, your subconscious conditioning defines your thinking. Your thinking determines your decisions, and your decisions will determine your actions, which finally determine your results.

There are four major elements of change, each of which is important in reprogramming your financial blueprint. They are simple but very powerful.

First is awareness. You cannot change something unless you know it exists.

The second element is understanding. By mastering your way of thinking, you can know that it has to come from outside you.

The third aspect of change is disassociation. Once you understand a specific way of thinking, you can distance yourself from it and decide whether to retain it or let it go depending on where you want to be tomorrow.

The fourth aspect is the reconditioning. This involves rewiring your subconscious mind on a cellular and permanent level.

Wealth Principle 4: Get Deeply Motivated

Money is a superficial motivator to push you to achieve success.

The challenge is that financial wealth is an external goal with advantages restricted to the world outside of you. Money can buy things, but it cannot buy happiness. It can build for you a beautiful prison, but it cannot get you out of prison.

The underlining limits of external goals similarly reduce how motivated you will be when looking for them.

To succeed in creating wealth, you want to be pushed by internal goals more than just external trappings of wealth.

You want a reason that will generate transformation to your life and drive you deep enough to overcome all the problems that come in between you and financial freedom.

Internally-driven goals that might concentrate your attention enough to succeed consist:

1. Charity. The more you have, the more you can give.

2. Freedom. Pull out from unnecessary events to have more time to grow, and live your maximum potential.

3. Growth. When you have financial freedom at hand, you have enough time to seek personal freedom. The riches in your external world become a reflection of the wealth in your inner world. The principles that result in financial wealth can also result in true wealth by impacting other areas of your life.

4. Leadership. Grow your wealth in the right way so that you can be a good example to friends and family.

Why you must have deeper causes is because creating wealth isn't easy.

You will encounter many challenges that you must overcome along your course to financial freedom. You must be ready to pay the price to reach your goal.

To remain in the course long enough to succeed, you must be driven by a commitment that runs deeper than just the lifestyle that money can buy.

Wealth Principle 5: Live with 100% Integrity

Make sure that you do things that will make your parents proud.

Don't encroach on other property, destroy the environment, or violate moral law. Don't lie or even cheat in search of financial freedom.

The rule is simple. If it doesn't feel right, then it perhaps isn't. If you don't feel okay telling your spouse, parents, and children what you are doing, then you probably shouldn't do it.

Never go for expediency over integrity because no size of financial wealth can replace a good night's sleep, a peaceful mind, and a clear conscience.

Wealth Principle 6: Offer More Value Than You Take

Adding value to society by giving more than you receive makes everyone better off. That's how you create wealth. You improve the lives of others by improving yours.

While the world is full of people who have amassed wealth by exploiting others or the environment but taking value can never result in happiness.

Exploitation may generate riches, but providing value brings fulfillment and riches.

When you give more value than you receive, success becomes a measure of how much you have given. The wealthier you're, the more you're giving to others.

It's a perfect way to live.
343

Wealth Principle 7: Be Disciplined

Becoming a millionaire is the cumulative effect of many small things combined and compounded over a lifetime. In other words, your daily habits will make or break your success.

Investing, saving, growing, and reinvesting your financial and business intelligence are important wealth creation habits that require continuous effort.

In short, wealth creation requires discipline.

Without discipline, you risk beginning procrastination. You must start the right habits today without delay. It calls for discipline to overcome procrastination by beginning today and to persist tomorrow.

Another great obstacle to a disciplined daily routine is "magical thinking." This refers to the false belief that financial security will magically happen without a specific action or plan.

You must know from today that wealth happens because you do what it takes to make it happen. The appearance of immediate wealth is based on the ground of years of disciplined daily routine. Remember, luck comes to those who make their own breaks.

Wealth Principle 8: Establish Supportive Environments

If becoming wealthy was easy, then everyone would have been wealth. Yet, only a few achieve financial freedom, although anyone can create a means to become wealthy.

The distinguishing factors are persistent and focused action. Life is full of distractions to damage your plans for wealth.

The solution is to develop a support system that helps you remain focused and brings you close to wealth.

Wealth Principle 9: Use Leverage to Create Wealth

Leverage is a great tool for generating wealth. You cannot become wealthy if you trade time for money, and it's difficult to do it alone.

You must choose to work smarter rather than harder by using the principles of:

1. Financial leverage.

2. Marketing leverage.

3. Time leverage.

4. Network leverage.

Leverage allows you to generate more wealth than you could ever by incorporating resources that extend beyond your abilities.

It is important to grow wealth without being obstructed by your abilities.

Wealth Principle 10: Treat Your Wealth Like Your Business

You cannot build a business without a business plan. So why should you build wealth without any plan?

Write down your wealth plan based on quality business principles that result in success. Some of these principles consist of accurate record storage, accountability, and leverage.

Manage your money like your business, because that is exactly what it is.

Also, your personalized wealth plan should take into consideration your unique interests, resources, and skills.

When done, your wealth plan will be rooted in your unique life situation, while respecting the proven success principles that no wealth plan is complete without it.

Wealth Principle 11: Steward Your Wealth

You are a servant to wealth the same way wealth is your servant.

Through your wealth legacy, you have the chance to bless yourself and your family's life now and in the future. And you can go past that by expanding the network to include the lives of all who follow you.

As a successful wealth creator, you'll be in a perfect position to organize for charities that achieve great social good.

Keep in mind wealth is not something that you own, but a flow that has a temporary house in your hands.

Wealth Principle 12: Be Courageous

Wealth doesn't come from the crowd. It comes from doing what others are unable to do. Therefore, it takes courage to put that extra commitment and effort.

In short, it takes courage to establish wealth. So be courageous in everything you do.

In summary, these are wealth building principles that result in true wealth. The goal is not just to become rich but to develop a balanced and satisfying life.

Chapter 6: Discover your Emotional Why

Emotions are a force to remember. For example, have you ever allowed the fear of failure to delay you from doing something you know you need to do, like creating a budget or even investing? What about buyer's remorse after a huge purchase, or any purchase for that reason? If you have experienced any of these reactions, you understand how great the power of emotions plays in our financial lives. Psychologists term these emotions and beliefs we have about money as "money scripts."

The Foundation of Your Money Habits

Do you ever feel like the discipline to make well-thought-out financial decisions must be too good to be true? Because regardless of how hard you try, you cannot make to stick to it? Well, I know others feel the same way. These feelings are not strange and are probably likely because of the emotional and psychological weight we all carry around associated with our money, also referred to as the money scripts. And these scripts usually begin showing up at a very young age.

While we may not know about it, we spend our childhood thinking of how our parents and other role models relate to and handle cash. Over time, our brains are subconsciously trained to respond in the same way. If your parents were sure of their ability to make wise investments, you would probably invest with confidence. On the other hand, if you saw your parents quarreling over expenses, you might experience some strong feelings of guilt when completing certain purchases.

The seeds of money scripts created in childhood, watered by observation, and finally grow to impact your emotional beliefs about finances as an adult. As a result, it is important to be diligent in speaking to your kids about money and teaching healthy financial behaviors. It's just as critical to take the time to analyze yourself and understand your money scripts and how they affect your financial behavior.

The Negative Aspect of Money Scripts

In general, not all money scripts are bad. Some behaviors we acquire are beneficial emotions about finances. But, other behaviors like money avoidance, concentration on financial status, or the worship of money, can be detrimental. Unhealthy emotions and belief patterns can result in all types of financial problems, such as compulsive buying, financial independence, and pathological gambling. Specific money scripts have been linked to reduced levels of net worth, lower-income, and higher amounts of evolving credit.

That may look extreme, but have you ever allowed panic during a market downturn to destroy your long-term investing plan? Have you ever been unable to decide because you were affected by worry and anxiety about the future? Have you ever destroyed your budget for the momentary high of getting something you really wanted? All of those behaviors originate from your money script.

It's Possible to Change Money Scripts

We usually think that if we were rich, we wouldn't have any problems. But we experience money issues because of the way we approach money, not because we don't have enough. This is good news. We might not succeed in increasing our income rapidly, but we can learn to control our perceptions and attitudes. Our money scripts may be rooted in childhood, but they are not permanent. With concerted energy, they can be changed.

The first thing you must do in defeating your money scripts is to highlight them. To achieve this, you must be aware of your emotional responses to common financial situations. Start to stop and discover your emotional responses to these common experiences:

- Purchasing things

- Volatile markets

- Healthy markets

- Earning money

- Saving for the future

- Making financial decisions

- Budgeting and tracking expenses

- Thinking about your financial future

- Interacting with a financial professional

How do the following things make you feel? Anything that triggers strong emotions requires further reflection. Remember that negative emotions aren't the only ones that can destroy your financial life. Some positive emotions, such as self-confidence, and optimism, can generate negative results if left unchecked.

Emotional Wealth

Do you ever dream of becoming wealthy?

What do you always imagine your life would look like if you became a multi-millionaire? What would you do? How would you spend your day? Who would you spend it with?

Often, we think that wealth is all about the amount of money in the bank. However, wealth is about the increased options that having a lot of money affords. It involves being emotionally wealthy.

The more money you possess, the more options are available to you. The more options you have, the more freedom you command in your life.

But did you know that you can be emotionally wealthy? And it doesn't need you to have millions in the bank.

You might be asking yourself why you would go for emotional wealth?

Put simply, all wealth is emotional.

Control Emotional Money Decisions

The secret to changing your money scripts and developing healthy money habits is learning to deal with your emotions. You can still create some new, healthy habits that secure you financially and apply them to your life. Disciplines and habits like taking advantage of automatic savings, scheduling regular family budget meetings, and involving the assistance of someone reliable to keep you alert are great places to start. Finally, you will discover how to respond to emotional triggers, and you can then take steps before you make any decisions.

Lastly, you need to be ready to forgive yourself when you make mistakes. Leave the past in the past and progress with the new knowledge you have acquired. Choosing to forgive yourself for past mistakes frees you up to be more effective with your new tools. As you start to gather victories, both big and small, you will probably find it easier to extend forgiveness.

Chapter 7: Create Your Millionaire Habits & Beliefs

Your behaviors, feelings, and thoughts will determine nearly everything you are or will be. Almost 95% of everything you feel, think, and will be decided by your habits. The secret to becoming successful, and living a great life is for you to acquire the habits of success that help you accomplish everything that you can.

Luckily, all habits are learnable. If you have bad habits, or if you have not yet developed the habits that you should become who you are capable of becoming, you can establish these habits by adhering to a systematic process of practice and repetition, the same way you learn any other topic.

It's difficult to learn good habits, but easy to live with. On the other hand, it's easy to acquire bad habits, but hard to shed away. In either way, once you have mastered a habit, it becomes automatic. You will find it easier to handle thoughts, behaviors, and feelings that are in line with the person you want to be and the goals you want to accomplish.

Where Habits Originate From

A habit is a "conditioned response to a stimulus," but what's its origin? A habit arises because of your specific response to a given stimulus, often beginning early in life. It is very similar to driving down the road and branching in one direction or another. Whichever direction you choose, good or bad, largely determines your final destination.

Fortunately, you aren't born with any habits. All the habits you acquired from infancy. Habits take different periods to develop. Therefore, if you want to overcome or acquire some, it will take time. However, there is a credited system that you can use to boost the process of new habit pattern development.

Behavioral psychologists use the term "operant conditioning" to refer to the way people learn specific automatic behaviors. Sometimes, they point to the "SBC Model" of new habit pattern development. SBC stands for Stimulus-Behavior-Consequences. This means something has first to activate a thought or feeling. In response, you behave a certain way. Then the result is you experience a certain consequence. If you repeat this process several times, you acquire a new habit.

Expectations Theory

According to this theory, people are inspired to behave in a given way by what they expect to occur more than any other factor or influence. In short, you do the things you like to do because of the effect you feel you will experience. Expectation theory describes small things like what you do and says in a social gathering and large things such as capital movements in the international financial markets.

Did you know that you can create your expectations? It's possible to develop the habit of expecting good things to occur, regardless of how things may look at the moment. Your expectations then affect your attitudes and how you treat other people. Your expectations, attitudes, and behaviors will then have an inner influence on the way things turn out. In effect, you can dictate a large percent of your future by expecting things to take place positively.

Unfortunately, negative expectations also translate to self-fulfilling prophecies. If you expect something to become poor, this will damage your behavior and attitude. Your negative attitude then boosts the probabilities that you will experience the negative result that you anticipated. If you repeat this always, you will acquire a negative and pessimistic attitude. This method of thinking will grow into a habit.

Development of New Habit Pattern

How long does it take to acquire a new habit? The period can be any length from a single second to several years. The rate of new habit pattern development is largely defined by the strength of the emotion that goes along with the decision to start acting in a given way.

Many people desire to lose weight and become physically fit; however, they don't take the initiative to start. Not until the doctor says, "If you don't reduce your weight and improve your physical state, you might die early."

The thought of dying can be so frightening and serious that the person immediately changes his diet, starts to exercise, stops smoking, and becomes a fit person. Psychologists describe this as a "significant emotional experience." Any experience of strong pain, accompanied by a behavior, can trigger a habitual behavior pattern that may persist for the rest of a person's life.

Experts say that it takes around 21 days to develop a habit pattern of moderate complexity. By this, they refer to simple habits such as exercising every morning before you start, going to sleep at a certain hour, planning every day, starting with your most critical tasks each day, or finishing your tasks before you begin something else. These are habits of moderate complexity that can be developed in 14-21 days through repetition and practice.

Well, how do you develop a new habit? Over time, a simple, powerful, proven formulae has been generated for new habit development. It's much like a recipe for cooking a certain dish in the kitchen. You can apply it to develop any habit that you like. As time goes, you will find it easier to develop the habits that you want to include in your personality.

Steps to Acquire a New Habit

1. **First, decide**. Make a decision that you want to start acting in a certain way 100% of the time, anytime that behavior is required. For example, if you choose to wake up early every morning and exercise, set your clock for a specific time, and when the alarm goes off,

get up, wear your exercise clothes, and begin your exercise session.

2. **Don't create an exception** in your new habit during the development stages. Don't create an excuse or rationalizations.

3. **Notify others.** It is important to notify others that you are starting to practice a specific behavior. It is surprising how much more disciplined and determined you will become when you realize that others are looking at you if you have the willpower to monitor your resolution.

4. **Visualize yourself**. See yourself acting in a certain way in a particular situation. The more you visualize and imagine yourself behaving as if you already had the new habit, the more rapid your subconscious mind will accept this new act.

5. **Develop an affirmation.** Repeat an affirmation daily over to yourself. This repetition dramatically accelerates the speed at which you learn a new habit.

6. **Resolve to persist** in the new habit until it becomes automatic and easy that you can feel uncomfortable when you don't do what you have chosen to do.

7. **Reward yourself.** Every time you reward yourself, you reaffirm and reinforce the behavior. Soon you start to connect, at an unconscious level, the beauty of the reward with the behavior.

Take It Easy on Yourself

Where do you begin in new habit pattern development? When people first learn the significance of new habit pattern development and the way positive patterns of thought and behavior can have a great effect on their lives, they usually make the mistake of choosing to create several new habits at once. They choose to improve in every part of their lives simultaneously. They excitedly create a list of new habits that they wish for their work, their financial lives, their relationships, their health, their business, and their organizational skills. As a result, they quickly hit a snag, and no improvement happens at all.

Here is the rule of creating new habits: be patient with yourself. It has taken you a whole lifetime to become the person you are. You can change everything overnight. Therefore, you need to select one habit that you feel can be more helpful to you at the moment than any other habit. Write it down and develop a positive affirmation of yourself behaving exactly as if you already had that new habit.

You then start immediately and don't create room for an exception. Talk to yourself positively and reaffirm to yourself that you already have this habit. Imagine yourself acting as though you had already mastered this behavior. Tell others. Reward yourself every time you engage in the new behavior. But only try to change one habit at a time.

Thinking in a Given Way

You must form a clear and exact mental picture of what you want; you cannot transform an idea unless you have it yourself.

You must possess it before you can give it, and many people fail to impress because they have a general concept of the things they want to achieve, have, or to become.

It is not sufficient to have a general desire for wealth; everybody has the same desire.

It's not enough that you need to travel, live more, or see things, etc. Everybody has the same desires. If you're going to send an electronic message to a friend, you will not send the letter of the alphabet in their order, and allow them to compile the message for himself. You would instead send a complete sentence, one which implied something. When you try to impress your desires, keep in mind that a complete statement must fulfill it. You must know what you want and be definite. You can never be wealthy by sending out unformed vague desires.

Go over your desires, determine what you want, and develop a clear mental picture of what you want to look when you get it.

That clear mental picture you must often have it in mind, you must maintain your keep your face close to it all the time. You should not lose sight of it.

It's not a must to take exercises in concentration, nor to set apart special moments for prayer and affirmation. All you need is to understand what you want and to want it strongly so that it will remain in your thoughts.

Spend as much of your leisure time as you can in thinking about your picture, but no one needs to exercise to focus his mind on a thing which he really wants. It is the things you do not really care about which deserve effort to fix your attention upon them.

Not unless you want to get rich so that the desire is intense enough to hold your thoughts directed to the purpose.

The clearer and definite you set your picture then, and the more you concentrate upon it, the stronger your desire will be; and the stronger your desire, the easier it will be to keep your mind fixed upon the picture of what you want.

However, something more is needed than merely to look at the picture. If that is all you do, you are only a dreamer and will have no power for achievement.

Being and Becoming

Know that you're special in the whole world. There has never been, nor will nor will there ever be, anyone just like you. And what sets you apart is your unique mind. You can decide, think, and act.

The eventual result of your thinking and experiences in your past is held in your actions of today. In your habitual methods of reacting and responding to other people, only your actions that show who you are and what you have become.

The best thing is that you are not just a human being. You are always in a continuous state of growth and change, eliminating old habits and ideas, and establishing new ones. It doesn't matter where you are coming from; all that matters is where you're going. And where you're going is only determined by your imagination.

Permanent Fixtures of Your Mind

Old habits do not die. They do not disappear. When you stop practicing them and discipline yourself to act in a new way, they become weak and get into your subconscious mind. Your new habits may replace the old habits, but you never forget them completely. They hide below the surface, waiting to reemerge at a later time when the stimulus that initially builds them is repeated.

Self-Made Millionaire Beliefs About Money

Self-made millionaires all have one common thing: they know becoming rich starts with what you believe about money. The way they look at money varies from everyone else.

Most people think that the wealthy have an unfair advantage. But the fact is, anyone can acquire wealth. But one of the biggest factors is your thoughts about money.

Many people believe that the only means to make a lot of money is to work longer hours. However, millionaires don't think about money in these terms. They focus on chasing what provides the highest returns instead of thinking they trade their time for money. But, many of us grew up with the beliefs about the money we may not know our parents are the cause for them.

In fact, some of these beliefs are passed on through many generations. One of the most popular belief is that it's selfish to want a lot of money. Another is that money is a rare resource, and it's hard to earn. Shedding away, these beliefs about money is important. Instead, you need to think about it in terms of freedom, abundance, and possibilities.

The fact is, you don't need to launch a startup tech firm to become a millionaire. What you need instead is the correct mindset and some financially savvy habits. If you want to be wealthy, you may have to begin changing how you look at money. Below are some lessons from those who are already wealthy.

1. Purpose of being rich

Many people desire to be multi-millionaires, but they are not committed to what it takes to be a millionaire. Steve Siebold is a self-made millionaire who spent approximately three decades interviewing other millionaires around the globe. After that, he wrote a book, How Rich People Think. According to Steve, the wealthy are committed to taking action, while others wait to win the lottery or seek for prosperity. They think rich people are dishonest or lucky.

Many millionaires will tell you that you must be ready to make sacrifices and delay gratification. Additionally, you must have great expectations if you want to be like them. You need to be ready to take some calculated risks that will pay off in the long run. You cannot sit in your comfort zone and expect some external force to come help you.

Relaxing without doing anything will send a message to your unconscious mind that you are not serious about becoming wealthy. It will divert your attention and stop you from looking for new ideas. After all, getting serious and taking a logical step-by-step approach is necessary to change your relationship with money.

2. Start being paid what you're worth

Grant Sabatier says that there is nothing more critical to your future than being paid what you're worth. He moved from earning a few dollars in his bank account to a million in a span of five years. Sabatier believes that many people don't get what they're worth. He recommends running an analysis of what other people in your industry with the same level of expertise and years of experience are earning. Forward this information to your boss when requesting a raise and highlight what you're bringing to the company.

If you're working as a freelancer, increase your rates to raise your revenue. As you improve at what you do, you offer more value, and your rates should increase. But hiking your rates is easier said than done. A lot of thoughts run in your head, and you imagine what will happen if your clients take their business elsewhere. In most cases, your fears limit you from earning what you genuinely deserve.

Negotiating to start getting paid what you're worth can be difficult. There will always be people who are ready to work for less than you do for the same task. The answer is to ignore them and concentrate on what you deliver that makes the amount you're asking worth it. Be firm on your fees once you've made up your mind what they should be. The fact is that some clients can afford you, and others can't.

It's also important to have an idea of how much you spend. If you can determine your net every month, you can see whether your financial worth is staying the same, improving, or getting worse. And once you have all the data, you can make changes to increase your income.

3. Learn how to save

Despite their commitments to budget, some people still can't get a word on their spending. When you examine the lifestyles of the rich and famous, you probably imagine Lamborghinis and yachts. But the fact is, many are wealthy because they know how to spend and save money.

Remember, it's not so much about the money you make as it is the money you save. You don't need to earn big to start saving or investing. Anyone can find a way to set aside some of their income. But the secret is to start saving as early as you can to reap the profits of compound interest.

You must make a mental shift and find happiness in saving money. You should enjoy saving and get as much satisfaction out of it like spending. If you develop this mindset, you will not care about spending any more.

Think of budgeting a game and setting a new challenge every week. Many millionaires often consider earning and saving a game. And it's a game they want to win, so they put all their attention into it. They attain great satisfaction when they see that needle moving upwards. So, remember, it's all about shedding away that negative perception about money.

5 Ways to Develop a Millionaire Mindset

1. Be Hyper-Responsive

If you read accounts of how millionaires act, you'll see a repeating theme. They're proactive, highly responsive people who always behave in dynamic ways. For instance, if they encounter a problem and discover that it's difficult to find a solution in the present market, they move on and start a business that addresses this very problem.

Similarly, when they're running a business. They look at trends around them and behave accordingly. They change marketing strategies, they spend more on methods of marketing their work, and they aggressively seek growth on both a professional and personal level.

In contrast, the average person without a millionaire's mindset will instead be reactive. They will be making changes only to react to things that happen around them. So, they always wait until crisis point before being ready to do anything different.

The lesson here is that you need to be proactive. This will not only allow you to attract abundance but can also increase your vibration in a manner that attracts all kinds of good new things into your life.

2. Tune into your greatest strengths

You'd be forgiven to think that the millionaire's mindset may require overcoming all of your weaknesses-or even becoming good at most things. But it's good to find the things you're truly excellent in. Polish those skills and use them to guide you to success.

Instead of being distracted by attempts to improve in many places at once, intentionally play to your strengths. You'll finally discover your path to the greatest level of success you're capable of attaining. And in case you're not sure what your strengths are exactly, think of the things that make you feel inspired and excited, and the things that attract the most praise from others.

3. Become an expert in your field

No matter which industry you've chosen in your quest to become a millionaire, you have to command an in-depth knowledge and understanding of all its features.

For example, you must understand that the industry's history, its current path, its most critical obstacles, and so forth. It's becoming an expert that will provide you the edge you deserve to succeed where your competitors fail. Doing so demands hard work, determination, and focus. In general, it's what can open the way to acquire the abundance of a millionaire.

4. Learn to love yourself by increasing your self-esteem

You might be surprised to discover that self-conception is important when you're trying to become a millionaire, but it really plays a big role. If you depend on the notion that you'll become confident and happy with who you're once you become rich, you will realize that you never quite hit the level of abundance you want to reach.

375

To achieve financial success, first, you need to cross barriers to healthy self-esteem and create a level of self-love that offers you the conviction that you need to be abundant.

Here are several things you can do to create a better relationship with yourself.

- Look after your body

- Hold strong boundaries concerning how others treat you.

- Learn to forgive yourself for past mistakes.

- Actively concentrate on your special gifts to the world.

5. Rewrite your beliefs regarding money and wealth

Lastly, many of us hold negative and harmful assumptions about money. These can affect the Law of Attraction work on a significant level.

Therefore, to create that millionaire mindset you're searching for, try to run an inventory of these limiting beliefs by challenging yourself to write down as many as you can imagine:

Some are quite common, such as:

- "Rich people are immoral."
- "It's just impossible to succeed in today's economy."
- "People like me don't become millionaires."

Then, for each of the above beliefs, write down a new sentence that more accurately reflect what you believe is right. For instance:

- "Anyone can be bad or good; it doesn't matter how much money they have."
- "I know I have the power to succeed."
- "I can be anything I want to be."

Think about converting these positive statements into affirmations that you say daily. Finally, you'll rewrite your beliefs, and they will stop holding you back.

Chapter 8: The Power of Positive Thinking and Happiness

You will agree with me when I say that the power of positive thinking is amazing.

The fact that your mind can change your world almost sounds too good to be true.However, I can assure you that focusing on the positive can generate good results.

Can you guess what millionaires and happy people think about all day long?

The answer is simple.

Wealthy, happy people spend time thinking about what they want and how to get it most of the time. As a result, creating a positive attitude can truly change your whole life.

When you think and talk about what you want and how to achieve it, you feel happier and in greater control of your life.

When you consider something that makes you happy, your brain truly releases endorphins, which provide you a generalized feeling of well-being.

For that matter, you establish a positive attitude.

As your income grows, you cannot forget your happiness. If you are not consciously protecting it, it can vanish. Remember that happiness results in success, not the other way around. Many people in the world often think that when they've tons of money, they are the CEO of a profitable company and have a lot of fame and fortune. They're going to be happy. However, that's not true.

The most common thing that prevents people from living an actual fulfilled life is the assumption that when they find success, happiness will follow. Take your life, for example. Have you ever felt like if you got a specific job or started your business, then happiness would emerge from it? Have you ever thought that if you made a huge sum of money, or once you get a wide or a husband that loves you, or once you lose weight, or once you buy a beautiful car, then you'll be happy? However, many people who think this way finally come to discover that they're wrong. It would be a big mistake if you didn't know of this secret. And yes, you can be a millionaire with the right habits, but why should you deny yourself happiness? Becoming a millionaire without fulfillment is useless. Let me help you accomplish it all.

Suppose happiness is the prerequisite for everything else? What if it is the answer to prosperity, success, love, passion, wealth, and weight loss? What if many of us don't know the way to be happy, but instead, we believe we will know once we arrive somewhere? Reflect on what you tell yourself: "All I want is to get my business running, and I'll be happy." Or: "As soon as I purchase that car, I'll be satisfied."

You see, many of us allow our desire for external things to control us. We feel like once we acquire that new car or that new job, then we'll be happy. But you know what? The excitement of outside properties vanishes. Have you ever thought, once I receive a pay raise of income, that is when the fun starts? Luckily, it happens, and you spend wisely, buy some new stuff, renovate your apartment, and think, I'm netting a lot of money, so now I'm happy! But a few months down the line, the extra income and what you bought no longer satisfies you.

As much as this book teaches you how to grow your wealth and achieve success using the right habits, no amount of money will make you happy unless you find internal satisfaction. But tie that with more money, and it is time for real fulfillment and next-level.

The thing is that the external world can only give you temporary happiness. We all want that ideal weight, next level of income, a great lifestyle, intimacy, perfect health, and more money. But all these fades away unless you learn how to be happy on the inside. And here's one crazy fact that you need to know. If you find happiness on the inside, then suddenly, all of those other things we want are more achievable. When you learn to create happiness internally, those things become a result of the happiness you're creating, which is the opposite of what many people think. Many people believe money, diamond rings, fast cars, and success come first, and then happiness will reveal itself. That is false, and the reason why so many people walk around feeling stressed and depressed.

Take a look at specific habits and thought processes that are the fastest way to happiness. These are just recipes, instructions, and ingredients that drive you to success faster.

1. Determine what happiness is and feels like to you

If someone was to ask you this question, "what makes you happy?' What would answer? Do you exactly know what you will say? This is a hard question for everyone. It is hard because so many times, people compare their definition of happiness to others. Simply because someone else's definition of happiness is a mansion, or an expensive car, doesn't mean it has to be the same for you! For sure, If you were to ask me the same question 10 years ago, I probably would have struggled to come up with a response. Back then, I didn't know exactly on what happiness truly meant to me. It would be easy to say, "Being with a beautiful woman," and that would be the default and not truly thought-out response. But you must get clear on what really makes you happy.

Take time and think through or even start writing down ideas about what makes your heart smile, your eyes brighter, and causes you to be alive with joy. What makes you happy? Don't divert to a few answers that have become your default response. Reflect on the time you were a kid in your life. When was your life at peace? What excited you? What brought a smile on your face? Is it going to a sporting event or going breathing fresh air? Is it spending time in the woods with your kids playing fun games?

Most importantly, what's on your list today? I know if you were to create this list 5 or 10 years ago, your responses would certainly be different. Some would be embarrassing, and some would be materialistic. So make sure you're reflecting on your present happiness.

Also, make sure you don't confuse happiness with goals. I know you still have financial goals, achievement goals, and materialistic goals. But you should know the difference between goals and what makes you truly happy.

The quest for happiness begins by thinking through and defining the phrase as it applies to your current life. So try to write down things without overthinking. Don't restrict your list to things you do, but include the thoughts that make you happy, blessings that you can be grateful for, and events that bring you joy. Write and write more. Then look at your list and circle around 3-5 items that you feel strongly about, and those are your best.

2. Stop overthinking

They say, "paralysis is caused by over-analysis." What prevents us from living the life we want is overthinking. You should have experienced this often especially when going to the next level in wealth and business. What eventually happens is that we overanalyze, overthink, and find ourselves stuck.

No matter your goal, you can overthink it to death. If there is a path to success, all you have to do is follow the path. Don't overthink things because by overthinking, you will never do anything.

It's good to obtain the knowledge you need to establish confidence, but then don't be shot down in endless questions, circular analysis, and second thoughts. If your heart is saying you act if your subconscious wants you to go for it, stop overthinking and swing into action.

3. Let the present be your friend

By present I mean now, this very moment you are living in. You have to be friends. Many people go through life looking forward to the next week, to next year, instead of making friends with them right now. We say to ourselves, "When I get this promotion when I start my own company when I lose weight-then and only then I'll be happy!" That kind of thinking is only an excuse for chasing happiness to some unknown time in the future. And when you do that. That time will never come. That is why you need to live in the present. Why not choose to be happy now?

When you use the word "when/then" too often-as in, "When I receive a promotion, then I can finally feel happy about my life" _ all you're doing is pushing your happiness to tomorrow because you're mentally living in a time other than right now. Let's be honest. How many of us are waiting to be happy until that one thing happens? What if you remove that mind-set and just make today your friend? What if today was a remarkable day? What if you stopped living in the past or the future but instead choose to be happy right this second? Suppose you started doing more of the things that make you happy and focused on more of the things that generate joy today? Right this moment. You can choose to do this; it is your decision.

How many times do you hit a snag thinking about what could have gone wrong in the future? How many times have you felt, "When I do this, then this might happen the following month or next year?" Then what happens? You switch on this slope of negative thinking, and you go snowballing down the hill of thinking what might go wrong someday. You're practicing the future and predicting a negative future. The fact is that you don't know where the future is going and how things are going to end up. Of course, living too far in the future with the wrong thoughts kills your happiness today.

Choose the present now. Recognize that each day is there for a reason and that every moment should be dealt with a present mind-set. As simple as this advice may appear, consider the consequences: Suppose you appreciated being alive and healthy and all the moments you have at this very moment?

When you can let the past fed away, you can stop concentrating on a fictional future and learn to live in the present. When you live in the now, you will finally discover the inner peace and happiness.

4. Focus on a positive result

This is a powerful technique to attract happiness into your life and achieve what you want early. Your energy is going to take any direction you aim it; you get to decide if it's spent on the negative or positive.

Know that the world has programmed us to think a certain way regarding situations we encounter. When something pops up, our minds want to switch to, "Oh no, this isn't good! What if this happens, or what if, what if." The answer is to monitor your thoughts. When what-if thoughts try to enter into your mind, say, "No, no, no. I'm not going to let my mind reach there." Remember the decision rest with you, either you focus on what might go wrong, or you focus on what might go right. Why not invest your effort in what can go right?

5. Let go of certain outcomes

This is not easy, but very effective. In most cases, we predict what different results should be, and we hung up on our predictions. "If I use this money to complete this deal, and I collaborate with this person, we should generate x amount of money, and here's how it's going to look." If it doesn't go like that, happiness disappears. You say to yourself, "That's not what I expected! That is not my prediction. This is not right."

Often, when an entrepreneur starts a business, the original idea fails to work. So then the entrepreneur changes the mind and discovers success in a different direction. For instance, that's how Twitter started. The original idea of Twitter was to be a podcast company. The success of Twitter would not have
388

happened if the entrepreneurs had given up because their initial idea didn't work out.

Once you let go of a certain outcome, the heavy nature of expectation decreases. You will become a better person immediately, and your happiness will rise.

Positive Millionaire Mindset

To become financially independent, you must create a millionaire mindset.

Wealthy people master the habits of becoming rich gradually rather than sudden. To achieve this, they believe in two rules. The first rule is that they should not lose money. The other rule is that if you feel tempted, then you should revisit the first rule.

Most wealthy people use most of their time to reflect than the average person. The very habit of thinking about their finances largely improves their decision-making ability. Wealthy people who spend their time organizing their finances perhaps make better decisions, and achieve financial independence.

Millionaires have other financial habits to ensure they don't lose money, and their money grows gradually over time. As you develop the millionaire mindset, the best financial habits which you can master is the habit of getting the right advice before you carry out any activity. In fact, looking for a financial advisor who has achieved financial independence is the best action. Your ability to choose the right financial advisors can a critical aspect in making the correct investment decisions.

Make it a habit to analyze anything before you start to invest. The general rule is that you need to spend a lot of time analyzing the investment.

Fast financial decisions are not the best. But if you set aside time to reflect and analyze every detail of the business, you will avoid any problems that might arise.

Don't let anyone force you to make an investment decision. Let no one convince you that a financial investment decision is urgent and should be made immediately.

Sometimes, successful investments are those that you never make a decision. Let it be a habit to understand an investment before you ever decide to quit.

Wealthy People Cover Their Assets

As you begin to become wealthy, don't forget to protect your wealth from unnecessary lawsuits. Get an attorney to help you protect your reaches and business.

Never Trust to Luck

An important factor in succeeding financially is insuring your property against any risk. It is interesting the way some people lose wealth which they have struggled to get. To avoid such problems, insure your wealth.

Many people don't like to spend their money on insurance, but it's one of the best things that you can do on your quest for financial freedom.

Chapter 9: Success Hacks

You are young passionate, confident, and you want to be a millionaire? Great!

Or maybe you want to take things a notch and launch that business you have been dreaming of, but you are scared of financial risks and not sure whether you want to release the perks of a salary and benefits.

The biggest question you could be asking yourself is: what are you ready to give up to establish the life and business that you really want?

In the modern world of powerful technology, the subject of success always seems complicated and overwhelming. Most people tend to be caught in a race to determine the "correct" formula within infinite possibilities.

It is possible to be trapped over which tool, whose method or what path to go to arrive at our destination the quickest and effective way.

At every turn, we are given articles, courses, tutorials, and videos that promise to provide us with the responses we are looking for.

This chapter is going to look at success hacks that you can adjust to suit your life at a moment's notice. Of course, there are a lot of habits or "hacks" that can help you along your journey to success. These are some of the best, and you can apply them into your life easily, and with a deeper effect than you may think.

1. Be honest to yourself

Ensure you're happy with the person you see in the mirror, with the person you are "being" every day. Are you the friend you want to be, the partner you want to be, or the parent you want to be? When you agree who you want to be, you are true to yourself.

2. Practice gratitude

Mobile phones can do virtually everything. Set a daily alarm to notify you to remain grateful. This is a cool, powerful trick. In the busy days we experience, it's possible to forget to practice gratitude.

Additionally, we can get annoyed, frustrated, overwhelmed, or even become pessimistic or unable to smile. Set your mobile alarm to go off at different times of the day, accompanied by a small description when the alarm rings. These reminders should make you take a 30-second break from whatever is happening and acknowledge everything in this world.

Practice the habit of appreciating everything. See the blessings and beauty of every moment. Thank God for keeping you alive.

3. Save money

You must make it a habit to save money. It doesn't matter how much you're earning per week, save some of it. There are some people in the world, and perhaps you might know some who will spend as much money as they earn. If they make $10, they are going to spend $12.

But you have heard this hack before. Financial advisers, parents, and spouses may have all emphasized that you begin saving.

This success hack isn't as much about money as it is about confidence.

When you have money set aside, it boosts your confidence. You will know in your mind that you can deal with any emergency that arises. If you have a bad month, break your hand, or bad three weeks, you can handle it. You develop a peace of mind knowing that you and your family are going to be fine until you're back on your feet.

Alternatively, if you have no money in your savings account, you're always going to be scared about your future, even if only subconsciously. And that is the worst feeling you can experience. All it does is kill your confidence and rob your peace of mind. You will start to say, "If I have another bad month, I won't be able to pay my rent. I got nothing saved for my retirement, and I have nothing in savings. I have nothing to fall back on!" Therefore, my advice is that no matter what your income is, create a habit of saving something every week of your life, even in the bad weeks. It's not about the money you're saving away as much as it's about the feeling of confidence that allows you to make better decisions moving forward.

4. Think solution not a problem

Many times when something wrong happens, people obsess about why it happened, whose fault it was, and so forth. But, you should learn from it, teach your brain to focus on the solution. Make a habit that when something goes wrong, you immediately think about how you can fix it. What actions can you take right now to reduce the damage? Create a habit to put all of your energy into the solution, not on why it happened or who's to blame.

5. Recover fast

Most wealthy people are millionaires because they have mastered how to bounce back from problems fast. Why not be one of them that rebounds from failure, or overcomes challenges faster than anyone else? Self-program this hack of bouncing back from challenges, and it will help you. Ask yourself how long you spend on an issue before you fix it? How long do you think over and over the situation in your mind? Learn from it, but select the pieces and move on with that experience in hand. The people who fail the fastest are the ones who find the fix quickly.

6. Identify the good in the bad

If you can develop a habit of finding something positive when things go wrong, your life will be changed. So many individuals have things going wrong in their lives, and they stagnate in them for years. Everything that happens in our life happens for us, and there is something good in all of it. If you can develop a habit of finding that good as early as now, then you will change your life.

7. Visit your happy place

Sometimes we find ourselves in challenges that require us to have hacks to set us free from our negative moods and set our minds and souls straight. When you experience difficult problems, you can try to remember that place which used to offer you the greatest happiness. Find that happy place and make it a routine when you're experiencing a tough moment, you start to imagine this place. Once your mind recollects, you can start to think straight again.

8. Keep investing in yourself

Learning is an endless process. You only stop to learn once you die. In life, you're either climbing the ladder of success or sliding. If you want to make a lot of money and become wealthier, then never stop investing in yourself. Acquiring more knowledge will change your life experiences into wisdom, and wisdom will offer you the guidance and insight to hit your next level. To attain the level of success you want, make sure that you keep learning from someone who has accomplished what you want. Find a mentor or a coach. Synthesize knowledge from those who have the path and the plan to success.

9. Spoil yourself randomly

This might contradict the hack about saving. But this is the point; you can save and spoil yourself in the right way. Choose wisely about the way you spoil yourself.

Reward yourself for your hard work, and you will even want to achieve greater success. Treat yourself to things that trigger a positive emotion, and if this involves creating a lasting memory, wonderful.

If you save money and spend less on things that don't mean a lot to you, when the time comes to spoil yourself on the things that matter, you will have the cash to do it. Treating yourself well can motivate you, provide you signs of what could be the norm, and push you harder to implement plans and make decisions to improve your life.

10. Think creative daily

We usually get into routines, and we live the same kind of life day after day. Sometimes we might feel we are on autopilot. When this takes place, your new ideas, dreams, creativity, and inventions don't get an opportunity to flourish.

Set aside 10 to 30 minutes every day, and use this time to think creatively. Don't respond to e-mail, don't text or look at social media. Just think. Focus on what's next for your life.

As you give yourself space to exercise creativity, you'll receive the juices flowing. Don't think that you're not creative, you are. If you're like most people, you don't appreciate yourself for your innovations. You have launched a new business, a new relationship, a game you play with your kids, a character that makes your spouse laugh, and a more effective way of completing your yard work. There is nothing in life that will come to us unless we reflect on it first. Look around you. That chair, that monitor, that table-someone thought about these things before being creative, and then those items became a reality.

If you forget to think creative every day, you're not feeding part of your soul, and you don't want it to fed away. In your creative time, there are lots of things which you can do; you can even decide to identify all those things that trigger your mind and fire you up to focus on the next level of life. Everyone has their definition of creative time. It can be writing, digital design, or painting. Whatever it is, set aside time to do it daily.

11. Learn to detect hidden emotions

While you spend more time polishing your technical skills, don't forget to master your people skills. One of the most effective ways to understand people is to learn how to identify micro expressions. They are unconscious facial expressions that express inner emotions.

Chapter 10: Ways Millionaire Think and Act Differently from Middle-Class People

In the process of manifestation, your thoughts lead to feelings, feelings, trigger actions, and actions trigger results. Everything starts with your thoughts, and your mind generates your thoughts. Now our mind is the basis for our life, and many of us have no idea of how these powerful apparatus work?

In everything that happens, you normally rush to the files of your mind to determine how to respond. Let's say you're considering a financial opportunity. You automatically jump to your file labeled money, and from there, you decide what to do. The only thoughts you can harbor about money will be what is kept in your money file. That's all you can consider because that's in your mind under that subject.

You make a decision depending on what you think is sensible, logical, and appropriate for you at the time. You make what you believe is the correct choice. The challenge, however, is that your correct choice may not be successful. What makes sense to you may regularly generate poor results.

1. **The rich believe "I create my life." The middle-class people believe "Life happens to me."**

If you want to build wealth, you must know you are the driver of your life, especially your financial life. If you don't hold this belief, then you need to inherently believe that you have little or no control over your life. Therefore, you have no control over your financial success. That is not how the rich think.

Did you know that most poor people are the ones who spend a fortune to play the lottery? They believe that their wealth is going to originate from someone choosing their name out of a hat. They spend the whole of their weekend staring at the TV, watching the draw, to see if they are going to win and become wealthy.

Although everyone wants to win the lottery, and even rich guys play it for fun once in a while. But first, they don't spend half of their salary on tickets, and winning the lottery is not their major strategy for building wealth.

You must believe that you are the one who determines your success, that you are the one building your struggle around money, that you are the one establishing your mediocrity and success. Whether conscious or unconscious, it's you.

Rather than taking responsibility for what is happening in their lives, poor people decide to play the role of the victim. The main thought of a victim is normally "poor me."

Well, how can you know that someone is playing the role of a victim? You will see three open clues.

Clue 1: Blame

When it comes to why they're not rich, most victims are experts at the blame game. The purpose of this game is to identify the number of people and circumstances you can point the finger at without looking at yourself. It's interesting for victims. Unfortunately, it's not fun for anyone who is around them. The reason is those close to victims are easy targets.

Victims tend to blame the economy, they blame the stock market, they blame the government, they blame their employees, they blame the head office, they blame their broker, they blame their spouse, and everyone else. It's always someone else or something else that is to receive the blame. The problem is anyone or anything but them.

Clue 2: Justify

If victims are not blaming anyone, then you will see them justifying or rationalizing their circumstances by mentioning something like, "Money is not really important."

Think about this, would you have a car if it wasn't important to you? Of course not. In the same way, if you don't see how money is useful, you won't have any.

Let me tell you something, anyone who says money is not important doesn't have any. Wealthy people understand the purpose of money and the position it has in our society. Alternatively, poor people validate their financial ineptitude by applying irrelevant comparisons.

The fact is this; money is very important in the areas in which it works, and not important in the areas in which it doesn't work.

Clue 3: Complaining

Complaining is the worst thing you could ever do for your wealth or health. What you focus on grows. Now, when you're complaining, what are you focusing on, what is going well with your life, and what is wrong with it?

Do you know that complainers normally have a difficult life? It looks like everything that might go wrong does go wrong with them.

Therefore, it is important to make sure that you do not stay close to complainers. If you need to be, make sure you have something powerful to protect yourself. The perfect solution is to stay as far away from complainers because negative energy is infectious.

Justification, blame, and complaining are like pills. They are nothing more than stress alleviators. They reduce the stress of failure. Consider this. If a person was not failing in some way, or form, would he or she need to blame, complain, or justify? The answer is no.

From now, as you listen to yourself, blaming, complaining, or justifying, stop immediately. Say to yourself that you're building your life and that at every stage, you will be attracting either success or crap into your life. You must choose your words and thoughts wisely.

2. Rich people have decided to be rich, and poor people want to be rich

Ask random people whether they want to be rich, and they will stare at you like you were crazy. The fact is that most people don't want to be rich. And the reason is that they have a lot of negative wealth thoughts in their subconscious mind that reminds them something is not right with being rich.

Poor people have a lot of reasons why getting and being rich could be a problem. They aren't 100 percent sure they want to be rich. Their message to the universe is filled with confusion. And this confusion arises because their message to their mind is confusing.

There are three levels of "wanting." The first category is, "I want to be rich." Wanting alone is not enough. In fact, wanting doesn't necessarily result in "having." And wanting without having results in more wanting. Wealth doesn't come from just wanting it. Billions of people want to be rich, but only a few become.

The next category of wanting is, "I choose to be rich." This involves deciding to become rich. Choosing is much specific and goes hand in hand with being accountable for building your wealth.

The last category is "I purpose to be rich." In other words, you give 100 percent of everything you have to become wealthy. You are ready to do whatever it takes to become rich.

Many people rarely commit to becoming rich. That is what sets apart rich people and poor people. The poor will not commit to being rich, and most likely, they will never.

Are you ready to work over 15 hours per day? Rich people are. Are you ready to sacrifice your weekends? Rich people are. Are you ready to sacrifice your hobbies and relations? Rich people are. Are you ready to risk all your energy, time, and capital with no guarantee of returns? Rich people are.

For a period, hopefully, not a long-time rich people are ready to commit and do all of the above. What about you?

It is important to mention that once you do commit, the universe will listen and be ready to support you.

In other words, the universe will help you, guide you, and even create miracles for you. But first, you must commit.

Chapter 11: The Challenge

Now you have learned the success habits of the richest people in the world. So it's time for you to reach new heights. You can have everything you've dreamed about: a great business, a wonderful job, and good relationships. It doesn't need to be a powerful thought. It can be your reality, and all of it is within reach. So what is preventing you from becoming a millionaire?

If you're like most people, you read the following words, got motivated about what's possible, and discovered where you could go. Probably you had a clear vision. Your thoughts may have comprised of all the positive things that may happen. If you don't allow the villain within, you destroy you and if you convert your story from limited to limitless. You can see how this change would affect your life. You attain success habits, success hacks and happiness habits. It all makes sense, and the stories of people motivate you just like you who had changed their lives.

So why is it that some people struggle to get started?

One reason is that the thought of making changes in your life can be scary. Therefore, your subconscious finds a place to be safe and doesn't want to divert. However, safe doesn't mean financially prosperous or fulfilled. On a conscious level, you have a lot happening. You have bills to pay, chores to tackle, and jobs to do. As much as you would like to start implementing these success habits, you need to take action. You have to do stuff.

First Thing's First

Have you ever tried to talk to yourself into changing using the sheer willpower? That method can work for some time, but still, it's not enough. You need to concentrate on one thing at a time, and what's possible and feel the change you're imagining. This is where your passion will emerge, and this is how you will get into action.

To start on what's doable, first, you must visualize your life in the next 12 months and, if possible in the next 12 years from now. Then create a sprint to reinforce your life.

Break down the 12 months into 90 days and imagine your life what it will be in the next 90 days.

You can use the following questions to challenge your mind.

- Whom are you spending your time with?

- What specifically will happen in the 90 days?

- What is your condition of mind?

- With all your positive changes, how do you feel emotionally?

Think like you were there in the future. Then use your pen to write down specific actions you need to take to make this imagined scenario a reality.

Keep in mind, these action steps are meant for the next 90 days. They are not supposed to achieve your general goals. They're to guide you in the right direction. So focus on what you need to do to accomplish that great job or start a new business. What will get you moving in the right direction? Respond to that, and you have created for yourself a map and transportation to get to the right place you want to be.

You Have Great Potential

Maybe you're saying to yourself I don't know you. You are not special, like Bill Gates. The truth is that you have massive potential. The question is, will you achieve this potential?

I believe you will, but you need to overcome one of the biggest myths that most people hold: some are gifted and have advantages, making their road to success easier than your path. Yes, some smart people are intelligent mathematicians and can perform complex calculations in minutes that many of us would struggle for hours.

You will realize that the words "lucky" and "gifted" are often misused. If you research those who do well, who move to the next level of life and attain their maximum potential, you will see two very critical things that best achievers have in common. They believe in themselves and their vision, and they practice hard. They have the grit to achieve the results they wish instead of waiting on the sidelines hoping they were "gifted."

The success habits shared in this book don't work unless you have worked on them. The difference between those who apply them and those who only think about taking advantage of them is that the former display grit. They demonstrate the readiness to go the next mile to achieve whatever they want.

How badly do you want to achieve that next level of life? Do you feel depressed knowing there's a lot that you can accomplish, yet you haven't?

The good news is that you can get everything you want and deserve as long as you do it.

Disapprove the Critics

Those who accomplish the most are the ones who push through challenges, even when no one else stands with them. They do what it takes to implement these success habits quickly, and if something doesn't go as planned, they don't give up. If you explore businesses that have experienced massive growth, at one point, they were at the brink of closing, and most of the founders of the same business were told their ideas would never work.

The thing is that critics are judgmental individuals that successful people have learned to ignore them. Critics are pessimists who give up on their dreams. Their bitterness makes them tell others why they cannot have or be something. If you want to experience abundant life, then you must first believe in yourself, and not depend on others for support. It sounds harsh, but it's your path to freedom. Once you breakthrough, you can expect a new group of supportive individuals to appear in your life.

Don't hate them, but learn to go against them if they insist you cannot do something. They may be work colleagues, family, friends, and others who tell you can't succeed for their reasons, not based on what you're capable of accomplishing. You may need to stand up to some of your peers and tell them you appreciate their opinion, but let them not tell you what you cannot do. Maintain confidence in yourself that you can accomplish anything you fix your mind to.

Discover the why of your life and fix your eyes on the goal regardless of who gets in your way, and no matter who says it's foolish. This is the thing; once you know where you want to go, you have to sacrifice and do everything you can to reach there, no matter what others might say.

In fact, you may have to act differently from what most people close to you are doing, and it will perhaps look odd. But if you proceed to do what the people around you do, you will continue to receive what they get. And they are not living the life that you would like; then you will have to do the opposite. You are going to have to distinguish yourself from your peers.

That aside, remember also that the habits that helped you achieve something at one point in your life may not help you today. The habits that took you to England are not the habits that will take you to Paris.

Getting Into the Right Business

Success, in any given business, depends on you having the correct faculties needed in that business.

Without good musical instruments, you cannot succeed as a teacher of music. Without well-developed mechanical equipment, you cannot achieve great success in any mechanical business. But to own a well-developed facility in any field of business does not guarantee success. They're musicians with amazing talent, and yet they live poor, some carpenters have excellent mechanical ability, but do not become rich.

It is important to have the right tools, but the tools must be used in the correct way. One man can have a sharp saw, a square, a great plane, and so forth, and build beautiful furniture. Another man can have the same tools and start to work to copy the furniture, but his result will be ugly. He does not know how to use good tools in the right way.

The different sections of your mind are the tools in which you must conduct the work, which is to make you rich. It will be easier for you to succeed if you jump into a business for which you are well prepared with mental tools.

Overall, you will do your best in that business, which will make use of your talent — the one for which you are naturally suited.

You can become wealthy in any business, for if you don't have the correct talent, you can develop that talent. In other words, you will have to create your tools as you go along rather than limiting yourself to the use of which you were born. It will be easier for you to succeed in a job position for which you already have talents in a well-developed state.

It is easier to get rich by doing something which you have previous experience, and you enjoy it. However, you will get rich most if you do that which you are passionate about.

Doing what you desire to do is the point in life. There is no real satisfaction in life if you were compelled to be forever doing something which you do not like to do, and can never do what we want to do. It is possible that you can do that which you want to do. The desire to do it is evidence that you have within you the ability to do it.

Desire is a reflection of power.

The desire to create a mechanical device is the mechanical talent seeking expression and development.

Where power lacks to do a thing, there is never any desire or wish to do that thing, and where there is a strong force to do a thing, it is evident that the power to do it is strong, and only requires to be created and used rightly.

In general, it is better to choose a business for which you have the best-developed talent, but if you have a strong desire to do any particular work, you should choose that work as the final one which you aim.

However, you can do whatever you want to do, and it's your freedom to follow the business, which will be most attractive.

You're not compelled to do what's unpleasant to do, and you should not do it except as a way to bring you to the doing of the thing you want to do.

In case there are past mistakes whose results have pushed you to enter an undesirable business, you may be obliged for some time to do what you do not like to do. However, you can make the doing of it attractive by understanding that it is making it possible for you to come to the doing of what you want to achieve.

If you feel you are not in the right business, do not be too quick to opt-out. The perfect way to change business or environment is by growth.

Don't be scared to make a radical or sudden change if the opportunity comes to you, and you feel after careful analysis that it is the right one. However, never take sudden changes when you are in doubt.

There is no hurry on the creative plane, and there is no lack of opportunity.

When you step out of the competitive mind, you will realize that you don't need to act quickly. No one is going to beat you to the thing you want to do, and there is enough for all. If one space is taken, a better one will pop up for you a little farther on. There is a lot of time. When you are full of uncertainty, wait. Go back to the drawing board and rethink your vision, and boost your faith and purpose.

A day or two spent rethinking the vision of what you want, and in thanksgiving that you are receiving it, will attract your mind into such a close relationship with God that you will make no mistake when you do make a decision.

Conclusion

Those who become wealthy are the ones who overcome challenges, even when no one trusts them. They do what it takes to implement these success habits in place, and if something doesn't go as planned, they don't give up.

I know you want more, and you are ready to focus on achieving it. The evidence that is right in front of you, and if you can read a book to the end, it says a lot about you and your future.

So right now, here's a challenge for you to try something that will start that change in motion and not allow you to fall back to your old habits. And that's a 90-day sprint. It breaks this big, heavy chore of change and breaks it down to a doable goal.

Description

If you want to be a millionaire, then keep reading. If you've been struggling to amass wealth, then keep reading. Do you want to learn the secrets of becoming a millionaire? Do you feel stuck in a rut and ready to learn new habits?

While we've all dreamt big such as driving big cars, and splashing money on luxuries we have always wanted, chances are you've considered this as a daydream despite moving on to purchase a scratch card every time you step out to buy milk.

However, becoming a millionaire isn't difficult and unattainable as you may think. Many people prove every year that you don't need to be working in a bank or win a lottery to build up your wealth to seven figures.

And for many rich-listeners, becoming a millionaire is more a matter of lifestyle and not having to be scared about your finances, than how much you have kept in the bank.

To live like a millionaire, you don't need to have a million pounds saved in the bank. In fact, 99% of millionaires don't. To become a millionaire, you will, for sure, require to be on top of your finances and investments.

Becoming a millionaire can mean all sorts of things, but in this book, we're typically mapping out a realistic path to growing your wealth past £1,000,000.

This book quickly walks through the whole of your life, reviewing the steps you can take to become a millionaire.

To go straight to the point, successful people have successful habits, and unsuccessful people do not.

In this book, you will discover the million-dollar habits of men and women who started from rags to riches in one generation. You will discover how to think more effectively, make better decisions, and take more effective actions than other individuals. You will discover how to plan your financial life in such a way that you accomplish your financial goals quicker than you imagine.

One of the most critical goals you must accomplish to become happy and successful is the development of your character. You want to become a great person in every area of your life. You want to become that person that others look up to and admire.

In each case, the crucial factors in the accomplishment of each of these goals that we all share in the development of specific habits that result in what you want to accomplish.

Remember, if you keep doing what you've always done, you will never break away from your job slavery. You will continue to live your life on autopilot.

Millionaire habits teach you every strategy to develop millionaire habits for breaking free from your job and start earning today.

Discover which habits you need to apply and how to get started?

How will the success process change your entire life?

Inside this book, you will learn:

- How to change your habits, and avoid procrastination?
- The millionaire strategies

- The secrets to success

- Discover your emotional why

Now is the time to begin getting serious.

Stop blaming others for your failure and take deliberate steps.

How to Create Wealth

Live the Life of Your Dreams Creating Success and Being Unstoppable

Nathan Bell

information, will be done as an illegal act regardless of the end form the information ultimately takes. This includes copied versions of the work, both physical, digital, and audio unless express consent of the Publisher is provided beforehand. Any additional rights reserved.

Furthermore, the information that can be found within the pages described forthwith shall be considered both accurate and truthful when it comes to the recounting of facts. As such, any use, correct or incorrect, of the provided information will render the Publisher free of responsibility as to the actions taken outside of their direct purview. Regardless, there are zero scenarios where the original author or the Publisher can be deemed liable in any fashion for any damages or hardships that may result from any of the information discussed herein.

Additionally, the information in the following pages is intended only for informational purposes and should thus be thought of as universal. As befitting its nature, it is presented without assurance regarding its prolonged validity or interim quality. Trademarks that are mentioned are done without written consent and can in no way be considered an endorsement from the trademark holder.

Introduction

Taking your success into your own hands is one of the best gifts you will ever give yourself in this lifetime. All too often, people allow themselves to be led around by others and find themselves spending a lifetime supporting someone else in achieving success, rather than leading themselves to success. This particular behavior leads to them never realizing their own greatness and truly reaching their full potential because they are constantly living up to the ideals of everyone else.

I can already tell that you are not the type of person who wants to sit around and spend your life living up to everyone else's standards. You have no desire to walk in someone else's shadow and experience mediocrity because you have your sights set on something far more magnificent and meaningful than most. You have your sights set on something a lot higher. You want more.

In order to achieve more, you need to not only be willing to take control over your own destiny but you need to be ready to implement the steps required to help you create the destiny that you desire. You need to find it within yourself to turn your dream and willingness into an action plan and then see that action plan through so that you can start truly living in those dreams you have dreamt for yourself. When you take your drive and energy and turn it into a plan you can follow, you develop a reality where you will achieve nothing less than everything you have ever dreamt of. This reality can only be achieved through you, and you alone, though. This is not a destiny you will ever reach by sitting around praying for someone else to put the necessary opportunities and experiences in your lap for you to get there. No one is coming to save you from mediocrity, except for yourself.

Because I understand the hunger and craving that you have in your heart that has you wanting more, I want to give you the blueprint you need to turn that into your reality. I want to take this book and show you how you can turn your dream into a goal, and your goal into a tangible plan that you can follow step-by-step to help you see the results you desire. In showing you this information, I am giving you everything you need to stop talking about what you want in life and start showing up for it. All you have to do is follow these steps to make your own step-by-step map, and then follow that map through until you see the results you desire to see.

While this process may sound simple, I have to warn you that it is not for the faint of heart. You are going to find yourself feeling overwhelmed, frustrated, and even incompetent at times. These feelings and experiences are extremely normal and every single one of us has them on our path to greatness. The one thing that separates those who succeed from those who don't is the willingness to keep going no matter what. If you have that true hunger in your heart that has you craving more and that will not let you rest until you achieve it, you have exactly what you need to take this blueprint and turn it into your own success. Nothing will stop you from achieving what you want because you have decided that nothing will, and as such you will keep going until you get to exactly where you want to be.

If want to start developing your own plan for personal and professional success, I encourage you to grab a pen and a notebook and get started. Please make sure you take your time and complete every step as thoroughly as possible so that you set yourself up for success from day one. People who are destined for success know that their plans must be rock solid in order for them to work, and they do all of the necessary research and planning beforehand to get to where they want to go. This is going to require you to do a great deal of personal discovery, as well as professional and practical research, so be ready to put in the work to create a foundation that will be strong enough to get you where you want to go. If you feel that you are ready to begin this journey, please, read on!

Chapter 1: Success Can Never Happen Without the Right Mentality

The number one thing you can do for yourself when it comes to establishing a strong foundation to begin to build your success is to check your mentality and prime your mindset. Your mind is the strongest tool you have, and it offers you the biggest advantage when it comes to achieving anything you want in this lifetime. If you learn how to understand your mind and use it to your advantage, you will always have the upper hand in every area of your life because you will be equipped with the strongest tool there is. There is absolutely nothing in this world that has not been accomplished by a strong mind; every single progression and achievement humankind has made has been driven by someone who knew how to activate and harness the power of their mind. If you want to achieve great things in this lifetime, you need to learn how to activate and harness that very same power.

Your mindset is and always will be the number one difference you have from the people around you, and it is something that will stay with you no matter what. While other things could fall apart or unexpected problems may arise, your mindset will always keep you moving forward. Because of how powerful it is, it is absolutely crucial that you master your mind before you move on to developing your personal and professional plans. Doing this beforehand ensures that your dreams are truly personal to youand that they actually offer you what you truly want in this lifetime. This way, you do not develop dreams based on someone else's desires or someone else's beliefs.

Another big reason behind why you want to develop your mindset early on is that it will support you with creating an incredibly powerful plan that has the potential to take you where you want to go. If you do not take the time to master your mindset first, your plan may be ridden with weaknesses and downfalls that prevent it from being strong enough to help you discover your desired results. In order to make sure that your foundation is truly as strong as it needs to be, we are going to start by identifying what mentality you need to have and what perspectives you need to foster to help you succeed.

The Leader Mentality

When it comes to cultivating success in your life, you need to start by having a leadership mentality. The leadership mentality does not necessarily mean that you are going to lead other people, although many people with the leadership mentality do step into the role of leaders and happily take these roles on in their lives. What the leadership mentality does mean is that you are going to take on the role of being a leader in your own life so that you can lead yourself to the greatness and success that you desire.

The leadership mentality is something that we create, not something we are gifted with. Every single leader you see and that you may admire right now has spent time learning how to become a leader by nurturing their mindset and discovering the mentality that comes with being a leader. As they continue to educate themselves on and acknowledge this practice, they find themselves becoming better and better at leading themselves and, consequently, at leading others, too.

The mindset of a leader is characterized by many different things, but there are generally seven key characteristics that absolutely every single leader must have in order to be successful in their lives. These characteristics includeopenness, ambition, a desire for ROI, belief that it is important, fear of the consequences of inaction, soul-searching, and a commitment to self-improvement. If you can develop and work on these seven characteristics in your life, you can develop your own personal role as being a leader in your life so that you can lead yourself to greatness.

Openness or open-mindedness is important because it provides you with the opportunity to always remain willing to see beyond your current perspective. Leaders know that they themselves are not the only ones privy to good ideas or good information, and they know that the way to get their hands on more good ideas and good information is to remain open. As such, they are always focused on maintaining an open mind and keeping themselves as receptive to new ideas and new possibilities as they can.

Leaders remain ambitious in that they are always open for improvement and they are always trying to advance themselves in as many different ways as they possibly can. They are hungry for opportunity, for growth, and for advancement and so they are always focused on moving forward in as many ways as they can. Often, a truly powerful leader is growing in many ways at any given time because they know they have the energy and potential to do so much more than any one thing in their lives. If you do find yourself leading a team, you should also be focused on developing ambition in your team as well so that as you lead them you are also supporting them in becoming leaders in their own lives, too.

A desire for ROI essentially means that a leader is always willing to work hard but they must know that there is going to be a reasonable payoff for the work that they are doing. Leaders are not just interested in small ROI's, either. They want to know that they are getting the absolute biggest payoff from their investment possible to ensure that they are investing in the smartest ways they can. This includes utilizing time, energy, money, knowledge, effort, and anything else they might invest in something. Because of that fact, if a leader invests in you, you should know that it is because they see potential in you and they believe that you are going to have a high "payoff" in the long run.

In addition to knowing that they will get a high ROI, a leader also needs to know that what they are investing in is actually important. True leaders will never invest in something if they cannot see the importance of it because, no matter how much they may get in return, it seems pointless if there is no real value behind what they are investing in. Leaders are often committed to at least one major cause or purpose in their lifetimes that keeps them moving forward and creating whatever it is they believe holds enough value to be worth their investment. In a sense, this is the long-game ROI where they are investing their ultimate amount of time, energy, money, knowledge, and effort into one major overall thing that they hope will have a huge payoff in the long run.

Aside from being highly driven *toward* something, leaders are also highly driven *away* from something, too. They are driven away through the fear of what the consequences might be if they never take action on something. They are afraid that if they don't act, the consequences will be much higher than the risk of taking action, and so leaders will always act in spite of risk because they know it is better than sitting around wishing they had tried. Of course, they will always do what they can to minimize the risk, but they will still move forward in spite of any risks that may exist so that they can enjoy the possible benefits of the action they took should it payoff in the long run.

Soul-searching is something that often seems surprising to people who have not yet dug into their personal leadership style, yet it is highly important in regards to becoming a leader. Soul-searching allows people to continually learn more about themselves and what they truly care about or what they want to accomplish in the world. Often, you will hear about leaders going on some sort of journey or trip that resulted in them doing soul-searching and learning extremely intimate and important facts about themselves along the way. This process of getting to know yourself and learning to deeply understand who you are and what drives you is what allows you to better understand how you can lead yourself and how you can lead others.

In addition to soul-searching, a leader should also always remain committed to self-improvement. Self-improvement is how you take the findings of your soul-searching and turn them into something that results in you evolving and becoming even better over time. Through self-improvement, you can offset any flaws or faults you may have and launch yourself toward greatness by regularly pushing for better and better. Through this, your results grow massively and you are able to continually move forward in life. Only fellow leaders will understand why consistent growth matters, as it seems like anyone who is not a leader seems perfectly fine remaining stagnant in the same comfortable conditions all of their life. To a leader, especially one that has taken the time to develop their leadership qualities, remaining stagnant and comfortable is possibly one of the worst things they could ever experience. They crave growth, even if they cannot always explain why.

Entrepreneur VS. Employee

Getting into that mindset of a leader requires one major change that has to take place in order for you to really lock into this leadership mentality and move forward. If you want to lock into this leadership mentality, you need to stop playing the role of the employee and start stepping into your role as an entrepreneuror a leader. Especially if you want to pave your way to financial freedom and really transform your life in massive ways, entrepreneurship is the only way forward. Entrepreneurship serves as the ultimate form of leadership, as you put your finances, your responsibilities, and your entire lifestyle into your own hands for you to shape and mold as you see fit. When you possess the power of an entrepreneur, you possess the ultimate power to transform your life and move forward in a major way.

Employees and entrepreneurs or leaders with an employee mindset never truly tap into their full potential because they are always focused on how they can serve someone else's dream. They are always waiting for instruction, hoping someone else will tell them what to do and expecting success to just fall into their laps. These individuals never fully take accountability for their success because they are unwilling to accept all of the responsibility and commitment that is required in order for someone to actually become successful.

Many leaders and entrepreneurs are surprised to realize that despite some of the changes they have made in their lives, they may still be committed to the employee mindset. If you find yourself sitting in the position of an entrepreneur or leader but still waiting for someone to tell you what to do, or still waiting for success to fall into your lap, you have not successfully changed your entire mindset over yet. Waiting on success to come your way, blaming other people for your lack of success, or expecting someone to carve your path out for you is all a sign that you are still sitting in an employee mindset. If you are fine with only ever living up to the expectations and dreams someone else has set out for you, that is completely fine. However, if you want to step away from mediocrity and have a say in your life and have the capacity to really make changes for yourself, then you need to allow yourself to really own your entrepreneur mindset.

You need to become willing to take total responsibility for yourself, your thoughts, your words, and your actions. You need to be willing to hold yourself accountable, even when you have to do so in a way that feels painful or requires you to address parts of yourself that are wildly underdeveloped or underperforming. In fact, you *especially* need to be willing to hold yourself accountable when you come across these weaker parts of yourself. In doing so, you need to be willing to see yourself as someone who has the power and the capacity to not only acknowledge these weaker parts of you but also turn these weaker parts into something magnificent. By teaching yourself how to either heal your weaknesses or develop new skills that offset your weaknesses, you ensure that you are always able to grow and become a stronger and better version of yourself.

In addition to learning how to manage yourself, stepping from employee to entrepreneur allows you to learn how to manage others, too. By managing others, I mean teaching yourself how to help others and support others in their growth without affecting yours. The reality is: if you become an entrepreneur, chances are you will have employees that you need to lead, and you need to be able to lead those employees without risking your own growth. You need to know the perfect balance of delegating and guiding so that you can show them how to grow and how to do tasks on their own without taking away from your energy to grow within yourself or make improvements within yourself. When you learn how to really guide yourself to your own growth and guide others to growth, too, then you have started to master the real art of what it means to be an entrepreneur.

Going from employee to entrepreneur is not for everyone, and it can take some time to get used to even if you do genuinely believe that this transition is for you. Like with everything, this transition takes time and effort and it will require you to really look at who you are and what you are capable of and decide whether or not you want to put the effort in to make that happen. If you do, you need to give it your all and be willing to do anything and everything in your power to help yourself step away from the lifestyle of being ledby others and into the lifestyle of leading yourself to your own results.

The Art of Always Learning

Entrepreneurs and leaders have one massive thing in common and it is that they are always learning. To always be learning means to have a growth mindset, and a growth mindset is indicative of a successful leader and entrepreneur. With your growth mindset, you can see the world as a place that is abundant with opportunity and potential and as a place where you can exist to learn from those opportunities and that potential. You discover ways that you can become even better, and you find opportunities to always grow within yourself and within the world around you.

When you have a growth mindset, you believe that all of your abilities and skills can be improved upon and you believe that you have the potential to do so. This means that you are always open to the possibility that even things that come hard to you right now can be improved so that you can do better and they can become easier for you in the future. With a real growth mindset, the belief does not extend just in any one area of your life, but rather in all areas of your life. People with a growth mindset genuinely believe that they can improve upon anything they want to and that if they are willing to put the energy in they can develop skills in any given area of their lives.

To have a growth mindset is important, and you should strive to develop your own growth mindset within yourself. In doing so, you keep yourself open to the potential and ability to learn more as you go, which means that you will always have access to the knowledge that you require to get the results you desire. This essentially leads to you having an open mind, but in a way that means you are not only willing to learn more but you are also willing to *try* more. Which is, in fact, another key difference between leaders and non-leaders.

Being willing to learn more is great, but you should also be willing to implement any new knowledge or lessons that you come across along the way. To be able to do this, you first need to be able to decipher which lessons or skills are worth learning, and which are not going to be worth your time. This is where it is helpful to be able to use a need for a high ROI and a need for what you are doing to be important. If you are able to identify the high ROI from the lesson or practice *and* you can clearly recognize its importance, you have a lesson or practice that is well worth the effort for you to give it a try.

After you have decided to try something new, you also need to be willing to monitor that new thing as you go. You need to implement it thoroughly and to the best of your ability, while also monitoring it to make sure that it is actually giving you the results you desire. If you find it is not, you can pivot and try to adapt your approach to improve your ability to get the results you desire. If after a few attempts and pivots, however, you find that it is not giving you the results you need and you cannot see how it possibly couldbe willing to peacefully let go of that practice and move onto something that is likely to give you a better payoff.

Knowing the difference between what is a good idea and what is not, and what is working and what is not, is incredibly important when you are trying to develop as a person. In being

445

able to decipher this type of information you give yourself the opportunity to make sure that you are always trying new things but that you are never wasting your time on any practices that are not serving you. The real key here is knowing how long to put your effort in, as you do not want to give up before you have a chance to get results, but you also do not want to hold onto something that is not going to give you results in the first place. You can find that sweet spot through regularly reviewing new practices and even working with mentors on them to make sure that you are using them properly before giving up on them.

How To Perceive The Planning Process

When it comes to planning, I want you to really focus on the mindset you foster. Having the right mindset with planning is important as it ensures that you are going to approach your entire planning process in an effective manner that actually leads to you getting the results you desire. Since the rest of this book is largely focused on planning and executing plans, you can see why this is an incredibly important mindset for you to understand and implement in your life.

The thing about planning that most people do not realize is that plans are a much stronger tool than people often give them credit for. Having strong, well-developed plans is the key to having success in anything in your life, and knowing how to rely on those plans and follow them through is important, too. Ideally, you want to see your plans as being the foundation for absolutely everything going forward, and as with any foundation, you need that foundation to be as strong as possible to make sure it can handle everything you are building on it. If you do not take the time to build your plans to be a strong and powerful foundation, then chances are you are not going to be able to build anything significant off of your plans.

When it comes to approaching your plans, you need to respect them for being the strong foundation they are meant to be. This means you need to be ready to immediately start by not only developing plans but refining those plans and researching everything you need to in order to make sure that those plans are as strong as they possibly can be. When you have completed your plans, you should feel absolutely confident that everything you have put in them is thoroughly researched and is true to the best of your ability so that when it comes time to follow those plans you can follow them without having to think about them. This way, rather than wasting time wondering if the plan is strong enough or trying to refine your plan along the way you can invest all of your time and energy into seeing that plan through and making it work for you. As a result, you are far more likely to make results from your plan because you will have made one that was designed to get you the results you desire.

447

One thing you need to be particularly careful about when it comes to planning is making sure that you have planned well enough but that you are not finding yourself stuck in analysis paralysis when it comes to your plan. If you find yourself planning too long, you may just turn the planning phase into an excuse to procrastinate rather than using it as a tool to help you create the results you desire. The sweet spot is spending enough time on your plan that you feel confident in itand accepting the fact that it will never be perfect and that if you absolutely need to you can adapt it at any point in the future to help you get the results you desire. In fact, if you do find yourself succumbing to analysis paralysis you might just find that you benefit from scheduling a few "reviews" into your plan so that you know when you can review your plan to see how you are doing. Knowing that these reviews are in the future may just give you the motivation you need to move past analysis and planning and into the process of actually starting to implement your plan and move forward in achieving the results you desire.

While planning is largely something that has a clear and easy-to-follow beginning, middle, and ending to it, it can help to adapt planning techniques and styles that may make planning even easier for you. The more you can adapt your planning strategies to suit your needs, while still upholding the primary purpose and benefit of planning, the better you will become at planning and the stronger your plans will become, too.

448

Chapter 2: You Will Go Nowhere If You Don't Know Your Long-Term Plans

Now that you understand the foundational mindset behind making plans for yourself, it is time for you to start making plans for your own future! Creating the plans for your dreams is a step that needs to be taken if you are going to find your way to the results you desire. As you begin to create these plans, there are many layers that you need to consider to ensure that they are strong enough to really get you where you want to go. I encourage you to take your time with this entire chapter and really work through the step by step process of creating your long-term plans so that you can see exactly what it is that you want to accomplish in your lifetime. If you work through this chapter properly, not only will you come out with powerful plans that will lead you to the success you desire but you will also come out with immense clarity that will help you truly know exactly what it is that you are working toward.

The steps you are going to need to take to create these long-term plans include: identifying what it is you really want for yourself, envisioning how each part of your life plays into this, recognizing what you can do to bring this into reality, and outlining your plan for moving forward. By the time you are done with all of this you should also find yourself feeling highly motivated with the realization that everything you want is far more achievable than you may have thought. Through this, you should have plenty of strong energy behind you to get you going and building the momentum you need to create the results you desire!

Step One: Your Masterpiece

To develop your master plan, you need to start with creating your masterpiece! Your masterpiece is the vision you have for yourself and for your life, and it is one that you will likely evolve over the span of your lifetime, always creating new elements to it and developing it in new and improved ways. Despite the fact that it will be ever-changing, the core dream you have will likely remain the same throughout your life, and you need to know what that core dream is. The clearer you are on what that dream is, the easier it will be for you to develop a plan that takes you in the right direction. If you ever find that you really do not resonate with that dream anymore you can always change it, so try not to put too much pressure on this step. This should be exciting, enjoyable, and powerful enough to give you a foundation to start on.

To begin developing this masterpiece dream you want to enlist the power of visualization, imagination, and curiosity. You want to combine these three skills with the realization that in your dreams there are no limits on what you can or cannot do, too.

Ideally, you want this dream to capture what you really want if there was nothing stopping you from what you could have, largely because the plan you will create next should help you smash through any limitations that prevent you from having exactly what you want.

You can start your practice easily by simply closing your eyes and allowing yourself to dream about exactly what you want for yourself. Begin by focusing on just one area of your life, such as your career. Imagine what it would be like if you were to have your dream career. What would your career look like? What would your roles and responsibilities be? What type of success would you feel you achieved as a result of your career? Get as clear as you can with what you currently know about yourself and your desires when it comes to identifying what you want your career to be like.

Next, start focusing on your wealth. What do you want your finances to look like? If you were to have absolutely zero limitations in your life, how much money would you be earning and what would you be doing with that money? What would it feel like for you to have that money? Again, get as clear as you can with identifying what you want for yourself and how you want that to fit into your reality.

Now you are going to start focusing on things that fall beyond the scope of career and finances, but that are still incredibly important to your masterpiece. These areas of your life include your health, relationships, romance, relationship with yourself, hobbies, and your spirituality or your religion. Focus on each one of these aspects of your life one at a time and allow yourself to really consider what it is that you are trying to create for yourself and how you want to create it. You should be focused on developing an idea of what it looks like, what it feels like, and how each element incorporates into your bigger picture.

Allowing yourself to dream beyond your career and finances and into the rest of your reality ensures that you are going to be able to create a career and a level of financial security that really allows you to develop the lifestyle you want. After all, if you are going to take your life into your own hands and create your own reality, you *should* give yourself the opportunity to create a reality that is really worth pursuing. By incorporating all aspects of your reality, you ensure that you are creating a reality that excites you and fulfills you and that genuinely gives you all that you desire in life.

After you have developed your masterpiece, I encourage you to write it down. Keeping track of what you want and highlighting key feelings and elements of your masterpiece is important. This way, anytime you find yourself struggling to stay on track you can review what it was that you wanted for yourself and what you really wanted to experience in your life. Ideally, reviewing this plan should motivate you. However, you can also use this as a way to track your evolution and to keep track of any changes you might have around how you want to feel or what you want to experience. Keeping track of these changes can be a fun and useful way to witness your growth through your life which can be useful for so many things, ranging from serving your nostalgia to showing you where you can improve in your life.

Step Two: The Practical Pieces

Now that you have identified what it is that you want for yourself, you need to go ahead and identify what the practical elements of what you want are. This means that you need to spend some time researching what needs to happen in order for your dreams to become your reality. This is the part where many people may feel intimidated and overwhelmed, as they may not know where to start. Often, when it comes to bringing your dreams into your reality there are many moving parts that need to come into play in order for you to experience the results that you want to experience. For example, you need to develop the skills and the knowledge required in order to bring those dreams into your reality, and you also need to acquire certain things or tools that will allow you to bring those dreams forward, too. By identifying all of the different elements that are needed for your dreams to come to life, you can begin to establish your plan in a way that allows you to create a clear-cut path for how you can make your dreams a reality.

To help minimize the overwhelm you might experience when it comes to identifying all of these different steps, I want to help you really organize these practical pieces and put them together in a way that supports you with creating the exact life you desire. The best way to get started is to identify each part of your life as a separate goal that contributes to the greater goal of you living your dreams. To remind you, these areas of your life are: career, wealth, health, relationships, romance, relationship with self, hobbies, and spirituality or religion. You want to take each area of your life and identify your overall dream or goal for that area of your life and begin to identify the practical things that need to happen in order for that goal to become achievable.

Start by identifying what skills you need within yourself. The skills we are talking about right now include intrapersonal skills such as your self-esteem, your open-mindedness, and your ability to remain aware of your own thinking and behaviors. Often, we struggle to identify what needs to change within ourselves because it requires us to take an honest account of who we are and what we are capable of. For many people, acknowledging their weaknesses and becoming willing to take responsibility for how those weaknesses have affected their life is challenging because it also means accepting some level of responsibility for unwanted life experiences. Naturally, this is incredibly challenging. However, if you want to cultivate any growth in your life you are going to need to be honest about what you are really capable of, what skills you presently have, and where your weaknesses presently lie. When you are able to be honest with yourself about where you truly are in life, reaching a point of growth becomes easier because you find yourself willing to really integrate the necessary skills to grow.

Next, you need to think about skills that you need to develop that may be less personal. These are skills that are more along the lines of interpersonal, such as your ability to actively listen to others, your ability to work on a team setting, and your ability to be dependable and reliable. Working on these skills ensures that you are going to have what it takes to confidently work together with other people to achieve your goals which, believe it or not, is incredibly necessary. When it comes to achieving the life of your dreams, more often than not these dreams are not compiled of you being alone, nor are they compiled of you being in low-quality relationships. You will likely want to have friends, family, and lovers around, as well as people like team members and employees. The better you can work together with others and establish and cultivate relationships with the people in your life, the better you will find yourself moving toward turning your goals into your reality.

The next layer of skills you need to look at is in relation to your abilities. These are your more practical skills, such as your ability to put a ball if you want to learn golf or your ability to use a computer if you want to develop an online business. Knowing how to incorporate these practical skills will ensure that you are not only developing the personal tools needed to achieve your goals but that you are also going to be able to take the practical steps to achieve them. The combination of these intrapersonal, interpersonal, and practical skills will result in you having everything you need to get started on developing the results you desire.

After you have focused on the skills layer of your plan, you need to focus on the tools. The tools are the last element you really need to make sure that your plan is developed enough to allow you to pursue it. When it comes to identifying what tools you need, you are still considering the practical element of your plan as these tools are going to practically help you move forward to what you desire. Any physical *thing* you might need should be considered as a tool toward you developing the life of your dreams, which means anything from money to tennis rackets or even a stylish wardrobe can be considered as practical tools. You will need to identify what the practical tools for your dreams are based on what your specific dreams actually are and what it is that you are trying to accomplish in your life.

Step Three: Putting It Togetherand Creating Your Plan

This is where you get to turn all of your research and brainstorming into an actualstep-by-step plan that you can follow to help you turn your dreams into your reality. You are going to now take all of the action steps you have brainstormed and align them so that you can create the outcome you desire for yourself. Here, you are essentially going to be drawing yourself a map from where you are to where you want to be.

To begin creating your plan, you first need to get incredibly honest about where you are right now in your life, particularly in relation to where you want to be. This is where you are going to honestly assess every aspect of your life and realize where your current strengths and weaknesses lie and where you need to improve upon yourself and your circumstances to help you reach your goals. Here, you need to be as honest with yourself as possible as this is how you are going to cultivate the best plan that will help you move forward. If you are not honest with yourself either by pretending you are further ahead than you are or by discrediting where you are at by pretending you are further behind than you are, creating a plan will be incredibly challenging. You will find that as you attempt to create this plan you find yourself struggling to honestly identify what steps to take because you have inaccurately identified where you are at right now.

Once you have accurately identified where you are at right now, you want to consider where it is that you want to be and then start reverse-engineering your goal from where you want to be to where you are now. Document every single thing that needs to happen ranging from your personal growth and skill development to certain circumstances that need to be created in order for your goals to be met. Continue working on developing this plan all the way until you reach back to where you are right now.

As you create each step in your plan, make sure that you are completely thorough about what those steps include. You want to keep those steps as carefully planned out as possible to ensure that when the time comes for you to enact that step you know exactly what you need to do to succeed. Remember, your plans need to be as thoroughly developed now as they possibly can be so that you can reasonably rely on them to help you create the results that you desire to create.

After you have created your plan and you have incorporated each step, do your research to ensure that you understand the skills and tools required for that step to be completed. You are going to double-check all of this later on, so simply take the time to make sure you have been as thorough as you possibly can be and that you can clearly see how each step needs to play out in order for you to be successful with it.

Step Four: Validating Your Plan

Now that you have the rough draft of your plan drawn up, you need to start creating the official plan that you are going to follow. This is the phase where you get to start validating your plan to ensure that your plan really is strong enough and reliable enough for you to commit to. By taking the extra time to really validate and strengthen your plan you ensure that you will not have any reason to have doubts in your plan later on, meaning you will be less likely to stray away from your plan and more likely to actually commit to your plan.

You will first validate your plan by looking it through from start to finish to make sure that you have not skipped any steps. Previously, you developed your plan through reverse engineering, which means that ideally, you should have incorporated all of the necessary steps into your plan. However, there is always the chance that it does not make quite as much sense when you look at it in the proper direction. If you notice any significant gaps or areas where your plan may need reinforcing, use this as an opportunity to identify those extra steps and put them into place to make sure there are no obvious gaps in your plan.

Now that you have filled in any obvious gaps, you want to meticulously comb through your plan to make sure that each part of the process makes sense. This is where you want to make sure that each tool and skill work together from one step to the next to build into what you are looking for. If you find yourself feeling as though there may be something missing or like you may benefit from adding additional tools and skills into your plan at this point, this is a great time to incorporate them into your plan. Again, the more thorough you can be, the better. You also want to do your research on each step, especially the ones you might be nervous about to make sure that you have everything in place for your success.

Lastly, you want to add deadlines to each of the steps on your plan so that you are motivated to get into action and achieve each milestone within a reasonable amount of time. Even if there are no external deadlines pressuring you to create the results you desire, creating personal deadlines is a great way to make sure that you hold yourself accountable and keep yourself motivated to reach the goals you set for yourself. The more you can work toward these deadlines, the more effectively you will make progress toward your goals as you move forward.

Finally, with everything done you want to review your entire plan from start to finish one more time to ensure that you feel absolutely confident and aligned with what you have planned for yourself. By now, you should feel as though all areas of your life have been reasonably worked together to create a larger plan for yourself to help you get where you want to go. As long as you have done it properly, you can feel confident that you have a plan that you will not need to obsess about, doubt, or worry about later on. Instead, you will be able to follow the plan you have laid out for yourself in a way that allows you to place all of your attention and energy into enacting the plan, rather than into worrying about the plan.

Step Five: Reviewing Your Plan

Just because you have meticulously created a plan that you can feel confident in does not mean that you should never review your plan. Every leader knows that plans are powerful tools, but that they are also flexible and should regularly be reviewed to ensure that they are still serving their purpose. While you do not want to review your plan too frequently, as this may cause you to doubt yourself and stray away from your path, you do want to review your plan consistently to ensure that it is still guiding you toward what you desire.

The best set plans will have certain review dates weaved into them so that you can look over the plan and make sure that it is still operating as strong as it possibly can. Ideally, you should review your plan every 6-12 months so that you can see how well it is working as well as directly track your progress against your plan to see how well you are doing. You can choose whichever review interval feels best for you based on how confident you feel in your plan and how well you understood the steps you were incorporating into your plan. Once you have chosen it, make sure you do not review the plan any sooner unless you absolutely must: for example, if it is absolutely not working or you have reached an impasse as a result of one of your steps and you truly cannot move forward with the plan any further.

During review periods, you are going to take the time to first look over your progress and see how well you are doing compared to your plan. At this point, you want to see if you are on track to succeed with your plan or if you are falling behind. If you find yourself way ahead of the plan, you may want to adjust your milestones and deadlines to encourage yourself to stay motivated to keep moving forwardand to make your goals more realistic for yourself.

After you have measured your progress and adjusted your timeline accordingly, you want to review the steps themselves to make sure they still appear to be the best possible steps forward.

It is not unusual to come across new information as you grow and move through each of the steps, and often this new information can help you improve the rest of your plan so that you can either achieve even better results or achieve your results faster. During reviews, you can implement this new information to ensure that each of the steps you will be taking going forward is concise and effective in helping you achieve your goals.

When you do go through the process of adjusting your long-term plan using new information, make sure you follow the exact same steps you followed upon building the plan itself. In other words, make sure you check the plan forward and backward to ensure that it gets you where you want to goand make sure you have thoroughly researched these new ideas to ensure you have incorporated them properly. The more effectively you can incorporate all of this information and all of these steps into your plan, the more successful you will likely be in reaching your desires.

After you have finished your review, you should feel absolutely confident in your ability to move forward with the plan for the foreseeable future. As long as you feel confident that you have made your plan effectively and that you know exactly what you need to do next, you can start moving forward with your plan again and pursuing it until the next review period. Then, once again, you can go through the same process of reviewing your plan, tracking your progress, and implementing any new strategies you may have found that will help you create the results you desire.

Chapter 3: Follow These Steps to Properly Manage Your Money All the Way to Financial Freedom

Before you move forward with the professional and entrepreneurial aspects of your plan, I want to discuss the important topic of managing your money. Every single person should take time in their lives to learn about important money management skills and, if you are in the process of building your own business, you will want to do this sooner rather than later. The sooner you can develop the skills to manage your own money effectively, the easier it will be for you to manage your personal money and the money belonging to the business that you are building your wealth through.

There are two elements to managing money that everyone needs to know about: what to do with the money, and how to get the most out of the money you have. Knowing where to put your money, how to use your money, and what to expect from your money is an important step when it comes to wealth management because it allows you to know that your money is working for you. This way, not only do you have some saved but you also have some of your money developing more money through the form of investments, meaning your money is effectively protecting you against things like losses or inflation. You also need to know how to get the most out of the money you have because, to put it frankly, no truly successful entrepreneur has ever let a lack of finances hold them back from achieving their success. Many massive entrepreneurs from Jeff Bezos to Steve Jobs were largely broke when they started their businesses, and yet through effective use of their money, they were able to get their businesses going and develop massive funds as a result. Knowing what to do with the money you have right now, and then what to do with the wealth you developwill go a long way in helping you have a strong experience with your money. This way, you do not find yourself mismanaging your money and ending up broke in the long run, or ultimately bankrupting your plan due to financial mistakes that could have easily been avoided.

Have A Budget

A budget may be one of the most basic wealth management tools a person can use, and yet many people overlook the idea of budgeting and instead attempt to manage their wealth spontaneously. This is not effective in helping you create the long-term wealth you desire because it results in money being mismanaged, misused, and misplaced. Often, people without budgets find themselves spending money they should not have, carrying unnecessary expenses, and failing to save any money because they have no idea what they have the capacity to save. Rather than having any long-term success, they end up draining their financial assets every time they come upon them and, as a result, find themselves struggling in the long run.

Creating a budget is not difficult and allows you to know exactly where your money is going and what you are doing with your money. Ideally, you should have budgets planned out for 3, 6, and 12-month intervals. Your 3-month budgets should be extremely detailed with your earnings and expenses all clearly written out to the dollar. Your six- and twelve-month budgets can be projections of what you anticipate you will have and what you anticipate you will be able to do with that money. Having all of these budgets created ensures that you have a clear understanding as to what you are working toward so that you can always make financial choices that are on track with your long-term financial plans and goals. After you have these longer goals in place, you should focus on reviewing your budget every month, as well as every single time you receive money whether it is expected or unexpected. This way, you can ensure that your budget accurately reflects all the funds you have and makes the most out of the money that you have earned.

Understand Your Expenses

Through creating your budget, you will realize that you have many expenses you need to account for and consider on a monthly and yearly basis. Understanding what your expenses are and how they are affecting you is important as it allows you to know exactly what you are spending your money on and why. You would be surprised how many people do not know what their expenses are or how much they owe on a monthly basis, and as a result, they find themselves missing payments and having services shut off because they mismanaged their funds.

Keeping track of all of your expenses is incredibly easy, but it is also incredibly important. You can do so by going through all of your statements and identifying every single expense you are paying on a month to month basis and writing it down on your "master budget" list. This budget list should allow you to see exactly what it is that you are spending your money on so that you understand where your money is goingand why it is going there.

It is extremely important that when you start tracking your expenses, you track more than just your mandatory bills. You should also track your leisurely spending habits and any other spending habits you might have to make sure that you are getting an accurate representation of where your money is going. This is going to help you when it comes to shaping your budget by allowing you to see where you may be overspending, as well as what types of spending are most important to you.

Understand Your Income

In addition to acknowledging your expenses, you also need to acknowledge your income. You likely know exactly what it is that you get paid on a monthly basis, but you want to make sure you keep track of this number so that you can incorporate it into your budget. You also want to be aware of any additional funds you may receive, such as any form of expected or unexpected money that you receive from outside of your salary. Most people view this money as being "extra" and will happily spend it on things like extra clothes, extra visits to a restaurant, or any other leisurely expenses. If you are setting yourself up to build and maintain wealth, though, you are going to want to stop seeing this as being extra and start seeing this as being a part of your overall income. Then, you should incorporate it into your budget and use it wisely.

While applying some of your extra funds toward leisurely purchases is a great idea, you should refrain from placing *all* of your extra funds toward leisurely purchases. The reality is, your leisurely purchases are likely not as big of a priority to you as your budget goals are; however, in the moment, they may feel like a great idea. It is easy to experience impulses around money, especially impulses that bring about instant gratification. However, this instant gratification is often the number one thing that leads to people experiencing buyer's remorse and can even lead to or reinforce poor spending habits. The more intentional you are, the more effective you will be with your money. Always focus on building stronger spending habits, even in areas where it seems harmless or like it should just be a "one-time thing." The more intentional you are, the more impactful you will be with your finances.

Pay Off Your Debt

Debt is something that can actually be leveraged and used in an incredibly positive and powerful way if it is used properly. However, most people carry their debt as a burden and fail to make the most out of it and as a result find themselves struggling to manage their debt. In many cases, this also leads to poor credit ratings which can actually harm your financial outlook in the future.

If you want to start making stronger financial moves and using your money in a way that improves your life and the business you will be growing, you need to pay off your debt and then begin managing your debt properly. Ideally, you should pay off your debt as quickly as you can and as effectively as you can. Most wealth management advisors will suggest paying off all unnecessary debt first before even considering a savings account because your money will be costing you more on a credit card than it will earn you in a savings account. By paying off your debt you save massive amounts of money every month which means that you will be able to put even more away or use it for other important things such as business expenses.

After you have paid off your debt, you do not be afraid to develop new debt. However, you do need to be vigilant to make sure that you are using your debt properly and not burying yourself under debt that you may or may not be able to handle. Make sure that your debt is always manageable, and that you are only accumulating debt over things that are actually worth going into debt over. As well, always have a plan to pay off your debt before you get into debt so that your credit rating stays strong and your finances stay healthy. Often, there are debt classes you can take in most cities that will support you in understanding how debt works and how to use it, but you can also talk to a bank advisor if you are not entirely sure. The more you can educate yourself on this topic, however, the more likely you will be to use your debt to your advantage rather than feeling as though you are burying yourself under a mountain that you can't dig yourself out from under.

Remove Unnecessary Expenses

In addition to paying off debts, you need to start removing unnecessary expenses from your budget. Unnecessary expenses are any expenses that you are paying for things that you are not using or things that you are not getting enough value out of. Removing unnecessary expenses ensures that you are freeing up more of your finances to put toward things that actually matter, and it also helps you with cleaning up your budget overall.

If you cannot completely eliminate certain expenses, consider cutting them down to as low as they can possibly be so that you are not spending any unnecessary money on things that you should not be spending money on. For example, lower your cell phone plan or your internet or cable plan to make sure that you are not spending any unnecessary money. If you have streaming services or subscription services, make sure you pay for only the specific level of each subscription you actually need. It may seem ideal to get "the best," especially if the expense difference between a smaller subscription and a larger subscription is not a big jump, but the reality is that if you are not using the bigger subscription, it is a waste of your money. While $5 per subscription may not seem like a lot if you are paying for more than you need on just 4 subscriptions, that is $20 a month or $240 a year. While $240 may not seem like a lot, that may be an entire week of groceries or extra funds placed into an

473

investment. If you are running a business, $240 may even be enough to cover an entire years' worth of website hosting or another similar service that benefits your business and earns you money. When it comes to wealth development, no amount of money is insignificant, no matter how seemingly small it may be.

Keep an Emergency Fund

One of the first budget goals you should have for yourself is developing an emergency fund. Ideally, you should be developing your emergency fund alongside paying off debt as being your two number one priorities if you are new to wealth management. Emergency funds are necessary as they prevent you from dipping into debt pools to pay for emergencies that you may happen upon and, the reality is, there will always be unexpected expenses that you have to pay for. Keeping a reasonable reserve of funds available ensures that you can pay for unnecessary expenses out of pocket so that you are not going into debt over those expenses.

The size emergency fund you will need ultimately depends on who you are and what your lifestyle is like. However, it is generally recommended that you have an emergency fund of at least 3-6 months' worth of your income available to ensure that if anything ever went wrong you would be supported. For the average family, this means you should have about $30,000 aside in a savings account for your emergency fund. Of course, this may seem overwhelming or intimidating at first, but you do not have to put this money aside immediately. You can start by putting aside one months' salary, and then moving on to paying off your debt. Once your debt is paid off, however, you should make it a priority to get 3-6 months' salary aside as soon as possible. If you really want a strong savings account, you should be focused on getting that number up to 6-12 months' salary so that you can handle any unexpected expense that might come your way, including a job loss.

Your emergency fund should be something that is always kept as a liquid asset that is not tied up into any sort of term investment. Because of the nature of these funds you need to feel confident that you are going to be able to access them at a moments' notice without any concern. If you were to have those funds tied up in assets or term investments, accessing it could cost you and that would completely defy the entire purpose of those funds.

Plan for Your Future

In addition to having an emergency fund that can be accessed at any time, you should also have funds that are being set aside for your future. Setting funds aside for your future ensures that you will have enough money to retire and do whatever you want for the rest of your life. When it comes to setting funds aside for your future, you should be focused on setting aside at least 10-15% of your funds for retirement specifically. These funds can be invested inany form of investment that is going to protect your assets while also giving you a decent return on your investment. Some places have investment funds you can place your retirement money into that results in you earning a matched amount on your investment up to a certain amount, meaning that for every $1 you invest you are given back $1. Having these types of funds opened and otherwise investing into portfolios that are going to give you a strong return is a great idea as it ensures that your money is growing while it waits for you to retire. This way, you have far more than you ever invested and you are protected against things like inflation.

It is important to understand that once your debt is paid off and you have accumulated more wealth, you will want to take an additional percentage and invest it into things like higher risk investment portfolios. However, your retirement funds should always stay in either low or moderate risk investments to ensure that you are never risking your future. Let the other funds you invest take the risk and possibly earn you massive results, instead. That way, you are investing wisely and you have the potential to earn more without the risk of losing everything you have.

Monitor Your Own Credit

Assuming credit companies will monitor your credit and protect you against mistakes or flaws is a bad idea, and assuming that simply paying your debt off will give you a strong enough credit rating is also a bad idea. You need to regularly monitor your own credit scores and pay attention to how your credit report reads so that you understand what is affecting your credit and what you can do to protect yourself against that.

The best way to maintain your credit is to pay your debt all the way off, then keep your credit cards at 25% or less of their total capacity. For example, only carry a $250 balance on a $1,000 credit limit. This number is the sweet spot for a strong credit rating and will ensure that you never get yourself into a position that you cannot reasonably manage.

In addition to keeping your credit low, also make sure that you are incredibly honest with yourself about what type of debt you can handle going forward. Buying vehicles with a loan or taking out a mortgage, for example, is not a bad idea *so long as you can handle it*. Do not assume that just because you pass the credit score means that you can handle the debt that you are looking at taking onbecause in most cases it does not. Instead, look at your actual budget and see how much you can reasonably afford to put toward things like car loans and mortgages so that you can feel absolutely confident in the debt you are taking on.

Invest Where It Matters

As you go on in life, and especially if you plan on starting a business, you need to make sure that you always invest when and where it matters. Knowing how to prioritize your expenses and spend your money on what truly matters ensures that you will always have exactly what you need to move forward to the next step. Investing in exactly what you need does not mean that you will not get everything else, it simply means you are investing in exactly what you need to create the funds for everything else you want in life.

The best way to see where you really should be investing your money is to look at your long-term plan and *honestly* identify where you need to invest your money. Make sure that you start by spending your money on what is going to get you the furthest. For example: if you are starting out with an e-commerce business, invest $300 into a basic laptop, $150 into a self-managed and self-designed website, $50 into a good payment platform, and $500 into product or other necessary expenses, instead of spending $700 on a laptop, $200 on a website, and $100 on products. Knowing how to find the right balance and being willing to upgrade things later on ensures that you have everything you need to get started so that you can actually create the opportunity for you to upgrade in the future. If you start out poorly, you may never create the funds or opportunities required to upgrade, which means that you have ultimately wasted your funds on poor investments.

Even as you begin to make more money and are able to upgrade to better tools, it is important that you still continue to hold onto the mindset of investing in only what is necessary for you to create your next opportunities. In doing this, you refrain from spending too much money on things that are unnecessary and instead keep that money available for other more important purchases. Which is, in fact, a major "secret" of the wealthy and elite. Despite the fact that it may seem that they are living a lavish and luxurious lifestyle, most of the wealthy are incredibly focused on spending their money only on what matter and investing the rest elsewhere. Often, their investments into things like designer wardrobes are made purposefully so that they have a wardrobe that upholds their reputation and that will last. Both of which are necessary for saving or developing funds. Or, if you see them having expensive spa days or vacations, these are often the rewards they give themselves to help them stay relaxed and focused during the in-between times when they are focused on work and are essentially living with the bare basics. By knowing how and when to spend their money, wealthy people are able to easily create more wealth and maintain their wealth while also living a luxurious lifestyle.

Chapter 4: The Seven Stages of Financial Freedom

Because you are reading this book, I can all but guarantee that the words "financial freedom" made it onto your life plan at least once. Financial freedom is the ultimate goal that many of us have and with good reason: financial freedom can offer us virtually unlimited opportunities and potential in life. Financial freedom is a wonderful thing to desire, and it is not nearly as challenging as you might think it would be for you to achieve it. In fact, you can achieve financial freedom within the next 15 years if you start enacting the plan outlined within this very chapter.

Although 15 years may sound like a long time, understand that you will find yourself experiencing a reasonable amount of wealth much sooner than 15 years. However, 15 years is about how long it will take for you to create a true state of financial freedom which means that you truly will not have to worry about finances any longer after those 15 years. As well, the time is going to pass anyway, so why not let it pass as you do something productive such as set yourself up for financial freedom?

In order to create the financial freedom that you desire, there are seven stages of financial freedom that you need to acknowledge and incorporate into your financial plan. Acknowledging and incorporating these seven stages will ensure that you work toward your financial freedom in a methodical manner that allows you to create the results you really desire. This way, you are moving forward in a way that is attainable, rather than intimidating and overwhelming yourself right off the bat. The more bite-sized and manageable you can make this plan, the more likely you will be to create the results you desire with it.

The seven stages of financial freedom we are going to discuss include: gaining clarity, becoming self-sufficient, building a nest egg, creating stability, developing flexibility, covering your life expenses, and finally having an abundance of wealth. If you can follow these seven stages in order, you will have all of the wealth you need to experience true financial freedom within the next 15 years.

Stage One: Gaining Clarity

The first step in creating financial freedom iscultivatingclarity around what financial freedom even means to you. You need to have clarity both on where you are right nowand on where you want to be. Clarity is going to provide you with the opportunity to clearly understand why you are currently struggling to create the results you desire and what you need to do in order to transform your money story. It is also going to support you with having a clear vision of what you are working toward so that you clearly know what it is that you are trying to achieve. As you develop clarity, you also come across the milestones and goals that you need to achieve in order to create financial freedom in your life.

The first step in creating clarity should always be identifying what it is that you truly desire for yourself in your life. Identify what financial freedom would look like for you, and what it would mean for you, and let that be your big vision. Having your big vision created first allows you to assess yourself in relation to that vision so that you can clearly see where you are currently thriving and where you need to be working harder to create the results you desire.

As you create your big vision, make sure you do so in a highly specific manner. Get clear on what specific numbers you want to have associated with your financial freedomand what freedom looks like for you. For example, for your financial freedom might look like having $500,000 aside for your retirement, your mortgage paid off, and the ability to live the lifestyle you want without ever having to worry about running out of money. You need to get clear on what financial freedom really looks like for you so that you can start working toward that vision.

Next, you need to assess where you are and consider how your present financial landscape is affecting your ability to get to where you want to go. First, look at the simple facts: how much money do you have, and how much debt are you carrying? Get clear on these numbers and look at them in relation to where you want to be so that you can see what specific financial milestones you need to achieve in order to move forward. Once you have, you can start looking at your actual financial habits, cycles, and behaviors. Start paying attention to how you make money, manage money, and spend money and get clear on how these behaviors are impacting your ability to reach your big vision.

As of right now, you do not necessarily need to do anything with this knowledge, but you do want to make sure that you are aware of it. The clearer you can be now, the easier it will be to set the next six goals and actually reach them because you will know exactly where you need to focus your efforts and improve your skills in order to get to the next stage of financial freedom.

Stage Two: Becoming Self-Sufficient

After you have gotten clear on where you are and where you want to be, you need to start becoming self-sufficient. Self-sufficiency is where you are going to start learning how to properly provide for yourself, particularly when it comes to taking care of your personal finances. Here, you are going to take those specific numbers of where you are presently sitting with debt and income and you are going to make a budget for yourself so that you can start managing your money more effectively. Then, you are going to follow through.

You would be surprised as to how many people struggle with being self-sufficient, despite the fact that it is one of the primary financial goals that we should be striving for in our adulthood. Learning how to become self-sufficient will support you in getting your finances in order as it will prevent you from leaning on credit cards and loans to try to pay for a way of life that you cannot presently afford. It also forces you to become accountable and ensure that you really are putting the work into creating the right income for yourself so that you can cover all of your expenses.

You can begin to become self-sufficient by doing things like paying for food and transportation, paying for your rent, and covering your own bills. Although this may all seem incredibly basic, it is important to address it as you want to make sure that you are self-sufficient without relying on any forms of debt or loans to do so. Covering your basic costs of living is one of the first biggest milestones you can achieve in creating a life of financial freedom.

If you look at your bills and realize that you are not yet capable of being self-sufficient, you need to start setting goals that are going to allow you to become self-sufficient. This means doing things like cutting out all unnecessary spending to avoid unnecessary expenses, thus allowing you to have more funds available for your necessary expenses. It also means honestly assessing whether or not your present career path is helping you create the funds you need and then addressing what to do if you find out it does not. For example, you could start working on developing new skills so that you can earn a promotion or seek out a new job that is going to pay you more. Finding solutions such as this will ensure that you are setting yourself up to take care of your own financial needs which is essential, especially if you want to become financially free.

When it comes to covering your own finances, some people question how a partnership might fit into this. You might wonder, if you are with a partner: is it enough for you two to cover your expenses together? Often, this means one person will make more and one person will make less and together you will have enough to cover each other's expenses. While this may be perfectly fine, if you truly want to achieve financial freedom, you should ideally focus on achieving it for yourself. This way, you are secure in the finances you have earned and set aside and you do not have things such as money coming in between you and your partner. With that being said, there is no right answer here so you are going to need to discuss this with your partner and decide what feels right for you and for your relationship.

Stage Three: Building Your Nest Egg

After you have achieved self-sufficiency and you are no longer relying on other people to pay your bills for you, you can move up into creating a nest egg. This is where you can stop living the lifestyle you have to live based on your budget and start creating a little breathing room for yourself so that you can begin to enjoy the lifestyle that you really want to live. Breathing room essentially means that you are going to have enough to have a little spending money every monthand that you are putting away money into a savings account as aggressively as you possibly can.

If you really want to give yourself some reasonable breathing room, you want to be saving up enough to cover 6 months' worth of living expenses for yourself. This means that if you require $2,346 per month to live, you want to set aside $14,076 as quickly as you can. This breathing room is going to allow you to reasonably cover any emergency expenses you may need to cover, ranging from unexpected bills to unexpected job loss. For many people, the creation of this breathing room is enough to give them massive peace of mind around their finances. While they may still not have the purchasing power they desire, the realization that they no longer have to worry about things like job losses or unexpected emergencies means that they have more freedom to do what they want and need in life.

The reality is, many people in today's world have yet to actually accumulate any form of accessible savings for themselves. They may have pensions or retirement funds through their companies, but these funds are not accessible and are incapable of giving them the security they need in an event where they need funds *now*. Not being able to cover any financial expenses above and beyond your basic monthly expenses can be overwhelming and, in all reality, puts you one bad month or unexpected expense away from being in financial crises. It is crucial that you prioritize this financial nest egg and really put aside as much as you possibly can until it is thereand then set it aside for good. You should not plan on touching or tapping into this money at allunless a true emergency does arise. Otherwise, this money should not be seen as anything you can leverage or use: its mere purpose is to protect you in the event of unexpected financial circumstances.

A smart move to make with your nest egg is to put it into some form of easily accessible high-interest savings account. While these accounts are not ideal for helping preserve the growth of your money or having your money work for you, they do keep your funds immediately accessible and you will not have to pay the penalty for accessing the money should you find you need it. Having your funds in an account like this ensures that you are not only in possession of emergency money, but you are managing that money properly and that it truly is serving the purpose that you need it to serve.

While this money is going to give you a strong start in creating financial freedom, it can still run out so it is important that you stay focused on making this a milestone and not your end goal. If you really want to achieve financial freedom, you are going to need to look a lot further than 6 months into your future with your finances.

Stage Four: Creating Stability

After you have set aside enough funds to cover 6 months' worth of expenses, you need to start thinking even bigger. The next milestone for you to achieve on your way to financial freedom is setting aside one years' worth of expenses. This is where you really start to go from being able to cover any basic emergency to truly being able to cover any emergency you and your family are likely to come across in your lifetime. Should you face unexpected medical bills, job loss, or damage to your property, you will know without a doubt that you have the funds available to cover those unexpected expenses.

For most people, having an entire years' worth of expenses saved up is the point where they really start to feel rooted and they no longer worry as to whether or not they will be able to reasonably cover their expenses should anything happen to them. This is the point where you get to start feeling like you could reasonably withstand multiple emergencies and still have enough to cover your expenses. At this point, you are no longer worrying about what is going to happen to you financially so you begin to have the capacity to start really enjoying the life you want to be living because you know you are financially secure.

Getting to this point does not need to be quite as aggressively achieved as getting to your first 6 months of living expenses because you have already saved up should anything go wrong. However, you also do not want to dwindle and take your time in getting here as the sooner you achieve this milestone the sooner you can start moving on to greater levels of financial freedom that will bring with them even more flexibility and adaptability.

As you save up these funds for yourself, you may be wondering where and how you should store and manage your funds. When it came to the first 6 months' worth of funds, keeping it somewhere immediately accessible is important as you do not want to have to pay penalties or feel pressed to wait a specific time period to access your money. However, there are not many circumstances you may run into that would require more than 6 months' worth of income that could not wait at least a little while. For that reason, you may want to reserve the remaining half of your funds in a conservative investment fund that will allow it to grow without risking your ability to access those funds in an emergency. Often, there are simple portfolios with terms that last between 1-3 months that are a great option for you to store these additional funds in. Should you ever find yourself come across an immediate and expensive emergency, you might find yourself needing to withdraw sooner. However, the likelihood of that happening is fairly slim and therefore it makes sense to allow that money to work for you by growing, even if it is growing at a slow and conservative pace.

Stage Five: Developing Flexibility

After you have saved up an entire years' worth of expenses to support you in any unforeseeable emergencies, you need to go even further to really give yourself flexibility in your life. This is where you are going to take it even further and save up an entire two years' worth of expenses for yourself. At this point, you are no longer worrying about emergencies but instead you are giving yourself ample freedom to live the lifestyle you desire to live, and you are providing yourself with a massive amount of flexibility.

Saving up two years' worth of expenses may take some time, but if you stay devoted to this goal it will not be challenging as you have already successfully saved up plenty at this point. By now, the practice of saving should come naturally to you and you may have even found more ways to save your funds and increase your savings account. Either way, the more you can commit to creating this savings account, the better.

As you continue to add these additional savings into your nest egg, you will want to explore more reasonable ways to store these funds. The additional year of funds ideally should be invested in some form of conservative to conservatively moderate investment portfolio so that you can store it while allowing that money to grow and earn even more income for you. In doing so, you can start to look into 6-12 year portfolios which will give you a greater returnbut will also result in you needing to wait longer to reasonably access those funds. With that being said, the chances of you actually needing to tap into those funds is unlikely unless you plan on making a larger purchase, in which case having that time period of having to wait is a great opportunity to give you time to vet the idea. Typically, needing to wait a few months to really consider making a large purchase is a great opportunity to help you make sure that you are making purchases that are actually important to you and that are worth the investment. As well, after you make that purchase you should seek to recover the expenses by saving them up again and placing them back into your savings account.

When you have successfully saved up two years' worth of earnings, you need to start focusing on reassessing your priorities and your financial goals. At this point, you have made huge strides and you are well on your way to financial freedom, so you owe it to yourself to celebrate your success while also reassessing to make sure that you are still on track for what you really want. At this point, you may find that your financial goals have changed, that you desire to make a new large purchase, or that you have some other priority that you want to consider for the time being. In either case, being able to sit back and make sure that you are still on track is a great opportunity to keep yourself aligned with creating the financial freedom that you truly desire in your life.

Stage Six: Covering Your Life Expenses

At this point in your financial freedom pursuit, you have already set aside more than enough money to help you cover unexpected emergencies, unforeseeable expenses, and any larger purchases you might want to make in your lifetime. However, there is plenty more that you can do to start allowing yourself to see beyond the immediate future and into the long-term future. This is where you get to really start thinking about the rest of your life

493

and securing your lifestyle for as long as you live. As long as you manage your finances properly, you will be able to continue to have a strong sense of financial freedom and financial flexibility within your wealth.

According to many financial advisors and wealth management experts, there are two key ways to effectively create the wealth you need to support your lifestyle for the rest of your life. One way is by saving up a million dollars; the other way is by investing in assets that are going to pay out consistently. You can choose which one you desire, or you can even choose both if you really want to protect yourself and set yourself up for a luxurious and financially flexible future.

If you choose the option of saving up a million dollars, essentially you are going to save that money and invest it into the most conservative portfolio possible that will still give you plenty of money to live off of. In this case, you are going to be living off of the interest of your one million dollars for the rest of your life. If you can get a portfolio that returns at even 5%, that's $50,000 per year to live off of. With that being said, the average rate of return is 8.7% which means you would actually be living off about $87,000 per year, which is plenty to afford you any lifestyle you want to live. In fact, many people do this and then live off of the interest alone and never work a day in their life. As a result, they are able to retire young and pursue the life of their dreams instead of spending their entire lives working.

The alternative option is to invest in things like real estate, which is known as being an income-producing asset. In this case, you have invested in something that will reasonably continue to cultivate an income for you so that you can continue to earn funds every single month off of that asset. While this is a great idea, you do need to make sure that you understand the risks you are taking as income-producing assets are not guaranteed to consistently produce an income and, in some cases, may also cost money to maintain. If you choose this route, do your research and make sure that you are doing everything you can to choose income-producing assets that will continue to pay off for a long period of time.

Stage Seven: Having an Abundance of Wealth

The final stage of developing financial freedom is achieving the point where not only are you going to be financially supported for the rest of your life but you are also going to be able to live the exact lifestyle you wantwhile leaving behind a financial legacy. At the seventh stage of financial freedom you are able to set aside money for your children, you can give through charitable donations, and you can start to use your wealth to bless other peoples' lives in a strong manner.

Having an abundance of wealth at this point often comes from you earning significant interest off of your investment portfolio while also having income-producing assets that you can continue to invest in and earn money from overtime. Ideally, you should continue to re-invest any money that you are not actively in need of so that you can continue growing your finances and earning your way to higher and higher levels of financial freedom. Through doing this, you ensure that you and your family or whoever you may wish to bless with your funds will never have to worry about finances again. At this point, you really have made your way through to the point of true financial freedom, and you have ample choices of what to do with that freedom to create the life and legacy that you want to have.

Reaching all the way to the seventh stage of financial freedom is certainly not an overnight change, and it will require you to consistently place effort into creating and maintaining your wealth. The idea is that each time you reach a new level of financial freedom, your understanding of producing and managing wealth also becomes clearer and more secure. As you continue to increase your skills around making and managing money, you will find that it becomes even easier for you to stay disciplined and reach your next level of financial freedom.

You will likely also discover that financial freedom is different from what you thought it might be. Many people believe that financial freedom is spending endless amounts of money without having to worry about running out. While people who are financially free can certainly spend great deals of money and still be financially secure, they often realize that by the time they reach financial freedom they have no desire to do so. Instead, they realize that along the way they learned discipline around money and, as a result, they are more likely to respect their purchases and only spend money on the things that matter. Chances are, you will find that the novelty of spending money passes for you and you find yourself spending money far more reasonably and responsibly once you achieve financial freedom, too. In the meantime, focus on learning how to foster healthier wealth creation and wealth management habits and stay devoted to achieving your financial goals. The more focused you can remain, the more likely you will be to achieve financial freedom within 15 years or less.

Chapter 5: The Number One Tool You Need to Create Consistent Wealth Is A Business

When it comes to creating financial freedom, one of the best ways that you can create consistently recurring income is through creating a business that is going to provide you with the opportunity to actually create that consistent and recurring income. If you have ever looked at anyone who has a significant amount of wealth, you will likely recognize that at one point or another they have become involved in entrepreneurship. Creating a business is an incredible way of putting your wealth in your own hands by creating an income-producing asset that has virtually unlimited earning potential. This is why this particular route of wealth creation is so desirable by people who are focused on increasing their finances: it gives them direct control over their ability to grow and manage their income.

Creating a business with the intention of becoming wealthy is something that you need to be particular about. Unlike creating a business purely out of the passion of running your dream business, creating a business to become wealthy requires you to honestly assess the profitability of any business you consider developing. You need to make sure that you are considering your long-term financial goals as well as your passions so that you are more likely to choose an avenue that will be enjoyable and successful for you, while also being massively profitable.

If you find that you are not particularly passionate about anything aside from wealth creation, there are plenty of routes you can take to bypass this seeming lack of passion so that you can continue to generate success and earn great money through your business. We are going to discuss all of these keys in this chapter.

Developing A Business with Your Goals in Mind

When it comes to developing your business, there are really two ways that you can go about it: follow something you are passionate aboutor follow something that is going to help you achieve your goals. While there is really no wrong reason for pursuing your business, it is important that you really consider what it is that you are looking to get out of your business before you make any plans for yourself. If you are looking for a business that is going to give you a great hobby that you can passionately run and hopefully earn some money off of, running a passion-based business is a great idea. Many people even run passion-based businesses and find themselves making a massive amount of money off of those businesses and, as a result, they find themselves creating the best of both worlds. However, it is important to realize that if you do intend on turning your passion into your profits it will virtually always become highly time-consuming, and it may never pay off as you may find yourself making decisions rooted more in passion than profit. While there is nothing wrong with that, if your original goal was to earn profits so that you could develop your wealth and secure your financial future, this may be the wrong way of approaching business.

Instead of getting caught up with what you are passionate about, consider first thinking about what your long-term goals are for your business. What do you ultimately want to create with your business? Naturally, wealth is going to come to mind when you ponder this question, and that is a good topic to focus on when it comes to creating and validating a business idea. However, there are other things you are going to want to create for yourself from your business, too, namely around the topic of freedom. You may wish to have the freedom of being able to travel when you want, to take time off when you want, or to explore different skills or areas of life when you want. You may want to be able to afford your dream lifestyle and then some, or you may want to be able to use a profit-based business to run a passion-based business so that you can truly explore whatever it is that you want in life.

When you really take the time to identify what your goal is in your business before you begin building a business, it becomes easier for you to start to identify opportunities that are likely going to reach these goals for you. You begin to find opportunities that have the capacity to earn the wealth you desireor to earn the freedom you desire. As you look, you will be able to find things that are going to afford you the opportunity to run your passion-based business, too, or that will easily and seamlessly mesh into your passion-based business so that you can easily run both. The more you look into what you really want and really need from your business, the easier it will be for you to identify a great opportunity that you can pursue which will afford you everything you desire in life. The key here is to make sure that you pursue something that is going to be capable of either achieving all of your goalsor achieve your primary goals while setting you up to achieve the rest of them.

Once you truly understand what you want and need, you can start looking into these business ideas that would effectively fit the mold for what you are looking for. As you do, make sure that you can clearly see how the business idea would fit into your ideal lifestyle and would serve the needs that you have. You want to make sure that you pick a business that is going to meet the majority of your needs, as this is how you will find a business that is genuinely worth pursuing. When you can clearly see how it is going to support you in the bigger picture, and in the long run, it becomes easier for you to convince yourself to put your whole heart in your business and turn it into something successful.

If one of your needs is for your business to be something you are or could be passionate about, make sure you consider that and that you develop a business that you can find yourself putting your whole heart into. The key to choosing between profit and passion is that, if your goal is to increase your wealth, you need to always put profit *first*. Passion can be a high ranking second place, but it does still need to be the secondary priority as this ensures that in matters where you need to consider your profit versus your passion you can make the right choice and choose profits. By choosing profits, you allow your business to grow large enough and strong enough to support your passions, which means, in the end, you do win by having *all* of your needs met.

If passion is not a large priority for you, you do not need to worry about having a business that you will be passionate about but you should still consider yourself with creating something that you will be interested in. You can either choose a business you will be interested inor a role of authority that you will be interested in. In either case, by ensuring that you have interest in your chosen business you ensure that you are going to be able to easily pay attention to what it is that you are trying to create and stay committed to your efforts. If you completely lack any level of interest in what you are doing it will become too easy for you to be complacent and overlook your goals in favor of getting out of doing something that bores you. Naturally, this is not a strong mindset to be in when it comes to business, so at least having some level of interest in your business choice will support you in creating what you desire with your business.

Creating the Vision for Your Business

Addressing your priorities and getting your mindset straight around profit and passion and any other needs you have is important. However, once your mindset is adjusted to serve your goals, you need to focus on creating an actual vision for your business that is going to give you a clear image of what you are working toward. The clearer you can be with your image and your intention, the more powerful you will be in creating the results you desire because you will know exactly what you are working toward *and* you will be able to see how it will serve you in getting what you want.

Creating a vision for your business may be one of the most enjoyable parts of building a business because there is no pressure involved. Aside from making sure the business can meet your needs and goals, you get to have fun creating any image that fits for you and turning this into your end goal. Turning your vision into something clear and achievable is a multi-step process. Following these steps is going to give you the best opportunity to create a vision that really meets all of the necessary needs for you to turn that vision into a plan. You might be delighted to realize that the process you use for identifying your vision for your business is not dissimilar to the process you would use for creating your vision for your own personal life.

The very first step to creating your vision is thinking about where you want your business to be in ten years. If you had achieved every single possible goal and need in your business, and beyond, what would that look like? How would you be running the company, or who would be running the company? What would your annual income look like? What type of involvement would you need to have in your business in order for it to meet your needs? How would your business be supporting your non-professional life?

Get extremely clear on what it is that you want for yourself and how you want your business to meet your needs. Then, identify how you can start meeting your business's needs. What would you need to do in order to keep the business running? Who would you need to hire, what skills would you need to have, and what knowledge would you possess? How would all of this create your ultimate vision?

It is important to understand that your company's vision and your company's mission are not one and the same, so at this time you are not defining what you are aiming to do for your company, you are defining what your company can do for you.

Identifying your involvement in the company should only serve as a tool to help you identify how your business will serve you in giving you the type of professional life that you wish to have. You should also understand that a vision itself is not a strategy; it is merely a clear understanding of what it is that you are working toward and what you are trying to create.

After you have gotten clear on what everything looks like, you need to ask yourself if the vision you have created helps you actually meet your goals. Consider every goal you set into place previously and ask yourself if that vision genuinely shows you meeting each of those goals. If it seems like it would be too challenging for you to meet those goals, you need to step back and look at your vision again to see how you can adjust it to make sure that your goals will be able to be easily achieved by your vision.

In addition to considering your goals, you need to consider your values and the values that you want to carry into your company. Upon starting their first business, many entrepreneurs forget that their values need to be upheld within their company; otherwise, they are going to struggle to pursue that business. If you find yourself struggling with conflicting values, see if you can either adapt your vision or find a new way to perceive certain parts of your vision so that you can match your values. Then, be highly intentional in carrying those values into your business so that you are not defying yourself or betraying yourself as you build your company.

Next, you need to be able to refine your vision into something that is bite-sized and easy for you to reasonably follow. If your vision seems too complex or overwhelming, you are going to have a difficult time actually pursuing your vision because you will not fully understand what it is that you are trying to pursue. Ideally, you should be able to get your vision down to a two to three sentence explanation so that you can clearly explain your vision, and quickly. The clearer your vision is, the easier it will be for you to incorporate into a goal so that you can turn that goal into a plan andactually follow it.

Once you have created your vision, you are going to want to do one final review to make sure that it really fits for you. Write it out on paper and read the words you have chosen to use; do they feel right? Do they accurately reflect what you want to create, or could you use words that would be more concise and effective? Read it out loud to yourself, does it sound like what you really want? Can you clearly see how it captures your goals and your vision for what you are truly looking for, in your business and in your personal life? Does it sound like it is going to honor the rest of the vision you have for yourself by not being *too*time-consuming, and by offering you the opportunities you need to have the overall life you want? If you feel really confident in answering all of these positively, and you feel that your vision clearly reflects what you want and need out of your business, then you have successfully created a strong business vision.

Establishing Your Business Plan

Once you have a strong vision in place, it is time for you to start creating an actual business plan from the vision you have developed. This is where you get to take your vision and create a mission and a strategy from your vision so that you can actually bring that vision into life and get the results you desire from it.

Establishing your business plan is going to happen in three steps. First, you are going to need to establish your mission; then, you are going to need to define your strategy. From there, you need to define what exact steps need to happen in order for you to turn that vision into an action plan. Once you have these three steps completed, you will have a strong business plan in place that will allow you to successfully pursue your business and achieve all of your desired goals and outcomes through that business.

Creating your mission is your first step in narrowing in on your business, meaning you are now stepping away from how your business will serve you and you are starting to focus on how you will serve in your business. Or, how your business will serve *others,* namely your clients. Your mission statement allows you to define what the objective of your business is and what you are trying to accomplish through the products or services you are selling. By defining your mission statement, you clearly define what goals you have for your business itself, how you want that business to perform, and what you want to accomplish as a result of that business. Because of all of this, your mission statement needs to be extremely focused on your business itself and should have nothing to do with you or your goals for yourself personally.

Some great examples of mission statements include:

- Patagonia: Build the best product, cause no unnecessary harm, use business to inspire and implement solutions to the environmental crisis.
- Honest Tea: To create and promote great-tasting, healthy, organic beverages.
- IKEA: To create a better everyday life for many people.
- Nordstrom: To give customers the most compelling shopping experience.
- Tesla: To accelerate the world's transition to sustainable energy.

Note that each of these clearly defines the company's mission but does not generally include information about the products or services they offer. That is because in business the products and services you offer are a tool in a part of your strategyand not an actual part of your mission. You should do the same thing in avoiding defining the product or service you will offer in your business but instead define what the goal of that product or service is. For example, if you start a sustainable fashion company, your mission statement should *not* be something like: "To create sustainable fashion items for people everywhere." It *should* be something like "Promoting sustainable lifestyles across the globe."

After you have created your mission, you need to break into your strategy. Your strategy is where you get to define your products or services, your ideal business model, and your approach to getting your products and services to your clients. At this point you are going to take your vision and your mission and turn it into a tangible series of goals and strategies you can use to help you create the results you desire.

The first part of creating your strategy is to identify what actual products or services you want to offer and then tailor those products or services to meet your mission or vision. If you were making sustainable clothes, for example, you would want to identify what types of clothes you would be making and who you would be making them for. Then, you want to identify what materials you use, what suppliers you would go to, and how you

509

would get those clothes to market in the most sustainable way possible.

After you have created your product suite and strategized how you would get those products to market, you are able to start taking these pieces and turning them into an actual strategy. This is where you are going to define how these products are going to serve a need, how you are going to identify your target audience, and how you are going to get your products to that target audience. If you are not sure about how certain elements of your business should work, try looking at other businesses in your niche and seeing how they have structured their business. Pay attention to the strategies they use to create their products, get their products to market, and actually make sales with their products, then use that to start building your own strategy.

If you really want to get clear and specific on your plan, a great idea is to retrieve a copy of a business plan template from the internet and fill it in with information regarding your own business. Fill out each step ranging from what your business is and who it serves to what your entry and exit strategies are and everything in between. This way, you can feel confident that you have all of the information necessary to create an actual business plan for you to act on. If you have a hard time filling out any part of the business plan, working together with a mentor is a great opportunity for you to learn from someone who has done this before you and who can help you complete the plan as well.

Validating Your Business Plan

Any time you finish creating a plan for your life or for your business you should always invest time into validating that plan. In developing your life plan, you get the opportunity to validate it to ensure that you are actually going to be able to get everything you want in life through the plan you have chosen. When it comes to developing a business plan, you want to ensure two important factors.

The first important factor you want to validate in your business plan is related to yourself and your personal overall goals. Since you are going to be the one running the business and investing your time and passion into it, you need to regularly assess your business plans and operations to ensure that they are supporting you in creating what you want in your life. It is important that you feel as though your desires and needs are being met through your business, especially when it comes to wealth creationand the way in which you are creating that wealth. You should feel confident that the plan you have devised for your business is one that is actually going to enable you to create the income you desire, and that is not going to take up more time or energy than you are willing to invest in your business. Continually reviewing your business to ensure that it is continuing to meet your life and financial goals ensures that you will never develop your business in a way that results in you feeling drained or uninterested by it.

One of the benefits of being able to create your life on purpose and creating a business to fit into your life is that you get to decide what the rules for your life and business. This means that you get to decide how you can fit your business into what you want for yourself and what you are willing to do to make that business happen. Of course, there are plenty of things you will *have* to do in order to make your business work, but often there is flexibility in *how* you do them so that you can live a life you desire and make the money you want to make. Working within that realm of flexibility is a great way to allow yourself to successfully run a business as it ensures you remain in the mindset of "*I love what I do*" rather than "*I can't wait for this to be done.*" Naturally, the more you want to show up and do what needs to be done, the bigger your business is going to grow and the more success you are going to have.

It does not often come natural to people who are transitioning from an employee mindset to an entrepreneur mindset to really know what they want out of their business, much less to give themselves permission to run their businesses their way. For that reason, it is important that you regularly review any plans you make immediately upon making them and afterward to ensure that you have made plans that will be successful *and* reflect your true desires.

After you have factored yourself into your plans and considered how your business plan is going to serve you, you need to see how your business plan is going to serve your business. This part is incredibly important as you need to make sure that your business plan can realistically get your business where you want and need it to go. At this point, you may realize you need to put some more work in than you intended or that you are going to need to compromise on what you are willing to do in order to get your business to the point that you want to get it to.

Being realistic when it comes to making business plans is crucial as you never want to underestimate what it will take to get your business to the point you want to get it to. It can be easy to feel overwhelmed by identifying what "realistic" even looks like, especially if you are new to the businessso do your best and review your plan frequently to ensure that you really have found a realistic balance. This way, you can feel confident that your business plan will truly get you to where you want to go in your business.

If you are ever uncertain as to whether or not your business plan is realistic, two great ways to validate this fact is to ask yourself "Do I really think I can achieve this?" and "How often do other people in this industry achieve goals like this?" Asking yourself if you honestly feel you can achieve something first is a great way to make sure that you are creating goals and plans that are realistic with *your* skillset and abilities. Checking in on the statistics for your chosen industry is an excellent opportunity to ensure that you are making plans that are realistic for the industry you are in. You can review your plan every so often and update it with your own statistics based on the performance of your own company to see how you are doing and to adjust your plan as needed.

Once you have a strong plan in place for your business, you can feel confident that you are running on a strong foundation. Creating a strong foundation for your business is absolutely essential when it comes to developing plans that will serve you in starting your business; however, it is important that you also grow beyond your plans. Moving into putting those plans into action is an excellent way to ensure that you are actually going to grow a business that will give you the lifestyle and income you desire.

Chapter 6: If You Want Your Business to Be A Success, You Need to Do These Things

Turning your business into a reality is a three-step process that requires you to first build an entity for your business. After you have developed your business entity you need to get that entity to the public and then grow that entity so that you can reach your financial goals. This may sound incredibly simple in theory, but developing your business and turning it into a profitable resource is something that will require you to understand the intimate pieces that go into each of these three steps. Those who have truly mastered the art of business have been studying these practices for years, but I have one secret that is going to help you get beyond what even years of studying is going to do.

See, everyone thinks business is about knowledge and education. They think that if they get a great degree and do all of their homework that they will truly understand what it takes to run a successful business and make great money doing it. If this were true, though, then every single person who graduated from business school would go on to run the next Apple, Microsoft, or Gillet company. The reality is, while knowledge is important, it offers very little in comparison to the secret that real business masters have tapped into and started using in their businesses. That secret could be summarized in one sentence, but it is best broken down into four necessary pillars of business: branding, marketing, selling, and growing.

Branding Your Business

The very first secret of building a successful business is branding your business. This is where you take your business plan and develop a business entity that you are going to use to interact with your clients. People think that your brand has everything to do with what products or services you sell, but this is far from the actual truth. The reality is: your brand has everything to do with "who" it is and how it connects with your target audience and makes them feel. If you can brand your business properly, you will develop an entity that has zero problems in reaching your target client and developing strong relationships with those clients so that you can monetize on those relationships. People who are fresh out of business school will tell you that branding is about the look of your business, ranging from your logo and your color scheme to your chosen "style," whether it be sleek, classic, bold, chic, or masculine. The reality is: these are all elements of your brand, but the *real* secret behind your brand goes much deeper than just your image, and it is also much simpler to create than an entire brand package.

The secret behind branding successfully is becoming aware of the fact that while for you your business is all about earning money, for your client your business is all about feeling good.

This means that you need to start right from the very beginning by cultivating an entity that makes them feel good. Everything about your brand persona from how your brand shows up to what your brand says and how it says it will provide you with an opportunity to create a positive relationship with your target audience. If you can put together an entire "persona" that makes your clients feel good, they will quickly and naturally connect with your brand in a way that makes them want more.

As the mastermind behind your business, you need to set aside the concerns surrounding what your brand looks like and first get to the root of the problem: what does your brand need to do, have, and be in order to make people feel good about it? This is the point where truly successful business masters will sit down and really consider what it is going to take for them to make a brand that helps their clients feel good, especially when in the presence of the brand. Consider key words that identify how your clients want to feel when interacting with your brand, such as: "good, happy, healthy, smart, eco-friendly, luxurious, supported, cared for, awed, inspired" and any other words that describe how you want your client to feel. Get as clear as possible, and make sure that every word concisely represents what you want your client to feel when they interact with your brand specifically.

Once you know how your client wants to feel and how you want them to feel, you need to take that information and start developing a real persona that will allow your brand to create these feelings within your client. This is where you get to become somewhat of a storyteller in that you get to create your protagonist and the protagonist in the story of your clients everywhere. The protagonist you create needs to be the good guy or the hero. It needs to be the one that directly considers a need or concern of your clients and then brings them the exact solution they are looking for in the way that feels the best for them. If you are running a fashion company, your brand is the hero that helps fashion-loving people everywhere get access to the exact types of clothes they are looking for so that they can genuinely enjoy engaging in self-expression. If you are running a tech company, your brand is the hero that recognizes a specific need in the tech-related areas of your clients' lives and offers them the exact solution they are looking for. No matter what company you are running, your protagonist clearly identifies a specific need that your client has and then meets that need for them.

After you have developed your protagonist that meets your clients' needs enough to play the role of hero, you need to give that protagonist a name, which will be the name of your company. Then, want to turn your brand over to the hands of experts who can bring your protagonist to life. You want to hire a graphic designer who can create a logo and graphic package that clearly reflects the personality you are bringing to life for your business. From here on out, you should always seek to work with professionals who can create images and graphic elements that match your brand's heroic persona.

Next, you need to start learning about how your protagonist needs to speak in order to stimulate the desired feelings within your client. If you have the funds available to hire a team of writers, you can use writers to help you create written content such as social media captions and written advertisement content for your brand. If not, you are going to have to learn how to do this yourself. Either way, you are going to want to learn the language of your brand as you need to understand it first, as no one can help you build your vision if you are not clear on what it is yourself.

The key secret in branding that master business owner know is that it is not about the look of your brand or even the sound of your brand that matters. You could spend as many hours on graphic design and color scheme coordination as you wanted, and your brand could still completely fail to reach your target audience. The reason behind that is that you have not taken the time to adequately create a protagonist that is going to become the hero in your client's story. You have created a pretty image that your client might appreciate, but that they will not truly be able to relate to. If you want to elevate yourself from new business owner to business master, you must always look into the core of what matters and then enlist the support of masters to help bring those matters to life. In the case of branding, your sole purpose is to identify your protagonist and bring it to life.

Marketing Your Business

Marketing is the first step in getting your business in front of your client's eyes. At this point, you are moving from having a protagonist to letting your protagonist actually become the hero in people's stories. Marketing your business is a skill that will take time to develop and, contrary to popular belief, it is not a skill that you can learn straight out of a book or a blog post. In fact, your own mentor will be unlikely to have the answers to give you the step-by-step process for how to market your brand to your clients. The reason behind this is that marketing needs to be authentic and it needs to speak to your clients in a way that clearly communicates directly with *them*. Perfecting the art of communication between you and your client is something that takes time because there is a certain synchronicity that needs to happen between what you are saying and how you are getting that message out to your clients.

With all that to be said, there are plenty of resources you can rely on to help you begin to develop the basis for your marketing so that you can start getting your messages out there. Most of these resources will speak about three primary forms of marketing: social media advertising, print advertising, and word of mouth. On a practical level, all three of them are necessary. On a business master level, the secret is that these practicalities do not necessarily matter in the way that people seem to think they do.

Social media advertising is the strongest form of advertising we can tap into in today's age. With the way society is currently structured, virtually every single demographic is on social media somewhere and will be easily accessed through a well-placed, well-developed, and consistent online presence. Creating a social media presence for your brand is necessary even if you do not plan on running an entirely online business because this is how people find you and become aware of who you are. For many people, social media is also where you are going to be able to develop credibility as they realize that you are a real and legitimate business. When you start developing your social media presence, think about your protagonist and how they would show up online. Develop an online presence that genuinely feels like a customized platform for the protagonist of your business, or your brand itself. Creating your social media strategy in this way ensures that your presence begins to cultivate those essential relationships with the people who will be directly supporting your business.

Print advertising is the same as social media advertising, except it tends to cost more and is not always relevant for every business that comes into existence. If you have a limited budget, or if you are planning on running a business based entirely on e-commerce, do not waste your time or budget investing in print advertisements. You can move onto print advertisements once you are larger and it seems reasonable to move into this stage of advertising if it ever does. If, however, you are running a brick and mortar business where e-commerce is not the entirety of your operation, you are going to need to master print advertisements. Business cards, billboards, well-placed posters, and other forms of print advertisement will all give you a great opportunity to get in front of the eyes of your clients.

Word of mouth advertising is and always will be one of the most profound and powerful forms of advertising you will ever tap into. In fact, some brands run exclusively on word of mouth advertising and put very little effort into advertising their brands anywhere else because they have managed to leverage word of mouth advertising so effectively. Word of mouth advertising gives you all of the credibility and validation that you require to immediately gain the interest and trust of your target clients. If you get into the eyes of the right people, it can also result in you being seen by a massive audience that is far more engaged and warmed up than any audience you might gain through other forms of advertising. The popularity behind word of mouth advertising is exactly why so many brands encourage referrals, while also hiring influencers to help promote their brands to the public.

While all of these advertising methods are excellent, the fact remains that to a true business master the practical application of these methods is of little importance. The real question true business masters are always asking is: "how can my brand talk so that people listen?" Everything else just becomes a tool to get people to listen to you, then. Again, focusing on the core root of what it is that you are really trying to achieve is necessary in helping you create the type of results you desire to create with your brand. After all, all of the marketing in the world will not matter if no one is listening to what you are saying. In order for anything you do to work, you need to first get people to care about what you have to say, and you do that by speaking and showing up in a way that makes sense to them. Social media, print advertisements, and word of mouth are all simply tools in getting people to talk about you and listen to what you have to say. As they do, they become aware of your brand and start developing personal relationships with the protagonist you have cultivated.

Earning Massive Sales

The second stage of getting your brand to your clients is to actually earn sales. Or, preferably, earn *massive* sales. After all, this is all about building wealth and creating a lifestyle and business that truly serves in your financial freedom, right? There is one specific element that, if used right, can blow your sales numbers up massively and result in you creating the type of income you want rapidly in your business. When you learn what this element is and how to work it, you will discover that it is indeed powerful and that it can be manipulated and used to your advantage even more than you might think. That element is momentum.

While smooth-talking, excellently placed advertisements, and timely sales all contribute to the sales process, the real thing that is going to drive your sales numbers up is momentum. If you want to earn consistent sales in your company you need to build up momentum so that you continue to get your name out there faster and further. The more you can get people talking about your brand and the products or services they have bought from you, the faster you are going to get into the hands of even more people. As you continue to grow massive sales, you will continue to earn massive sales *revenue* which will help you grow your income and build wealth.

It is important that in developing your momentum you understand the two things you can do to help develop and grow your momentum over time. The first thing you can do is ensure that everything is in place for sales to happen. This means your brand needs to be well-developed, your marketing needs to be thorough, and you need to have the necessary steps in place for sales to actually happen. If you are an e-commerce business, this includes a sales channel such as a functional and well-branded website and a proper checkout page on your website. If you are a brick and mortar store this includes having sales personnel in place who can help your customers check out with their goodies that they are buying from you. Having everything clearly in place and displayed for your clients ensures that once they are ready to shop with you everything is in place for a smooth and enjoyable shopping experience. The experience you create through shopping should directly reflect the protagonist of your business, or your brand, as you want to make sure that you keep this persona consistent all the way through the process. This means if you have developed a hip and chic persona, the entire checkout process should cater to a hip and chic audience. Any type of persona you have developed needs to be honored through the sales process.

You also need to make sure that you have the power to back up growing momentum as you start to develop the momentum within your business. This means you should have enough product to fulfill orders or personnel to fulfill services, as well as enough resources to ship your products out quickly enough to fulfill your orders. You also want to have some level of customer support available so that if any problems happen during the shopping or shipping process there is someone on board to deal with that. While you can probably deal with it yourself early on, having someone there to help in the long run will ensure that you can stay focused on what matters: masterminding and running your business.

Once your sales channel is entirely fixed in place, the next step in your business development process is to get your sales funnel and marketing strategies working together in perfect harmony. You want to make sure that your marketing strategies are clearly driving people to your sales channel, and that your sales channel is matching the expectations of your customers when they find your marketing materials. As you grow you will want to continue nurturing this part of your business as you will need to continually adapt it to stay consistent and provide the best client experience possible.

The key way that a business master leverages the secret of momentum when it comes to making sales is in realizing that momentum does not just support business growth but it also supports you in closing sales. While the technical applications like shoppable websites and shipping strategies are important, a business master knows that these things are just tools in creating what truly matters: the client experience. The client experience should build on excitement, joy, and satisfaction as they go further through your sales channel. This means that from finding your well-placed marketing materials to charging their card for your products or services, your client needs to feel like each step of the process became even better than the last. Through this building momentum, they are much less likely to lose interest or back out of a purchase halfway through the process. As a result, you end up with massive sales numbers that support your massive income goals.

Facilitating Growth

Have you ever seen a business come out with a great product or service, sell that product or service like crazy for a period of time, and then completely disappear after the hype around that product or service wore off? This happens because many people fail to truly tap into the secrets of harnessing momentum so that they can grow their businesses. Instead, they ride on the momentum of a great idea and a fresh new launch to make sales, and then they never actually capitalize on that momentum by using it to create their next new launch, and then their next new launch. If said people were to master the process of harnessing and utilizing momentum, they would be able to continue to earn those massive sales numbers and grow their business exponentially over any given period of time. Since you are looking to have a business that acts as an income-producing asset, you want to make sure that you know how to harness that momentum and continue to grow it into a bigger and even more profitable brand.

Harnessing momentum in your business comes from knowing how to work with your audience to keep their attention while also creating attention on other great new things that you have to offer them. This particular part requires you to continually ask yourself what your audience needs and how often they need it. It also requires you to know how to use language and marketing to build anticipation, as anticipation builds up massive amounts of momentum, and that momentum will continue to increase your baseline momentum over time.

Look at it this way:

- You launch your first product in your business and, as a result of a successful launch, you find yourself earning huge sales numbers off of that launch. Let's say you sell 1,000 units per week at first.

- Shortly after your launch, let's say within 3 months, you are down to selling about 300 units per week. This is your "baseline" momentum. You can either prepare to launch a new product or service and grow momentum again, or you can let this momentum slowly trickle until you reach 0 units per week. (Let's say you choose to launch something new.)

- 4 months after your initial launch, you have a new product to offer. You start marketing it and by the 5th month it is officially available to the masses. Let's say you sell 1,000 units per week of this new product again. This momentum will also bring new attention to your original product, so let's say that increases your original product to 500 units per week. You are now selling 1,500 units per week.

- As momentum begins to stabilize again, you find yourself selling about 400 units of each product per week, bringing your new baseline momentum up to 800 units per week.

If you wanted to harness momentum and use it to develop massive sales while also growing your baseline sales, you would follow a similar structure of launching to help your business continually get into the eyes of your clients. By offering different products or services, relaunching old ones, or updating existing offers, you ensure that you are always giving your clients something new to look at. As a result, you tap into previous clients' by giving them something new to buy from you and you give yourself the opportunity to tap into even more clients. This is because with each launch more and more people will be talking about your brand and getting interested in what it is that you have to offer.

In addition to using a launch strategy to earn more sales, you can also use PR or public relations as a way to get your name out there even more. When it comes to PR, your key strategy is to talk to as many people as you can about your brand so that they, too, will talk to other people about your brand. The more you can focus on speaking to quality people, the better you will be at getting your name out there. You can do this by talking to bloggers, newspapers, other businesses, influencers, and anyone else who has a massive reach that will be able to possibly write about your brand and get your business in front of their audience. The more you can get your name out there, the more successful you will be and the more you will be able to create the results you desire.

So, the secret to growing your business that masters know about and you need to is knowing about how to use momentum as a way to increase your growing business. The more effectively you can harness momentum, the better you will be at getting your brand in front of the right people and growing over time. With each new launch and experience of building and releasing momentum you will increase your bottom line and keep your business growing overall, eventually allowing you to 10x, 100x, and even 1,000x your initial results as you continue to get your name out there.

Another bonus secret that I will offer you that business masters realize is this: when it comes to running a successful business, knowing what you are actually doing has very little to do with the success you create. Where success actually comes from is asking the right questions so that you can identify what truly matters at the core of everything you are doing. Then, you need to prioritize your attention so that you can fulfill those matters and get your business where it needs to be. Most of the successful business owners in our current world have almost no idea about how to actually run their business in that they are not marketing experts, sales experts, or even branding experts. Instead, they knew how to ask the right questions and find the right answers and then they enlisted the help of other people to bring all of that information to life. By knowing how to focus on what matters and then direct others to bring those matters to life, you give yourself the best opportunity at being able to run a truly successful empire that will earn you all of the money you need to create your financial freedom, and your financial legacy. That is the ultimate secret of business masters everywhere.

Conclusion

Financial freedom is something everyone seems to want, but very few people are on the right path to achieve it. Being able to create financial freedom for yourself requires you to know the right mindset and the right actions to take to help you make money, manage money, and create your financial legacy. If you are able to effectively master these three elements, you will find yourself on track with leaving behind a legacy that matches your personal goals.

When it comes to creating the right mindset, you need to learn how to take the pressure off of yourself and focus on what really matters. This means that you need to limit your pursuit of perfection in favor of a pursuit of curiosity and fulfillment. Every single mindset you need to cultivate in order to create the success you desire will come from first being willing to be curious and developing an insatiable craving to fulfill your curiosity. The more you can develop this within yourself, the more you will be able to mentally stay on track with doing what it takes to create wealth and a financial legacy.

Making and managing money comes from that same core mindset, except that you will likely find that you truly need to put yourself to the test and master that mindset in order to effectively make and manage money. The more you can master your self-discipline and self-control and work on yourself to allow yourself to master the art of making and managing money, the more money you will be able to make and manage.

Through this, you will find yourself effortlessly running a business, managing the money from that business, and living the lifestyle that you desire to live. This is key in being able to fulfill those lifelong plans you have for yourself, so if you really want to live within that vision, get committed and stay focused on developing self-discipline.

Creating a financial legacy is about so much more than just creating financial freedom. It is about creating financial freedom for yourself and anyone else whom you might want to help out, too. If you have children, grandchildren, or even a chosen charity that you want to support, being able to build enough money to tap into genuine financial freedom means that you can pour money into these areas of your life that you care about, too. As a result, you are able to truly leave behind a legacy that goes far beyond simply being wealthy yourself. With the right actions, you can also develop a business that serves as a legacy by having the capacity to not only pass on funds to your loved onesbut also an income-producing asset that will serve them in creating their own financial legacies.

Before you set out on your mission to create your own financial legacy, I ask you to please take a moment to review *How to*

Create Wealth on Amazon Kindle. Your honest feedback would be greatly appreciated, as it will allow me to continue to create great content to support you in achieving your life goals. It will also help others just like you find this excellent resource so that they, too, can begin to build their way to financial freedom through creating their own wealth.

Thank you, and best of luck! You can do it!

Description

Financial freedom seems like a distant and unachievable dream for most, but for someone like you it seems like a realistic goal. You know not everyone was made for greatness, but this exclusive club sounds like the exact place you were meant to end up. Mindset, freedom, and fulfillment are synonymous with your life-long goals, and you are ready to tap into the step-by-step process of bringing those goals to life. That is why you decided to read this book, and I assure you will find it to be a good decision.

Achieving financial freedom is something that, believe it or not, can be achieved by absolutely anyone. With the right vision, mindset, and goals in place you can earn, save, and strategize your way to leaving behind your own financial legacy. In order to get there, however, you need to know how to harness and focus your energy so that you can follow a clear-cut path to your success.

There is one rule that successful people follow that no one else does, and because of that they achieve all of their life long goals while many others find themselves continually believing that their goals are unrealistic. This rule is simple: do not reinvent the wheel. Aside from that, there are no rules.

The path to success is already carved out; all you need to do is walk it with your own sense of style. You need to learn how to follow that path in a way that will generate success in your life, without taking away from the freedom and experiences that you truly desire to have. As long as you learn to walk that path properly, *you make the rules*.

If this freedom lifestyle sounds like what you want, grab your copy of *How to Create Wealth: Live the Life of Your Dreams Creating Success and Being Unstoppable*today so that you can begin to build the life you want.

Some of what you will learn about in *How to Create Wealth* includes:

- The necessary mindset that you must have in order to create wealth (hint: <u>no one</u> will ever get wealthy without this mindset)

- The power of vision and why most people's vision never amounts to anything more than a pipe dream
- Why managing your finances is the number one way to accumulate wealth, as well as the seven stages of financial freedom and how to turn them into actionable goals
- The most important secret you need to know in order to create a successful income-producing asset that will pay for your dream life *(I'm still surprised that no one else seems to be talking about this!)*
- What you *actually* need to do to build a successful business
- And more!

If you are ready to say "YES" to your financial legacy and start living the life you know you are meant for, grab your copy of *How to Create Wealth* today and start enforcing these necessary steps into your life. I guarantee that if you follow them properly, you too will be amongst the exclusive club of people who _actually achieve greatness._

CPSIA information can be obtained
at www.ICGtesting.com
Printed in the USA
LVHW041218201020
669278LV00002B/132